A FALCON GUIDE®

Hiking California's
Golden Trout Wilderness

A Guide to Backpacking and Day Hiking
in the Golden Trout and South Sierra Wilderness Areas

Suzanne Swedo

FALCON®

GUILFORD, CONNECTICUT
HELENA, MONTANA
AN IMPRINT OF THE GLOBE PEQUOT PRESS

All photographs by Suzanne Swedo
Maps created by Trailhead Graphics ©
The Globe Pequot Press

Library of Congress Cataloging-in-Publication Data
Swedo, Suzanne, 1945-
  Hiking California's Golden Trout Wilderness: a guide to
  backpacking and day hiking in the Golden Trout and
  South Sierra wildernesses / Suzanne Swedo. —1st ed.
      p. cm. — (A Falcon Guide)
  Includes bibliographical references (p.).
  ISBN 0-7627-2655-5
    1. Hiking—California—Golden Trout Wilderness—
  Guidebooks. 2. Hiking—California—South Sierra
  Wilderness —Guidebooks. 3. Golden Trout Wilderness
  (Calif.)—Guidebooks. 4. South Sierra Wilderness
  (Calif.)—Guidebooks. I. Title. II. Falcon guide.

GV 199.42.C22G659 2004
917.94'86—dc22
                                    2003056979

Manufactured in the United States of America
First Edition/First Printing

In Memory of Tom

Contents

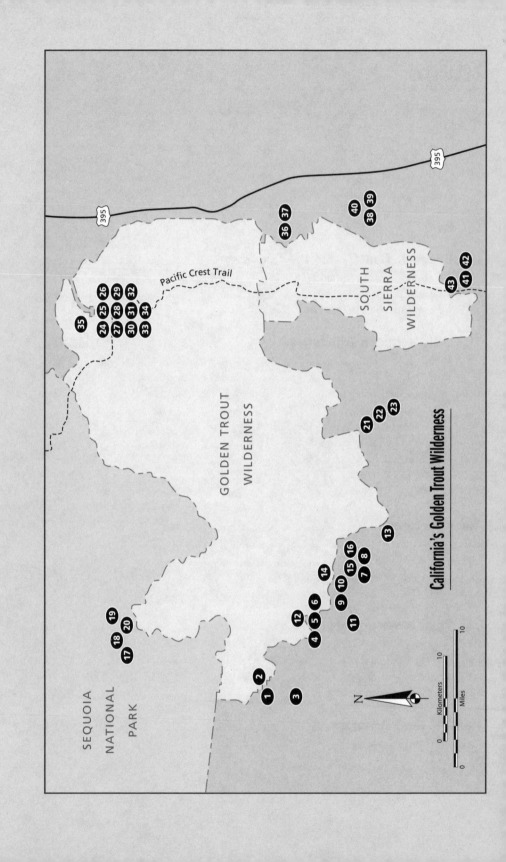

California's Golden Trout Wilderness

Acknowledgments

Thanks to the many USDA Forest Service people who patiently and cheerfully answered questions and supplied much valuable information and advice. Among those who went the extra mile and deserve extra-special gratitude are Marty Hornick, Jan Cutts, and Kathleen Nelson, along with Bill Prather of the Thacher School.

For help and company along on the trail and for patience and moral support during the days of struggle with the computer, great thanks are also due to Erica Crawford, Peggy Graham, Roxanne Hylton and Jim Willoughby, Melinda Goodwater, Sharon, Steven, Shemya, and Annette Lee, Meryl Leventhal, Pat Medley, and of course Rex Raymer.

Introduction

The Golden Trout Wilderness, created in 1978 under the Endangered American Wilderness Act, encompasses grand open hiking country, a quintessentially western landscape complete with clusters of range cattle and an occasional tumbledown log cabin set against a backdrop of craggy peaks and impossibly blue skies. While it is very much a part of the great Sierra Nevada range, the glaciers that sculpted the ridges and carved the canyons just to the north reached their southern limits within the wilderness. Beyond lies a land with a sense of great expansiveness and sweep, along with a more hiker-friendly surface with fewer steep ups and downs. The same factors that limited the reach of the ice, a more southerly latitude and slightly lower average elevation range, offer a further attraction to backcountry travelers: a hiking season longer by several weeks than in the rest of the Sierra. Backpackers homesick for the high country after a long winter will find many trailheads accessible as early as May, and can usually expect pleasant weather through October.

One hundred forty-seven miles of trails, including a section of the famous Pacific Crest Trail (PCT), wander through majestic forests of pine and fir, giant sequoia groves, vast green meadows, and wildflower gardens, along thundering rivers and tranquil meandering brooks. The lakes and streams are inhabited by several species of trout, including two subspecies of the rare and beautiful golden trout, the state fish of California for which the wilderness is named. Great granite peaks both invite casual rock scramblers and offer challenges to technical climbers. Geologically recent volcanic activity has added interest to the landscape in the form of colorful cinder cones and lava flows. Wildlife-watchers will find mule deer, black bears, marmots, squirrels of all kinds, and even (introduced) beavers, along with a marvelous variety of birds, especially raptors. There are soda springs for sipping and hot springs for soaking.

The wilderness occupies the broad sloping Kern Plateau, the southernmost portion of the true High Sierra just south of Mount Whitney, highest point in the continental United States at almost 14,500 feet. Elevations in the wilderness range from 4,700 feet at Forks of the Kern in the south to 12,900 feet at Cirque Peak in the north. To the east beyond the Sierra Crest, the land abruptly drops more than 5,000 feet to the unearthly desert beauty of the Owens Valley floor painted with eerie swirling patterns of color of the usually dry Owens lakebed.

The most striking topographic feature of the region is the formidable Kern River, one of the few in the nation that's free flowing and pristine enough to qualify for Wild and Scenic status under the Wild and Scenic Rivers Act. Most Sierra Nevada rivers begin near the crest of the roughly north–south trending range and flow quite sensibly down its eastern and western flanks. The main fork of the Kern, however, slices a straight deep gash down the spine of the mountains, following an

Golden trout, California's beautiful threatened state fish

inactive fault that runs north to south. It is a striking anomaly clearly visible on aerial photographs and relief maps. On the ground it forms an almost impassible barrier to east–west travel across the wilderness, except in two places where sturdy bridges have been constructed.

Hikers seeking solitude in the popular Sierra Nevada will find it here. With only one exception, the wilderness is not easily accessible from any major highway. Sequoia National Park and the John Muir Wilderness form the northern boundary, preventing motor access from that direction. The roadless South Sierra Wilderness forms part of the southern border, while the dramatic escarpment of the range on the east limits access from the Owens Valley and Interstate 395. Southern and western entry points are reached by secondary county and Forest Service roads, some unpaved. Hiking in the Golden Trout Wilderness requires some commitment; you won't find casual drop-in picnickers here. There are, however, many rewarding day hikes using one of the many campgrounds along the wilderness boundary as base camp.

A wilderness permit is necessary for overnight travel, but most trailheads are so infrequently used that only one of them has set a quota.

The Golden Trout Wilderness is administered by two different federal agencies. The Inyo National Forest on the east cares for two-thirds of the total 303,287 acres, and the Sequoia National Forest on the west is responsible for the rest. The northwest corner is included in the new Giant Sequoia National Monument, established in 2000 to protect the remaining giant sequoia groves not originally included in Sequoia National Park.

Geology

The Golden Trout and South Sierra Wildernesses occupy the southern end of the Sierra Nevada, a 400-mile-long dynamic classroom of geologic forces and features. The range was formed by the collision of vast plates of the earth's crust, lifting what had once been seafloor and offshore volcanic islands to become mountain peaks. Between about 150 million years and 80 million years ago, huge globs of molten material called magma from beneath the earth's crust began to force their way toward the surface. Most of the magma cooled and solidified beneath the surface to become granitic rock. After this, mountain building ended for a time. Wind and rain began to wash away almost all of the overlying ancient seafloor to reveal the gray granite that gives the Sierra Nevada its distinctive appearance today. The granitic rocks come in all shades, from nearly white to almost black, but share a more or less salt-and-pepper texture. In some cases the individual salt and pepper "grains" or crystals are minute; in others they might be several inches square. Crystals that are visible to the naked eye are what distinguish granite from volcanic rock such as lava, also present in the wilderness. The molten material that becomes lava rises to the surface, cools, and solidifies too quickly for individual bits to grow large enough to see, while if same material cools more slowly underground, it becomes granite. Both are igneous rocks—they originate as magma from beneath the earth's surface.

As the blobs of magma rose and cooled to granite, they cooked the surrounding and overlying seafloor sediments to a new kind of rock known as metamorphic. Marble, quartzite, and schist are examples. Metamorphic rocks are generally darker in color than granitic ones, sometimes beautifully striped in reds, blacks, and whites. They break along parallel planes rather than in right-angled chunks, and the layers are often intricately folded. Most of this older metamorphic material has been eroded away from the mountaintops, though a few remnants can still be seen in the Golden Trout Wilderness in the form of elongated septa, or screens of ancient rock that lie between two emplacements of younger granite. One outcropping occurs on the west side of Kern Peak, and another can be found along the steep eastern escarpment between Ash and Cartago Creeks. The largest one runs north to south, entering the wilderness near Bullfrog Lake and exiting near North Fork Creek. This is part of the huge Mineral King roof pendant, the bulk of which lies farther west.

About twenty-five million years ago, after a period of quiescence, the range began to rise once again, this time as a result of movement on the famous San Andreas Fault. For the most part the entire Sierra Nevada was thrust upward as a unit. There are surprisingly few faults within the range itself; most of the action

The steep faulted escarpment of Mount Whitney and the southern Sierra from the east

occurs along the eastern edge. The Sierra is still alive and growing. Hot springs steam and bubble along numerous faults, and earthquakes rattle local residents. As recently as 1872 an earthquake struck the town of Lone Pine just outside the wilderness, devastating the area, killing many of its residents, and lifting the mountains as much as 15 feet. Over time, this sort of faulting along the east side has caused the Owens Valley to drop downward as the Sierra rose so that the range is tilted upward from west to east, then abruptly drops away in a vertical cliff.

The one spectacular exception to the lack of faults within the Sierra Nevada occurs in the Golden Trout and South Sierra Wildernesses. The Kern Canyon fault, through which the Kern River flows, is more than 80 miles long and runs north–south, unlike all the other river valleys in the range, which run east–west. Its age is unknown, but because lava that poured into it after its formation has been dated at 3.5 million years, it must be at least as old as that. It has split the Southern Sierra into two parallel crests, the main Sierra Crest on the east and the Great Western Divide on the west. Unlike the faults along the eastern escarpment, the one that produced the Kern Canyon is no longer active.

The uplift of this massive mountain range caused climate changes of continental scope. When the mountains had become high enough to block the flow of the moist winds that blow from the Pacific, rain and snow began to fall on their western flank. Rivers and streams carved deep canyons, carrying great loads of silt down westward to fill the great Central Valley of California with rich and productive soil. The land to the east, now mostly deprived of precipitation, became desert.

The landscapes of the Golden Trout and South Sierra Wildernesses share another geologic feature that distinguishes them from the country farther north. Some very recent and quite spectacular volcanic activity occurred here in several distinct spurts. One of these began about 2.5 million years ago when violent explosions of rhyolite produced the conical domes of Templeton and Monache Mountains. The most recent phase of volcanism began less than a million years ago and continues to the present, though its most recent activity occurred 5,000 years ago—the age to which Groundhog Cone, the youngest in the region, has been dated. During this phase the lava was more liquid and faster flowing than before, pouring from openings such as the South Fork Cone, creating the eerie landscape of the Golden Trout Creek Volcanic Field. One of the most beautiful and interesting structures created by this flow can be seen at the confluence of Golden Trout Creek and the Kern River. Here the molten material cooled at such a quick and uniform rate as to produce a wall of wonderfully regular basalt columns like those of the Devil's Postpile to the north. Beneath the surface the earth cools very slowly. The inner heat warms groundwater that rises to the surface along faults. Jordan Hot Springs, where scalding water bubbles into cool Ninemile Creek, is a notable example.

Another Sierran rock type that builds up near hot springs like Jordan is called travertine. It is made up of calcium carbonate carried by underground water as it rises and evaporates, depositing its load of minerals on the surface. A natural bridge made of this material crosses Golden Trout Creek a few miles above the Kern River. At this spot a now defunct hot spring once flowed and deposited a mass of travertine on top of a bed of sand and gravel. Later the creek carved out the streambed and carried away the looser material, leaving the bridge above.

The artistry of the glaciers that put the finishing touches to the topography of most of the High Sierra began at about the same time as the volcanic activity in the Golden Trout Wilderness did. About two to three million years ago, the climate of the earth cooled just enough so that winter snows did not melt away during the summer, but accumulated to great depths, then compressed to ice. The ice, under its own weight, began to flow down previously cut stream courses, gouging them wider and deeper, scraping and polishing their bottoms and sides, sharpening the mountaintops into spires and horns, forming knife-edged ridges called arêtes, and carving out amphitheaters called cirques. Later the ice left in these basins melted, leaving thousands of sparkling alpine and subalpine lakes, many of which over time have filled in with silt to become flower-filled mountain meadows. There are no glaciers at all in the Golden Trout and South Sierra Wildernesses now, and those that did reach this far south before were waning in power and volume as they entered the region. They have left their mark, however, in the form of cirque lakes, the steep sides and flat bottom of the upper Kern River Canyon, and piles of glacial till, jumbles of unsorted rock shoved aside or dumped in ridges and piles by melting ice. And of course from every high point clear of timber, the ice-carved crags, some still sheltering small glaciers, march away to the north, providing a dramatic High Sierra backdrop to the gentler terrain of the Golden Trout and South Sierra Wildernesses.

Life in the Southern Sierra

The Southern Sierra Nevada of which the Golden Trout and South Sierra Wildernesses are a part is a land of remarkable diversity, allowing hikers opportunities to experience everything from desert to alpine environments within a limited number of miles. As in the rest of the Sierra, there are extremes of topography and therefore extremes of weather, temperatures, and soil. These provide habitats for a wide variety of plants and animals, many of them rare and endemic (limited to this region alone).

The lowest point in the wilderness is at Forks of the Kern at 4,700 feet, where vegetation on cooler slopes and along stream bottoms is mostly woodland made up of deciduous black oak and evergreen canyon live oak, along with smaller, shrubbier scrub oak species. Chaparral clothes the south-facing slopes with dense thickets of ceanothus and manzanita, bursting with life in springtime especially after a fire, to which this community is adapted. Manzanita blooms with bunches of little white bells that mature into applelike berries by early summer; frothy bunches of blue, lilac, and white ceanothus perfume the air. Gray pines with massive, knobby cones and insubstantial-looking foliage made up of long, gray needles overtop the lower-growing species. Most of the birds of these lower elevations are small and drab in color in order to blend in with the shrubbery for safety, but in spring they make up for their lack of showy plumage by their brilliant and complex songs. The two exceptions to this rule are the blue and bold squawking scrub jays and the clownish red, black, and white acorn woodpeckers with their *rackety-rackety* call. Bobcats, rabbits, coyotes, and foxes can sometimes be spotted, especially at dawn and dusk.

Spring and fall are the best times to visit these lower elevations, since summer temperatures can reach one hundred degrees. Still, even later on there are plenty of creeks and pools for wading, and the Kern River stirs up its own air currents that create a cool breeze along its shores. The snowpack is less deep and melts off earlier here, too, so you can get a jump on the hiking season before the high country is accessible, and can usually continue well into fall since snow from the first few storms seldom lasts long.

Between 4,500 and 7,500 feet, a mixed coniferous forest of ponderosa pine, sugar pine, white fir, Douglas fir, and incense cedar at first mingles with, then replaces the

Giant sequoias

oak forest. Black bears, mule deer, ground squirrels, tree squirrels, and chipmunks go about their business and are usually fairly east to spot. Brilliant blue Steller's jays scold among the trees from morning to night. Along the western border of the Golden Trout Wilderness grow the star attractions of this elevation range: the giant sequoias. The sheer size of these trees—dwarfing the white firs and flowering dogwoods beneath them—along with the filtered sunlight that dapples the bracken fern on the forest floor, lends their groves a hushed and reverent atmosphere unlike any other. Also known simply as Big Trees, these are the largest living things on earth, at least aboveground (an underground fungus is currently vying for that title). They are not as tall as the Coast redwoods but far surpass them in sheer mass, growing up to 300 feet high and 30 feet in diameter. They are among the oldest living things on earth as well, persisting as long as 3,000 years, though not as long as the 4,000-year-old bristlecone pines in the nearby White Mountains. Their wood is brittle and useless for building, but is tough and long lasting as well as resistant to fire and insects, so the trees have been decimated by logging for roof shingles and fencing. Even without human destruction, the trees are rare enough. They exist only on the western slope of the Sierra in fewer than eighty-five isolated groves where temperatures and moisture are exactly to their liking. They and their nearest relatives clothed great tracts of land on several continents millions of years ago when the climate was wetter and warmer than it is now. Big as they are, they are finicky about their environment and need perfect conditions in order to reproduce. One of the most important of these is fire. Their surprisingly small cones produce millions of extremely tiny seeds that must reach a forest floor burned free of litter so that they can germinate at once.

Fire also dries and opens the cones so the seeds can be released. Their thick bark makes them resistant to fire, and most show multiple scars from past blazes. Only an extremely intense conflagration will reach the crown and kill the tree—the kind of blaze likely to occur only when misguided forestry practices in the past suppressed fires and allowed too much fuel to build up on the forest floor. Animals contribute to the continued presence of the trees as well. Douglas squirrels, also known as chickarees, like to eat the scales of young green cones, allowing the seeds to be released. A wood-boring beetle causes more mature cones to open by laying her eggs between their scales. When the larvae hatch out, they begin to chew their way into the cones, cutting off their supply of water and nutrients. The cones soon dry out, fall apart, and disperse their seeds.

Lodgepole pines, with two needles per bundle, "cornflake" bark, and small, oval cones, dominate the slopes between roughly 7,500 and 9,500 feet. Red fir and western white pine (also known as silver pine) occasionally accompany the lodgepoles, but are more common farther north. This elevation receives the heaviest winter snowfall. The snow piles into drifts that remain well into July in shaded gullies. Forests have fairly open, bare floors because little sunlight reaches the ground, but leafless little saprophytic plants, including several kinds of orchids, thrive here, nourished by dead and decaying material in the soil.

Straddling this zone and the subalpine region above it is the Kern Plateau. The broad meadows found here are unique in the Sierra Nevada because they have not been scraped to bare bedrock or their margins polished smooth by the glaciers that melted just to the north. Instead, they are shallow bowls lined with sandy granite alluvium. Farther north lodgepole pines grow right down to the edges of the meadow sedges and grasses and eventually colonize them. Meadows on the southern Kern Plateau have sandy margins that will not support trees, but do host some unusual wildflowers. The extremely rare Ramshaw abronia, *Abronia alpina,* grows nowhere else in the world except near Ramshaw and Templeton Meadows. It is a low-growing sticky, glandular, white and pinky-lavender sand verbena that carpets the meadows' edges in wet years.

Through these meadows flow the cold clear streams favored by the golden trout, the state fish of California. These are also endemic species that live naturally only here, though they have been transplanted to lakes and streams elsewhere. (Tradition has it that the first transplanted fish were carried to Cottonwood Lakes in a rancher's coffeepot.) There are two subspecies of golden trout, the Little Kern golden trout and the South Fork golden trout. Both are small—about 6 inches long on average—but strikingly beautiful in speckled gold with a wide red stripe running along each side, blotched with vertical black patches. Their pinkish flesh is delicious. Their endangered status is due partly to their limited range, partly to hybridization with non-native rainbow trout, and partly to the muddying by cattle of the clear water they need to survive. They may be taken only with barbless hooks, and limits are small.

In the subalpine zone between 9,500 feet and timberline, the beginning of the true High Sierra, the landscape is more open and rocky and the views are the finest. The sky is intensely blue because the air is thinner. The limber pines that reach these elevations are often gnarled and stunted, forced to hunker down to avoid howling winter winds.

No hunkering for the foxtail pine, though. These pines do not form the sprawling mats called krummholz, but stand straight and tall, defying the fiercest gales on the exposed ridges they prefer. Their trunks are stout, up to 5 feet in diameter, and they rarely exceed 30 feet in height. They are easily recognized by their bundles of five short needles clustered along the ends of branches in long tails. They have an oddly separated range. One subspecies lives here in the Southern Sierra, radiating from an arc around the upper Kern River drainage. Another subspecies grows in the Klamath area of Northern California, hundreds of miles away. They are fairly closely related to the ancient bristlecone pines and are probably the longest-living pine in the Sierra, up to 2,000 years.

A favorite character in this zone is the Clark's nutcracker, a large showy gray, black, and white bird, one of the jays whose squawk can be heard all over this country. They

A Clark's nutcracker, a bold and noisy member of the jay family

are important to the maintenance of the high pine forests because of their food storage habits. They pluck the seeds from the cones of timberline pines such as foxtails and limbers, give them a shake to test their weight and condition, eat a few, then store the rest in a pouch under their tongues. Authorities cite the capacity of this pouch to hold from 80 to 150 seeds. The birds then bury the uneaten seeds in shallow holes on sunny south-facing slopes where snow does not accumulate too deeply to eat later. Of course, not all of the stored nuts are retrieved; many sprout to grow new pine trees.

The region of high peaks and passes above timberline is true arctic-alpine country. The temperature is low, winds high, and the growing season short, so plants keep their heads down. Most of the alpine wildflowers are perennials that wait underground for the few short weeks of sunshine and freedom from snow. Beginning roughly in mid-July and continuing through August, they burst forth to carpet high meadows and decorate rock crannies with masses of color. Across the late-lying snowfields, rosy finches chase insects that have been blown up from below. Pikas or rock rabbits scurry among the rock piles on fur-soled feet, gathering food to see them through the winter. They are the size of small plump squirrels, but are actually related to rabbits, with stubby tails and rounded ears. They are almost invisible when motionless, but if you sit quietly beside a high-elevation rock pile for only a few minutes, they will resume their activities, yelping now and then as they hurry back and forth clutching little bouquets of grasses and wildflowers in their jaws.

Beyond the crest, the mountains fall away all at once to the desert country of the Great Basin. On the steep eastern slope and in the gentler country in the southern end of the South Sierra Wilderness, mountain and desert species mingle in a rich and unusual flora. In some places eastern-slope piñon pines and western-slope gray pines grow side by side. Sagebrush and golden yellow rabbitbrush extend all the way to the subalpine region from the high desert, and an occasional beavertail cactus blooms with vivid magenta flowers early in the season.

From high points along the crest are stupendous views of the Owens Valley and the Coso Range and beyond to the Panamints that rise above Death Valley. Just out of sight lies Badwater, lowest place in the continental United States. From several of these same high points hikers can spot nearby Mount Whitney, the highest point in the lower forty-eight. Hikers are not likely to find a greater variety of landforms and life anywhere else in the world!

History

The first human beings in the Southern Sierra Nevada about whom we have any information at all were the Paiute or Shoshone people from the east side of the range and the Yokuts and Monaches from the west. They followed the seasons up and down the mountainside as food plants ripened, game migrated, and winter snow buried the high country or intense heat made the valleys inhospitable. They gathered an enormous variety of plants, trapped fish and small game, and hunted deer, bighorn sheep, elk, and pronghorn. The groups passed back and forth across the mountains to trade a variety of goods, especially acorns from the western slope and piñon nuts and obsidian from the east. Backcountry travelers can find evidence of these peoples' daily activities in the form of bedrock mortars in oak groves near streamsides where acorns were pounded into meal, the staple food. Only two or three decades ago, arrow points and other tools could be found here and there along Sierra trails, but these are extremely rare now. If you are lucky enough to spot such an artifact, admire it and leave it in place.

The eighteenth century brought a few Spanish missionaries to the mountains, but they made little impact on the life of the Native people in the beginning. Neither did the few white fur trappers who wandered through. The nineteenth century, however, brought explorers such as Joseph Walker and Captain John C. Frémont, who began mapping and describing the peaks and passes, making way for the influx of miners and settlers that would doom the Native Americans' way of life forever. Today most of the descendants of the Paiute and Yokut people live on reservations on both sides of the Sierra Nevada.

The view from the Sierra Crest eastward toward the usually dry Owens Lake

The 1849 California gold rush did not affect this part of the Sierra Nevada as much as it did the country to the north. Prospectors came to the Southern Sierra in the 1860s and did find some gold, but nothing like the riches that had been discovered elsewhere. Most of the action was found to be in the Coso Range across the Owens Valley, where silver, lead, and zinc brought a stream of miners and prospectors flowing across the Sierra. New roads and trails needed to be built across the range to carry people and supplies to mines like the Cerro Gordo, and to haul the ore back to San Francisco.

John Jordan arrived in 1861 and hired local Indians to guide him over some of their traditional trading routes and to help build a trail across the mountains from Visalia to the Owens Valley that could be operated as a toll road. Jordan was drowned in 1862 trying to cross the Kern River on a raft, but shortly thereafter another company bought the rights and completed the trail. A year later another trail, the Hockett, was completed just to the north of the Jordan Trail. This one carried even more traffic across the mountains. It was used for a time by the U.S. Army to send supplies to Camp Independence in the Owens Valley as well as by miners, but in 1864 the Walker Pass toll road was constructed, and work on the Jordan and Hockett Trails was abandoned.

Logging operations had a further impact on the mountain environment. Timber was needed to supply fuel for mining operations in the Coso Range, so the rare foxtail pines, along with lodgepoles and Jeffreys, were cut, then delivered by flume down Cottonwood Canyon, loaded onto a paddle-wheeled steamer, and shipped across Owens Lake. From the far shore they were hauled by wagon up to the Cerro Gordo mine. Further logging, including the cutting of the giant sequoias, was carried on along the western slope of the range to supply fencing and building materials for the farmers and ranchers in the Central Valley.

A severe drought in the early 1860s forced herders of sheep and cattle to drive their animals to the higher, moister mountain meadows of the Golden Trout country, where by the 1880s their unrestricted numbers had overrun and overgrazed the land, leaving desolate patches of sagebrush and deeply eroded gullies that have still not recovered from the trampling.

It was at about this time that the some farmers dreamed up the bizarre scheme to divert Golden Trout Creek into the South Fork of the Kern by means of a tunnel blasted through the ridge separating the two streams in the area now known as Tunnel Meadow. Fortunately, this effort failed (see Hike 30). The Tunnel Meadow Guard Station later became the communications center connected by phone lines to cow camps all over the area.

By the early twentieth century, the general public had succumbed to the lure of the wilderness, encouraged by writings of John Muir and others. Tourists arrived on foot or on horseback to angle for the beautiful golden trout or to socialize, dance, and soak in the pools at Jordan Hot Springs. In time three airstrips were built nearby to fly in visitors (see Hike 22). By the 1950s the Kern Plateau had become a favorite playground of motorcyclists, who further tore up vegetation and increased soil erosion.

Fortunately, the same impulse that brought many visitors into the wilderness for recreation led to efforts to preserve the region from further overuse. Sheep were banned from the mountains altogether, and federal grazing allotments were established to limit the number of cattle allowed to forage there. Still, environmentalists would like to see cattle banned completely from the wilderness, citing the silting up of streams that damages the habitat of the threatened golden trout, which need clear, cold water. They argue that the land cannot recover from past overgrazing until all cattle are removed and the damage from former overuse repaired. Hikers also object to muddy streams and trampled wildflowers, along with meadows strewn with cowpies and buzzing with flies. Cattlemen site historical precedent as well as more enlightened management of their herds. Time, public opinion, and the legal system will determine the fate of cattle in the Golden Trout and South Sierra Wildernesses in the future.

Zero Impact

While the primary aim of this book is to encourage people to experience and appreciate the beauty of the Golden Trout and South Sierra Wildernesses up close and on foot, the backcountry environment is fragile. Hikers can do their part to reduce their impact on the natural environment by respecting wilderness rules and practicing Zero Impact principles.

Although the Golden Trout and South Sierra Wildernesses have a long history of human disturbance, their relatively new wilderness status and the regulations governing it should allow some of the worst of the old scars to heal over time. However you feel about the question of whether or not cattle grazing should be allowed to continue in the wilderness, you as a hiker still have a responsibility not to contribute to the degradation of the land by your own actions. Please read and follow the suggestions and guidelines you will receive along with your wilderness permit.

On the Trail

Group size is limited to fifteen people. Hiking on already established trails leaves the least impact on the land, so all routes described in this book follow trails. To prevent damage to the trails themselves, do not shortcut switchbacks. They have been built to retard erosion as well as to create a more comfortable grade for gaining and losing elevation. When the trail is wet or muddy, try to avoid walking alongside it, trampling vegetation and wearing a parallel trail. Many of the wilderness's meadows are scarred by a series of wide parallel ruts across the landscape that look like the work of vehicles, even in places where no vehicles have traveled in the past. On the other hand, if you must cross a meadow with no conspicuous pathway and are part of a group, spread out so that you do not create a new rut by numerous feet passing over the same route.

Good manners and consideration for others, not to mention safety, dictate that foot travelers yield to pack animals on the trail. Step off the trail and stand quietly until the last horse or mule has gone completely past. Bicycles and mechanized travel of any kind are prohibited in the backcountry. Downhill hikers should yield to those heading uphill so that the climbers can maintain their rhythm and momentum.

Selecting a Campsite

You may camp anywhere you choose in the wilderness so long as you observe a few restrictions designed to reduce your impact on the land and on other campers. Choose a site at least 100 feet from water and, whenever possible, 100 feet from the trail, or at least out of sight of passersby. Pitch your tent or spread your tarp on sandy ground or pine duff, never on growing vegetation. In the afternoon sunshine green meadows are deceptively inviting, but they're cold, damp, and buggy at night. Use an established campsite, one that has been used before if you can, and do not modify the area in any way by digging trenches around tents, building new fire rings, or breaking limbs off trees.

Badly eroded trail through Mulkey Meadows

Campfires

In the Sequoia National Forest on the west side of the wilderness, campfire permits and shovels are required in addition to a wilderness permit. In the Inyo National Forest on the east, your wilderness permit doubles as a campfire permit. Campfires are permitted anywhere in the Golden Trout and South Sierra Wilderness except in the Rocky Basin Lakes and Chicken Spring Lake basins, or when special fire restrictions are in effect. At elevations near timberline fires are permitted, but discouraged.

If you must have a fire, keep it small and cozy and take only firewood that is dead and lying on the ground. Do not remove branches from standing dead trees. They provide homes for dozens of different creatures and are important parts of the ecosystem. Vegetation grows slowly at high altitudes, and the few trees that manage to hang on to life near timberline are evergreens that do not drop much organic material on the ground. The soil needs protection from compaction that the litter on the forest floor supplies. Compaction from tents and human feet prevents the soil from absorbing vital nutrients and oxygen and removes the source of organic material that is returned to the soil as it decomposes. Backpacking stoves are so light and efficient and modern fabrics so warm that fires are no longer needed for cooking or warmth, but for social atmosphere alone. Keep it small if you must have it, and of course, make sure it is completely out before you leave.

Housekeeping

There is one simple rule for good housekeeping in the wilderness: Do not put anything in the water. That includes soap, food scraps, and fish guts. Biodegradable soap is not the answer. *To biodegrade* means "to decompose"; that is, to rot. Biodegradable soap does not poison organisms in the water like detergent can, but it does encourage the growth of bacteria that can upset the chemical balance of the water to the detriment of the organisms that live in it. Hot water and a little sand do fine for washing dishes, but if you must use soap, wash and rinse everything at least 100 feet from any water source. The same goes for your own body. A refreshing swim in a mountain pond or a soak in a hot spring won't do any damage, and you can surely survive a few days in the wilderness without contracting some dread disease if you do not use soap, but if you feel you must, wash and rinse at least 100 feet away from water.

Keep your camp clean of crumbs and other edibles. Learn to take just what you need to eat, and pack out your leftovers. At regularly used campsites, jays, squirrels, mice, and marmots may come to expect food scraps and can acquire bad habits such as chewing holes into your pack or tent to investigate appetizing smells.

Human waste disposal is one of the most difficult problems in the backcountry. Bovine waste disposal is another, but we can at least take responsibility for ourselves. Find a spot 200 feet from water where there is some organic material on the ground and dig a hole about 6 inches deep, then cover everything. Take extra plastic bags along and pack out your toilet paper. A teaspoon of powdered bleach in the plastic bag will prevent odors. Buried toilet paper is sometimes dug up again by animals and can take years to decompose underground. Do not burn toilet paper; more than one serious fire has been started that way.

Bears

Bear activity in the Golden Trout and South Sierra Wildernesses is on the increase, but has not yet become the serious problem it is in the front and backcountry of the Inyo National Forest and the national parks to the north. To prevent losing your food to a bear or encouraging bears to vandalize your car at a trailhead, wilderness travelers are required by law to ensure that bears do not get access to food or refuse. Bear canisters are strongly recommended by the Forest Service, but are not required, though they may be in the future. The next best technique to protect your food is the counterbalance method. You can find illustrations and descriptions of this technique at ranger stations, but while it appears simple enough on paper, it is often difficult in the backcountry. Sometimes it is impossible to find a tree of proper height with a branch of the proper diameter over which to sling a rope, or to get your food sacks balanced perfectly. In any case the counterbalance method should be considered a delaying tactic only: Bears are much stronger, more patient, more determined, and much more intelligent than you think. If you can get it up there, they can get it back down again. Attach pots and pans or other noisemakers to your food sacks so that when the bear goes to work you will have some warning and can chase it away. While canisters are not perfect (they are bulky, weigh almost three pounds, and cost about $75), they are effective, easy and cheap to rent, double as convenient camp chairs, and go a long way toward preserving your peace of mind.

Horseshoe Meadow is the only wilderness entrance where you may not leave food in your car. Sturdy storage boxes are provided at the trailheads. Use them. Remember, if a bear gets your food or damages your vehicle because you did not store it properly, *it's your fault!*

A Few Words of Caution

Weather Patterns

While most Sierra summer days are clear and sunny, high mountains create their own weather. Hikers must be prepared for anything. Snow can fall at any time of year, including July and August, though it is not common. Afternoon thundershowers, sometimes accompanied by violent hailstorms, can build with amazing rapidity on summer days that begin without a cloud in the sky. They are usually of short duration, but long enough to drench and chill an unprepared traveler. Never set out without rain gear. Lightning can be a serious hazard on open ridges above timberline and in the middle of wet meadows. If a storm threatens, head downhill and/or into the cover of timber as quickly as possible. If you're caught in an exposed area with no time to descend, get away from your pack or any metal equipment and squat until the danger passes—do not sit.

Drinking Water

Despite the clear and sparkling appearance of most of the wilderness lakes and streams, water from even the most remote of sources has been found to contain *Giardia lamblia,* a microorganism that causes diarrhea and other intestinal upsets. In cattle country such as the Golden Trout and South Sierra Wildernesses, *Giardia* and as well as bacteria are especially prevalent. Giardiasis is not a life-threatening illness for normal healthy adults, but it is debilitating and persistent and must be treated with antibiotics whose side effects may be equally unpleasant. The symptoms do not appear for more than a week after exposure, so victims sometimes do not associate their malady with their wilderness experience. Treat all water with a water filter guaranteed to remove *Giardia,* with iodine, or by boiling. Since the bug is killed at temperatures far below boiling, even at high elevations, just bringing water to a rolling boil is treatment enough. Iodine is lightweight, convenient, and effective if fresh, but some people are allergic to it and some object to the taste.

Rattlesnakes, plentiful at mid and lower elevations, prefer to keep to themselves.

Wild Animals

Injuries caused by bears or other animals in the wilderness are almost invariably due to human ignorance or carelessness. Take care to avoid moving between a mother and her babies, whether bear or cow, and do not try to touch or feed an animal. Mountain lions have been spotted in the wilderness, but they are very shy, and attacks are extremely rare. If you should encounter one, do not run or you might be mistaken for prey. Hold your ground, wave your arms to make yourself appear larger, and shout. Then congratulate yourself on being given a glimpse of a beautiful animal in its native habitat.

You have a better chance of seeing rattlesnakes this part of the Sierra than elsewhere because temperatures are a bit warmer and elevation is slightly lower on average. There is more of brush to provide cover for the small animals like rabbits, squirrels, and mice that are the rattler's food. Snakes are most active at dawn and dusk and blend beautifully with their surroundings. They prefer to save their venom for catching their food and do not strike at people unless they feel threatened. Watch your step, do not stick your hand into a crack or crevice you can't see into, and remember that the chances of being bitten are extremely slim and snakebites are rarely fatal.

Always overestimate the depth and force of mountain streams when you ford.

Stream Crossings

This is one hazard that is not exaggerated, unlike perceived threats from wildlife. Few of the streams in the Golden Trout and South Sierra Wildernesses have bridges: The main fork of the Kern has only two; the South Fork, two; and the Little Kern, only one. Be sure to research trail conditions in advance if your proposed route involves a river crossing. Frequently it is the smaller creeks swollen with snowmelt early in the year that are the most dangerous because it is easy to underestimate their force. Some streams have log crossings that must be managed with great care. A stout stick is a great stabilizer. Be sure to plant it upstream so that rushing water does not grab it and pull it out from under you. Always unbuckle your pack straps so that if you should fall in, you can free yourself from being dragged and held underwater.

Whenever you have to wade, always overestimate the depth and strength of the current. Sierra streams are so clear that they are usually deeper and swifter than they seem. Do not wade through water higher than your knees. The recommended method is to remove your socks and cross in your boots, which will give you temporary protection against the numbing cold and more stability on underwater obstacles. Do not try to cross barefooted. Seek out the widest part of the stream, even though the temptation is to pick a narrower spot to make the crossing quicker. The widest spot is usually the shallowest, slowest, and safest. If you are not sure whether you can cross safely, you can try again early in the morning before the snow upstream has begun to melt in the morning sun. Do not take chances. You can always return another time.

Losing the Trail

Trail conditions in the wilderness vary wildly. Some get plenty of traffic and are quite well maintained, but high water, avalanches, rockslides, and fast-growing meadow vegetation and brush can obscure even these in a single season. The hooves of milling cattle are a special challenge to route finding, no matter how frequently a trail is cleared. Many of the trails here get only periodic maintenance, and some almost none at all. Hikers must have some degree of competence with a topo map. Learn to stay alert for trail blazes on the trees, made by cutting away the outer bark, usually in simple geometric shapes at approximately eye level. In open, rocky places watch for cairns, also known as ducks—piles of rocks that indicate the presence of a trail. Also watch for sawed logs, metal tags, or plastic strips. If you become confused or lose a trail, go back to a point where you were absolutely certain of your location, and start over. Do not continue to blunder ahead, hoping the path will reappear.

If you feel you are hopelessly lost, stay put, take some action to draw attention to your position, and wait for help. In the Golden Trout it is especially important that you leave notice of your planned itinerary with someone at home who can contact authorities if you do not return on time. If you are not perfectly confident in your own ability to find your way around, do not head out into the backcountry without a companion who is.

How to Use This Guide

The purpose of this guide is to help you choose and plan a backpack or day hike in the Golden Trout Wilderness or South Sierra Wilderness best suited to your time, energy, experience, and personal preferences. It offers a preview of what you are likely to see and experience along your chosen route: geologic features, historical sites, trees, birds, flowers, and mammals. It helps you anticipate places where the trail is faint, where it is clear, where and when rivers and streams are special sources of delight, or where they may be obstacles to travel.

Each trail description begins with a statistical section for quick reference to the characteristics of the hike. A general description opens each write-up and lets you know whether the route is a loop, in which you return to the place where you started without retracing your steps; an out-and-back hike, in which you return to the trailhead the same way you came; or a shuttle hike, in which you begin at one trailhead and end at another, requiring two vehicles or another driver to pick you up or deposit you at either end. An occasional hike will be described as a lollipop loop, in which you hike from the trailhead at Point A to Point B, then follow a loop that returns you to Point B, from which you retrace your steps to the trailhead. A final type of hike is called an upside-down hike, which begins by losing elevation and ends be regaining elevation.

Total distance is described in miles. Since the Golden Trout Wilderness is managed by two different national forests and straddles a number of ranger districts, trail signs and mileage aren't always measured or marked consistently. In some areas official government trail miles are rounded off to the nearest 0.1 mile. In other areas they are rounded off to the nearest mile, so that a distance of 1.49 miles will be given on a sign as only 1 mile. Trails have also been rerouted over time, and signs are not always changed to reflect changes in distance. I have walked every route described here and have combined official figures with my own experience, using a combination of measuring techniques, so all distances cited should be accurate within 0.25 mile.

The **Difficulty** rating is bound to be interpreted differently by hikers in varying degrees of physical condition, including their adaptability to high elevation. In general, easy trails can be negotiated by anybody who can walk. Moderate trails are of greater length or involve significant elevation gain and loss and may challenge those who are not accustomed to much physical activity. Strenuous hikes will challenge the most experienced and energetic of hikers.

Total climbing will give you a rough idea of how much climbing and descending you can expect. The figure included is the sum of all the hills on the hike.

Trail traffic: A rating of light means that you probably will not see another hiking party along the way. Heavy means that you will regularly meet others on the trail, and will have company on weekends at more popular destinations. Moderate covers the wide range between these two extremes.

The **Best months** section usually turns out to refer to the only time that trails are open and safe to use at all because roads to trailheads are impassable until then. Most trails in the Sierra Nevada are passable only on skis, snowshoes, or with special winter climbing equipment for much of the year. More specific times to visit areas especially noteworthy for their seasonal display of wildflowers or fall colors, or that are too dangerous to attempt during high water, will be mentioned here.

Maps: The maps in this book give a detailed picture of local features and the correct location of routes that might be in error or out-of-date on the USDA Forest Service or U.S. Geological Survey maps, but they won't give you the big picture needed to identify surrounding features from a mountain top or show where a nearby stream ends up. Trail descriptions are intended to be used along with U.S. Geological Survey topographic maps, available at wilderness outfitting and sporting goods stores and through the USGS at P.O. Box 25286, Federal Center, Denver, CO 80225; (800) USA–MAPS; or online at www.mapping.usgs.gov. Because the Golden Trout Wilderness was established after the publication of the USGS topo maps, the Golden Trout Wilderness and South Sierra Wilderness map, Sequoia and Inyo National Forests, published by the USDA Forest Service, should also be used. These are available at many ranger stations and outfitting stores in the area or from the Eastern Sierra Interpretive Association by calling (760) 873–2503. You can also fax this group at (760) 873–2563, or contact it online at esia@schat.com. The street address is ESIA, 798 North Main Street, Bishop, California Highway 93514. While the Forest Service map is less detailed, it is more current. Many of the trails that used to be used by motor vehicles or by sheepherders in the old days have been abandoned or deliberately obscured, and some of the others rerouted. Both the USGS and Forest Service maps have a few errors, and while these are mentioned in the text whenever I have noticed them, using both maps for comparison is helpful in case of confusion.

Trail conditions vary widely in the wilderness. Many trails are well and regularly maintained, others are maintained infrequently, and some not at all. Even those that get regular attention can be trampled to obscurity by cattle. The Golden Trout and South Sierra Wilderness map shows trails in various colors to indicate their degree of maintenance. Many of those indicated by fine dashed lines are not visible at all. I have only included hikes in which there is some vestige of a marked trail, and have ignored those that can be negotiated by map and compass alone and have become cross-country routes.

Permits are discussed in the section introducing each group of hikes.

Trailhead facilities refers to sources of supplies or contact with emergency services nearest the trailhead.

Finding the trailhead describes the most direct ways to reach the beginning of each hike. Some hikes can be reached from either the east or the west side of the Sierra, but if one approach is ridiculously long or difficult, it has been omitted. They may not be the only possible ways. All the approaches described here are suitable for regular two-wheel-drive vehicles. A few trailheads in the southern part of the wilderness are accessible by four-wheel-drive vehicles from the Monache Mountain area within the Sequoia National Forest. The Sequoia National Forest map available at ranger stations shows their location.

The Hike is the main text of the chapter and will give you the most detailed information about the trail, the flowers, the animals, and the views you will see along the way. These are also directions that are keyed to the mileage in the Key Points.

Key Points are landmarks on the trail, usually trail junctions. The distances between them are sometimes a bit inconsistent with figures shown on trail signs because trails have been rerouted over the years to avoid obstacles such as rockslides or washouts, or to protect fragile vegetation in boggy meadows. Again, all distances between points are accurate within 0.2 or 0.3 mile.

Map Legend

─────────	Paved Road
═════════	Improved Road
=========	Dirt Road
▬▬▬▬▬▬▬▬▬	Featured Trail
- - - - - - - - -	Trail
🚶	Trailhead
⛺	Campground
▌	Ranger Station/ Guard Station
🔲	Picnic Area
■	Structure
)(	Bridge
•—•	Gate
▲	Mountain Peak
— — — — —	Park/Wilderness Boundary
⬭	Lake
～～～	River or Creek
⚬	Spring
≈	Waterfall

Giant Sequoia Country and the Tule River

A short, blunt panhandle of beautiful country extends westward from the main body of the Golden Trout Wilderness to include the upper drainage of the Middle Fork of the Tule River. Sequoia National Park shares its northern border, and Mountain Home State Forest dangles from its southwest flank. The boundaries of the new Giant Sequoia National Monument, established by President Clinton in 2000 to protect the fewer than eighty-five remaining groves of giant sequoias not already included in existing national parks, overlap those of the wilderness. The Big Trees, *Sequoiadendron giganteum,* the largest living things on earth, are the star attractions of this part of the wilderness. They grow in fewer than eighty groves scattered along the western slope of the Sierra Nevada, and nowhere else. Their rarity alone makes them precious, but it is their monumental size that evokes a sense of spiritual awe in anyone who wanders through their quiet groves.

The hiking season here is longer than in some parts of the Golden Trout since elevations are relatively low. Trailheads are usually accessible by mid to late May. During the high point of spring snowmelt, however, the Tule River and many of its tributary streams become raging torrents, too dangerous to ford. Check with rangers about water levels before beginning an early-season hike. Autumn is an especially lovely time for hiking here, too. Streamside oaks and willows turn golden, dogwoods are purple, and hazelnuts, currants, rose hips, and acorns cluster in the branches, tempting both humans and wildlife preparing for the coming winter.

The only access to this part of the wilderness is through Mountain Home Demonstration State Forest, the first state forest in California, established in 1946. You can get there from Interstate 5 or California Highway 99 via Porterville and Springville on California Highway 190, or from Visalia on California Highway 198. Be sure to stop at forest headquarters to pick up a map of the area since some of the trails described in this section are not marked on the topo. Both wilderness permits and campfire permits are required for overnight visits and are issued in Springville. There are no trailhead quotas.

There are a number of beautiful campgrounds nestled in the sequoia groves in Mountain Home State Forest at the wilderness's edge from which to explore the surrounding area. These are free of charge and are available on a first-come, first-served basis. You can contact the state forest for further information at (559) 539–2321 in summer, (559) 539–2855 in winter.

1 Tule River to Eastside Trail Loop

A scenic low-elevation loop day hike among the world's largest trees with numerous short, steep ups and downs. Streams can be dangerous during spring runoff.

Start: Hidden Falls Campground on the Middle Fork of the Tule River.
Total distance: 8.2 miles.
Difficulty: Moderately strenuous.
Total climbing: 1980 feet.
Trail traffic: Light, except near campgrounds.
Best months: Mid-May through October.
Maps: Mountain Home State Forest map available (free) on a rack outside the state forest headquarters; USGS Moses Mountain and Camp Wishon quads; and the Golden Trout and South Sierra Wilderness map. The USGS and Forest Service maps are useful for topographic detail, but do not show parts of this trail.
Permits: None required.
Trailhead facilities: Water and toilets at Hidden Falls walk-in campground. Nearest gas, phones, and groceries in Springville.

Finding the trailhead: From the Tule River Ranger Station in Springville, 8 miles west of Porterville on California Highway 190, drive 4 miles northeast to Balch Park Road and turn left (north) toward Mountain Home State Forest. Go 4 more miles to Bear Creek Road, turn right (northeast), then drive for 23 winding miles to a Y intersection. The headquarters of Mountain Home State Forest is just 0.2 mile to the left. Pick up a map here, then return to the intersection and follow the right fork southeast, then north. In another mile reach another Y intersection with a sign directing you to the right on Summit Road toward Shake Camp and Hidden Falls Campgrounds. The road is not paved beyond this point but is fine for ordinary passenger cars. Follow the signs for 5 miles to Hidden Falls. The road crosses the Middle Fork of the Tule River just past the campground entrance, and just beyond the crossing is a day-use parking area on the right. Overnight parking is prohibited.

The Hike

This hike wanders along the border of Mountain Home State Forest and the Golden Trout Wilderness, upon which is superimposed Giant Sequoia National Monument. Don't be too concerned about the tangle of government agencies that administer the area; the trail itself is usually clear enough. The terrain it traverses resembles Paul Bunyan's washboard with numerous short, steep ups and downs, in and out of ravines cut by numerous creeks plunging down to meet the Tule River in a series of cascades and waterfalls. These can be dangerous to ford during the high point of spring snowmelt.

To begin, cross the road from the parking area to the sign that says RIVER TRAIL, REDWOOD CROSSING 1.5 MILES. Just a few feet up, the path splits near a stone water fountain. The left fork takes you to the riverside where anglers and others have fouled the otherwise lovely shore with litter. Follow the right fork uphill into the

silent beauty of the giant sequoia forest. Here the most delicate of ferns and flowers emphasize the almost incomprehensible immensity of the big trees. Even full-grown white firs, the usual associates of the sequoias, seem puny and insignificant beside their colossal neighbors.

At mile 0.6 watch for an unsigned junction on the right marked by a duck or cairn. Climb fairly steeply up this right-hand fork northeast to meet the Eastside Trail at a sign at mile 1.0. (If you should miss this junction, you can continue north along the River Trail to Redwood Crossing. Do not cross the river, but follow the trail to the right a few yards to a sign that directs you back to the Eastside Trail. You will only have come about 0.5 mile out of your way.) From the Eastside Trail junction, turn right (southeast); the left fork climbs northward to Summit Lake. The big trees thin out as you leave the moister river bottom, giving way to black oak, white fir, incense cedar, and sugar and ponderosa pine among which enormous granite boulders are scattered. The trail bobs up and down, allowing glimpses of the ridge that culminates in Moses Mountain across the Tule River Canyon. At one point the path drops into a rocky creekbed and disappears, but picks up again on the far side behind a fallen log. It negotiates several more little creeks lined with metamorphic rock outcrops that are extremely slippery when wet.

At mile 2.1 the McAnlis Trail, a shortcut down to the road and campgrounds of Mountain Home State Forest, joins this one on the right. The junction is signed, though the sign only mentions the Griswold Trail ahead and Redwood Crossing behind. Climb straight ahead to the high point of the route at 6,800 feet then descend to ford a little branch of Galena Creek, whose banks bloom with a dazzling display of flowers that includes fragrant leopard lilies and mints, and some very pungent wild onions. Pick your way carefully down a gravelly, slippery slope to cross the main fork of Galena Creek where it tumbles over more or less regular granite steps in a pleasing series of little falls. The sunny slabs beside the creek invite loafing, sunbathing, or lunch. If it is early in the season and if the water is high and swift, turn back. The wet rock is as slick as glass, and the force of the water will grab you if you lose your balance even for a second. If it is safe to cross, head up out of this drainage and pass over a hump on trail that has not been cleared of fallen timber for some time. Then descend steeply, sliding and kicking up dust, into the canyon of Silver Creek. Like most watercourses in the area, Silver Creek is lined with hazelnut bushes. The nuts ripen in late summer and make a delicious snack.

At mile 4.7 reach the Griswold Trail junction and turn right (southwest). There is no sign, but the way is clear, and from this point on, the Griswold Trail is shown on the topo and Golden Trout Wilderness maps. Descend a long series of switchbacks, reach a junction at mile 5.8 near the battered remnants of an illegible sign,

◀ *Hidden Falls on the Middle Fork of the Tule River from the campground*

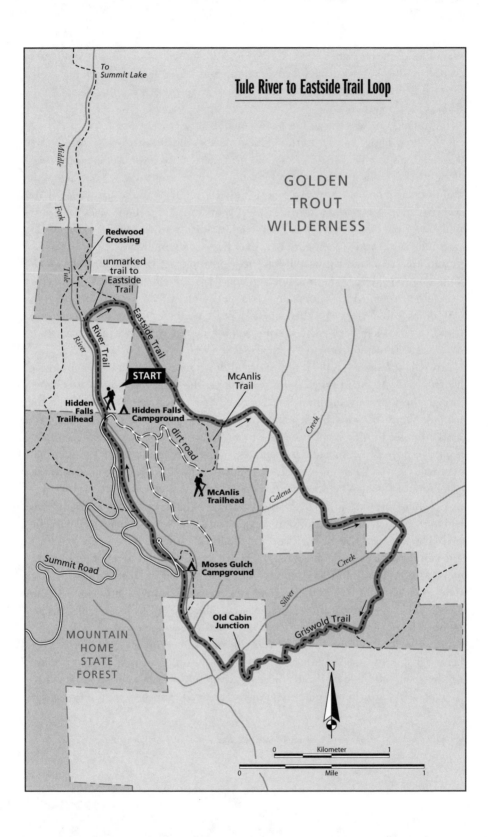

Tule River to Eastside Trail Loop

To
Summit Lake

**GOLDEN
TROUT
WILDERNESS**

Middle

Fork

Tule

**Redwood
Crossing**

unmarked
trail to
Eastside
Trail

Eastside Trail

River

River Trail

START

McAnlis
Trail

**Hidden Falls
Trailhead**

△ **Hidden Falls
Campground**

dirt road

Creek

**McAnlis
Trailhead**

Galena

**Moses Gulch
Campground**

Creek

Summit Road

Silver

**Old Cabin
Junction**

Griswold Trail

**MOUNTAIN
HOME
STATE
FOREST**

N

0   Kilometer   1

0   Mile   1

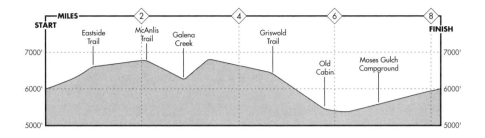

and turn right just before you reach the Tule River. After a very few more switch-backs past some old mine workings, arrive at Silver Creek once again and recross it on logs to an old miner's cabin. This is the lowest point on the route at 5,420 feet. In a short time recross Galena Creek. Beyond, the trail splits again. Either fork will take you across the river, the right one on a log, the left one over rocks. On the west bank now, turn right and follow the river upstream. Climb a few switchbacks to a dirt road at mile 6.9, on which you turn right again to the entrance of Moses Gulch Campground. Pick up the trail that skirts the left (west) side of the camping area and winds its way upward to meet the lower campsites of Hidden Falls Campground. Continue upstream through this campground past some pretty pools into which tumbles little Hidden Falls. The trailhead parking area is just beyond and above the falls.

Key Points

0.0 Hidden Falls Campground.

0.6 Unmarked trail to Eastside Trail, turn right.

1.0 Eastside Trail, turn right (southeast).

2.1 McAnlis Trail, continue straight.

4.7 Griswold Trail, turn right (southwest).

5.8 Old cabin junction, turn right.

6.9 Moses Gulch Campground road, turn right.

8.2 Hidden Falls Campground.

2 McAnlis Trail

A shorter loop day hike through the Big Trees with an optional visit to a waterfall. This hike avoids the numerous ups and downs and the many stream crossings of Hike 1, Tule River/Eastside Trail.

Start: Hidden Falls Campground on the Middle Fork of the Tule River.
Total distance: 3.6 miles.
Difficulty: Easy to moderate.
Total climbing: 1,380 feet.
Trail traffic: Light, except near campgrounds.
Best months: Mid-May through October.
Maps: Mountain Home State Forest map, available (free) on a rack outside the state forest headquarters; USGS Moses Mountain and Camp Wishon quads and the Forest Service Golden Trout and South Sierra Wilderness map. The USGS and United States Forest Service maps are useful for topographic detail, but do not show parts of this trail.
Permits: None.
Trailhead facilities: Water and toilets at Hidden Falls walk-in campground. Nearest gas, phones, and groceries in Springville.

Finding the trailhead: From the Tule River Ranger Station in Springville, 8 miles west of Porterville on California Highway 190, drive 4 miles northeast to Balch Park Road and turn left (north) toward Mountain Home State Forest. Go 4 more miles to Bear Creek Road, turn right (northeast), then drive for 23 winding miles to a Y intersection. The headquarters of Mountain Home State Forest is just 0.2 mile to the left. Pick up a map here, then return to the intersection and follow the right fork southeast, then north. In another mile reach another Y intersection with a sign directing you to the right on Summit Road toward Shake Camp and Hidden Falls Campgrounds. The road is not paved beyond this point but is fine for ordinary passenger cars. Follow the signs for 5 miles to Hidden Falls. The road crosses the Middle Fork of the Tule River just past the campground entrance, and just beyond the crossing is a day-use parking area on the right. Overnight parking is prohibited here.

The Hike

Cross the road from the parking area to the sign that says RIVER TRAIL, REDWOOD CROSSING 1.5 MILES. Just a few feet up, the path splits near a stone water fountain. Follow the right fork uphill. At mile 0.6 watch for an unsigned junction on the right marked by a cairn. Follow this right hand fork northeast to meet the Eastside Trail at a sign at mile 1.0. (If you should miss this junction, you can continue north along the River Trail to Redwood Crossing. Do not cross the river but follow the trail to the right a few yards to a sign that directs you back to the Eastside Trail. You will only have come about 0.5 mile out of your way.) From the Eastside Trail junction

Streamside hazelnut bushes provide crunchy snacks in late summer and fall.

turn right (southeast). At McAnlis Trail turnoff from the eastside trail at mile 2.1. The junction is marked by a sign pointing back toward Redwood Crossing and forward toward the Griswold Trail, but does not mention the McAnlis Trail at all. The turnoff is obvious, however. Turn right (south) and descend on moderately steep switchbacks to a clearing at mile 2.6. This is the McAnlis Trailhead and the end of a secondary state forest road. There are no signs of any kind, but there is only one way to go. Stroll down the road, really not much more than a wide trail. You are unlikely to meet any traffic. Keep right at each of the two unmarked junctions, and in an easy mile find yourself back at the River Trailhead and your car.

If you have time and energy, you might want to continue about 0.5 mile farther along the Eastside Trail past the McAnlis Trail junction to visit Galena Creek. If the water is not too high, the flat sunny rocks at the base of the little series of waterfalls make a good picnic spot. Just keep in mind that while this detour is short, there is some steep downhill hiking to Galena Creek that you'll have to climb back up again before you head back down the McAnlis Trail.

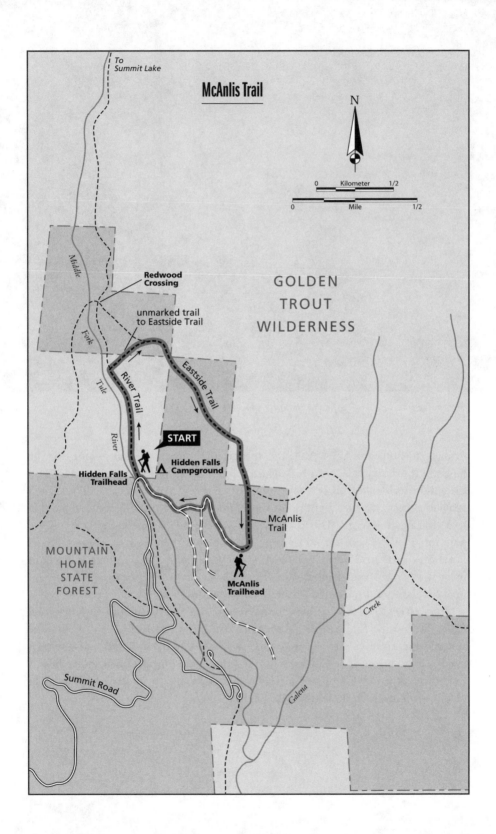

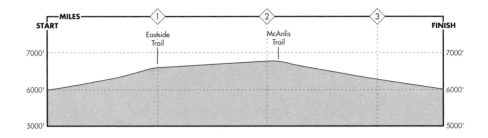

Key Points

0.0 Hidden Falls Campground.

0.6 Unmarked junction, turn right.

1.0 Eastside Trail, turn right (southeast).

2.1 McAnlis Trail, turn right.

2.6 McAnlis Trailhead/secondary road's end.

3.6 Hidden Falls Campground.

3 Shake Camp and the Tule River

A loop backpack or vigorous day hike exploring a significant portion of the lower Middle Fork of the Tule River drainage. It's a beautiful hike with lots of variety, but is much more strenuous than it seems since there are lots of steep ups and downs.

Start: Shake Camp Campground in Mountain Home State Forest.
Total distance: 10.6 miles.
Difficulty: Moderate as a backpack; strenuous as a day hike.
Total climbing: 2,050 feet.
Trail traffic: Light, except near campgrounds.
Best months: Mid-May through October.
Maps: Mountain Home State Forest map, available (free) on a rack outside the state forest headquarters; USGS Moses Mountain and Camp Wishon quads; and the Golden Trout and South Sierra Wilderness map. The USGS and Forest Service maps are useful for topographic detail but do not show parts of this trail.
Permits: None for a day hike. Required and available at the Tule River Ranger Station in Springville for overnights.
Trailhead facilities: Camping, water, and toilets. Nearest phones, gas, and groceries in Springville.

Finding the trailhead: From the Tule River Ranger Station in Springville, 8 miles west of Porterville on California Highway 190, drive 4 miles northeast to Balch Park Road and turn left (north) toward Mountain Home State Forest. Go 4 more miles to Bear Creek Road, turn right (northeast), then drive for 23 winding miles to a Y intersection. The headquarters of Mountain Home State Forest is just 0.2 mile to the left. Pick up a map here, then return to the intersection and follow the right fork southeast, then north. In another mile reach another Y intersection with a sign directing you to the right on Summit Road toward Shake Camp. The road is not paved beyond this point but is fine for ordinary passenger cars. Follow the signs for 3 miles, passing the pack station, to the trailhead just next to the Shake Camp Campground and a public corral.

The Hike

Set out northward past the big trailhead sign on the well-worn Long Meadow Trail beneath ponderosa and sugar pines, incense cedar, and white fir, alternating with open spots of gooseberry, ceanothus, manzanita, and kit-kit-dizze. Climb fairly steeply at first, then begin a rolling up-and-down progress along a slope, which, after about a mile, begins to lose more altitude than it gains. Giant sequoias begin to appear at about the same time you first pick up the rush of Tule River. By the time you reach Redwood Crossing, the volume has swollen to a roar and the size and density of the huge trees have increased to provide an appropriately grand setting for the cascading water. The river is fairly shallow here but flows with tremendous force early in the year, so ford with great care. There is an enormous downed sequoia just upstream that can be used as a bridge, but it lies on a steep slant and is somewhat slippery.

A miner's cabin among the giant sequoias along the Tule River

Just beyond the crossing an unmarked trail heads right, downstream, toward Hidden Falls Campground. Ignore this and continue a few yards up out of the riverbed to the official signed junction that points north toward Summit Lake and south toward Hidden Falls Campground. Turn right (southeast) and in 0.3 mile meet another junction with a sign that says (inaccurately) REDWOOD CROSSING 0.1 MILES. Continue straight ahead (southeast) along the Eastside Trail. The Big Trees thin out as you leave the moister river bottom, giving way again to mixed oak-conifer forest amid which enormous granite boulders are scattered. The trail bobs up and down, allowing glimpses of the ridge that culminates in Moses Mountain across the Tule River Canyon. At one point the path drops into a rocky creekbed and disappears, but it picks up again on the far side behind a fallen log. It negotiates several more little creeks lined with metamorphic rock outcrops that are extremely slippery when wet.

At mile 3.6 the McAnlis Trail, a shortcut down to the road and campgrounds of Mountain Home State Forest, joins this one on the right. The junction is signed, though the sign only mentions the Griswold Trail ahead and Redwood Crossing behind. Climb straight ahead to the high point of the route at 6,800 feet, then descend to ford a little branch of Galena Creek whose banks bloom with a dazzling

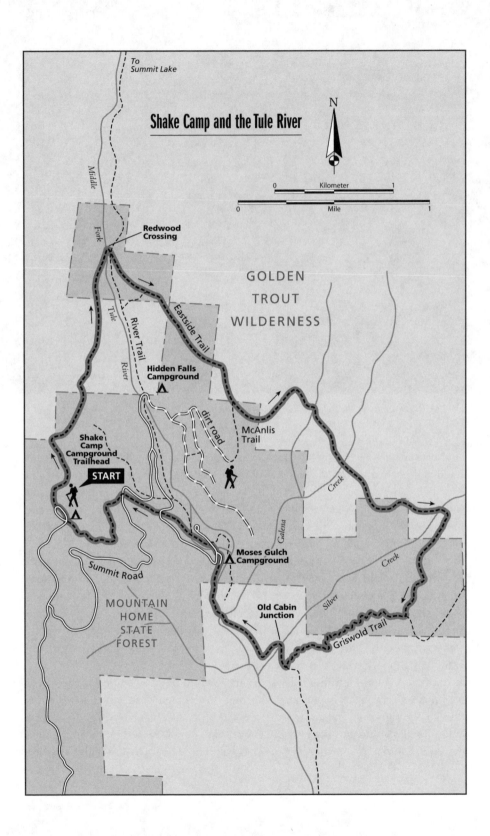

Shake Camp and the Tule River

To Summit Lake

N

0   Kilometer   1

0   Mile   1

Middle

Fork

Redwood
Crossing

GOLDEN

TROUT

WILDERNESS

Tule

River Trail

Eastside Trail

River

Hidden Falls
Campground

dirt road

McAnlis
Trail

Shake
Camp
Campground
Trailhead

START

Galena

Creek

Moses Gulch
Campground

Summit Road

MOUNTAIN
HOME
STATE
FOREST

Old Cabin
Junction

Silver

Creek

Griswold Trail

display of flowers that includes fragrant leopard lilies and mints, and some very pungent wild onions. Pick your way carefully down a gravelly, slippery slope to cross the main fork of Galena Creek where it tumbles over granite steps in a pleasing series of little falls. The sunny slabs beside the creek invite loafing, sunbathing, or lunch. If it is early in the season and the water is high and swift, turn back. The wet rock is slick as glass, and the force of the water will grab you if you lose your balance even for a second. If it is safe to cross, head up out of this drainage and pass over a hump on trail that has not been cleared of fallen timber for some time. Then descend steeply, sliding and kicking up dust, into the canyon of Silver Creek. Like most watercourses in the area, Silver Creek is lined with hazelnut bushes. The nuts ripen in late summer and make a delicious snack.

At mile 6.2 reach the Griswold Trail junction and turn right (southwest). There is no sign, but the way is clear, and from this point on, the Griswold Trail is shown on the topo and Golden Trout Wilderness maps. Descend a long series of switchbacks, reach a junction at mile 7.3 near the battered remnants of an illegible sign, and turn right just before you reach the Tule River. After a very few more switchbacks past some old mine workings, arrive at Silver Creek once again and cross it on logs to an old miner's cabin. This is the lowest point on the route at 5,420 feet. In a short time recross Galena Creek. Beyond, the trail splits again. Either fork will take you across the river, the right one on a log, the left one over rocks. On the west bank now, turn right and follow the river upstream. Climb a few switchbacks to a dirt road at mile 8.4, on which you turn right again into the entrance of Moses Gulch Campground.

At the upper end of the campground, the Griswold Trail splits at mile 8.6. The right fork follows the Tule River northward to Hidden Falls Campground. Follow the left fork toward Shake Camp on trail that parallels, then crosses the campground road, climbs steeply up a gully, crosses the road a second time, then loops north, south, then north again in a big S curve to reach the Shake Camp Trailhead just beyond the corral.

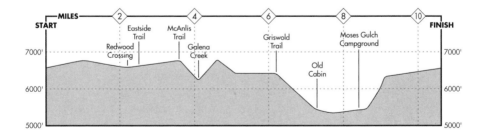

Key Points

0.0 Shake Camp Trailhead.

2.2 Redwood Crossing, turn right.

2.5 Eastside Trail, continue straight ahead (southeast).

3.6 McAnlis Trail, continue straight.

6.2 Griswold Trail, turn right (southwest).

7.3 Old cabin junction, turn right.

8.4 Moses Gulch Campground road, turn right.

8.6 Shake Camp/Hidden Falls junction, turn left.

10.6 Back to Shake Camp.

The Little Kern and Tributaries

The drainage of the Little Kern River (actually the west fork of the Kern) occupies the western slope of the Sierra. It is primarily forest country, but with what a variety of forests! The cooler, damper pockets at lower elevations shelter groves of giant sequoias; on drier sites grow more open stands of mixed conifers such as yellow pine, sugar pine, incense cedar, and white fir. Higher up are quiet red fir and lodgepole forests that finally give way to picturesque subalpine species like foxtail pines and junipers. Interspersed with these are lots of marvelously flowery meadows, sparkling mountain lakes (home to hungry trout), and some spectacular waterfalls.

While none of these hikes takes you above 10,000 feet in elevation, this is rugged country all the same. The innumerable tributaries of the Little Kern have carved deep gullies into of the mountainsides; most hikes involve lots of ups and downs that make total-climbing figures misleading. Allow more time than you think you'll need for hikes in this area.

Trail conditions vary in this part of the wilderness. Some of the trails are popular with anglers and equestrians, who use packers to take them to their favorite spots; these get regular maintenance. A few more lightly used routes get infrequent attention, and you will have to do some bushwhacking. That's the trade-off: The more solitude, the greater the route-finding challenge.

These midelevation western-slope forests receive the Sierra's heaviest precipitation. In a year of heavy snowpack, or even during a moderate year at the height of spring runoff, gentle burbling creeks can become raging torrents, impossible to ford. The Little Kern itself can be dangerous well into July. Be sure to check with rangers in advance of any hike, especially in the early season, for information about stream crossings. Roads to trailheads in the higher country are seldom clear before mid-June. The backpacking season doesn't really get under way until July—even after roads are open, snow can linger late into the season in the shady ravines, obscuring trails, making camping damp and uncomfortable.

You'll probably be checking in at the Tule River Ranger Station or perhaps at the ranger station in Kernville anyway in order to pick up your wilderness permit and campfire permit. The entire Little Kern drainage lies within the Tule River Ranger District of Sequoia National Forest. There are no trailhead quotas in effect, and you can request your wilderness permit by mail, but are required to pick up your campfire permit in person (whether or not you plan to have a fire). California campfire permits are available at most Forest Service offices and are valid for a year.

All of the Little Kern trailheads require a good deal of slow (though scenic) mountain driving, whether you approach from the west via Porterville or the east via Kennedy Meadows. The route along the Kern River from Kernville on County Road M99 is the most spectacular of all, but like the others is relatively narrow and winding. There are a number of small resorts along the way where you can get gas and supplies, but their hours are often limited. Make sure you have a full tank of gas before you leave the last town. There is no public transportation. Sequoia National Forest has fifty developed campgrounds, or you can choose your own spot. Some campgrounds open on a first-come, first-served basis, while others require reservations. Some have more elaborate facilities and charge higher fees. You can check them out by calling (877) 444–6777, reserve online at www.reserveusa.com, or consult the USDA Forest Service Sequoia National Forest map.

4 Maggie Lakes

An out-and-back backpack to a trio of classic glacial lakes with
While the net elevation gain for this hike is only 1,050 feet, the
and downs in between that you'll be gaining and losing at leas
much.

Start: Summit Trailhead.
Total distance: 18.6 miles.
Difficulty: Moderate.
Total climbing: 2,400 feet.
Trail traffic: Light on weekdays, medium on weekends.
Best months: June through October.
Maps: USGS Camp Nelson and Quinn Peak quads; Forest Service Golden Trout and South Sierra Wilderness map.

Permits: Required and available at the Tule River Ranger Station in Springville. A California campfire permit, valid for a full year, is also required and may be issued here.
Trailhead facilities: None. Nearest gas, phones, and groceries at Ponderosa, 2 miles south of Quaking Aspen on the Western Divide Highway.

Finding the trailhead: From the west, begin at the Tule River Ranger Station in Springville, 8 miles west of Porterville on California Highway 190. Drive 27 miles to a junction where California Highway 190 becomes County Road M107, the Western Divide Highway. Turn left (north) onto Forest Road 21S50, North Road. A sign points to several trailheads, including SUMMIT, 11 MILES. In 4 miles the road splits and becomes unpaved, though it's fine for passenger cars. Turn left here and in 7 miles reach the road's end at the signed trailhead in a clearing.

The Hike

This is the first leg of the Boy Scouts' Silver Knapsack Trail (see Hike 12). The large sign at the trailhead indicating the mileage to various local destinations is less accurate than the smaller sign above it that gives the distance to Maggie Lakes as 9 miles.

Beginning at an elevation of 8,250 feet, the Summit Trail descends gently through fir forest to cross the south fork of Mountaineer Creek as it tumbles down a notch through a profusion of wildflowers. As the path leaves the creekbed, it traverses a windward-facing hillside where the constant dampness of the prevailing breeze has clothed the trees in luxuriant fur coats of lichens in a startling shade of chartreuse. The route attains a ridgetop and rounds a little granite knob from whence the Little Kern River drainage and the Great Western Divide become visible to the northeast, Maggie Mountain appears to the north, and the smog creeps up from the Central Valley to the west. It drops down off the ridge to reenter deep, hushed, red and white fir forest. Little sunlight reaches the floor, so the only wildflowers that grow here—odd little coral root orchids, pinedrops, and snowplants—have no green leaves, but live on decaying material or living roots of other plants

beneath the surface. Now and then spaces between the trees reveal sunny and somehow mysterious little grassy clearings.

At mile 3.0 is a junction marked by dilapidated signs where a trail heads west down to Camp Wishon. Just beyond this lies Jacobsen Meadow, brilliant green and blooming with knotweed, senecio, corn lily, and yarrow. There is a campsite here, but the meadow is fed only by muddy little seeps that do not provide much water. At Mowery Meadow (mile 4.0) another seldom maintained trail coming from Grey Meadow joins this one on the right. Continue straight ahead (north) to reach oddly named Alpine Meadow, another green and pleasant camping spot that is not at all alpine. Now the Summit Trail climbs moderate switchbacks until it meets the faint Griswold Trail (mile 5.3), where all that remains of a sign are a few splinters. This route plunges downhill to the left (west) toward Mountain Home State Forest and Sequoia National Monument. A newer sign in a tree just beyond the junction identifies Griswold Meadow.

Climb another mile through the now familiar pattern of alternating forest and meadow to reach the top of a shoulder at about 9,300 feet, highest point on this hike, for a startling change of scene. Lonely foxtail pines cling stubbornly to great expanses of wind- and ice-scoured rock. A series of granite glacial cirques and peaks begins at nearby Maggie Mountain and marches off to the north to meet the Great Western Divide. Here the Summit Trail swings left (west), then drops on unstable footing to cross a year-round creek. Just beyond, at mile 8.3, is a junction with several campsites nearby. The right fork leads to private property in Pecks Canyon. The left turns west toward Maggie Lakes. The trail rises and falls over fingers of glacial rubble, between which lie depressions that can be unpleasantly boggy and buggy.

Lower Maggie Lake lies in a cirque beyond the final moraine at mile 9.3. Its dramatic backdrop is the conical sister peak of Maggie Mountain. (Maggie herself is hidden behind.) There are plenty of good campsites at the lake's north end; just be sure to settle at least 100 feet from the water's edge. There are good-sized trout in the lakes and plenty of opportunities for exploration. The smallest, middle Maggie Lake is tucked into a little pocket just beyond the low ridge below the center of the conical peak. To reach it most easily, follow the western shore around the lower lake. To continue to the largest, upper lake, head uphill to your right (west) from the middle lake and scramble toward the lowest point of the ridge above. You will probably pick up a well-worn use trail that leads to the lakeside. There are campsites at the north end of this lake, too.

Return the way you came.

Maggie Lakes in the cirque beneath a sister peak of Maggie Mountain

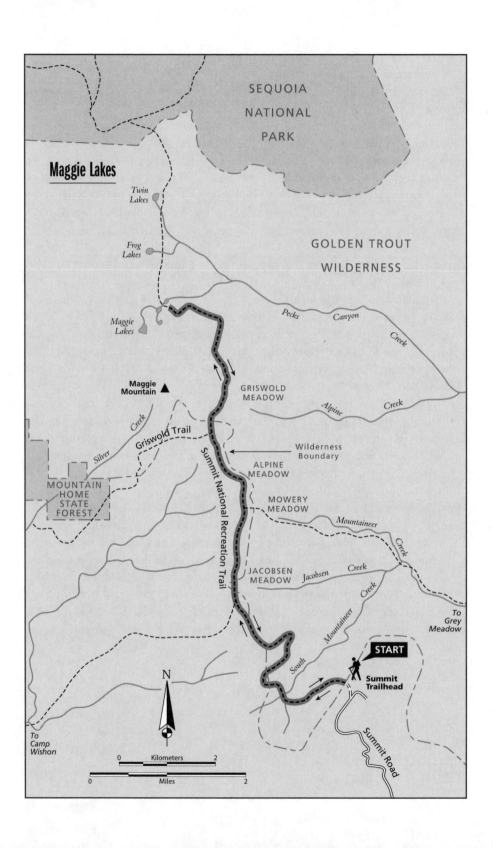

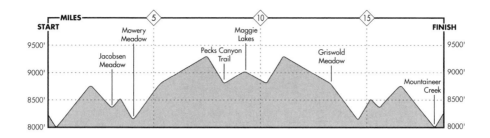

Key Points

0.0 Summit Trailhead.

3.0 Jacobsen Meadow.

4.0 Mowery Meadow and trail from Grey Meadow, continue straight (north).

5.3 Griswold Trail, continue straight (north).

8.3 Pecks Canyon Trail, south end, turn left (west).

9.3 Maggie Lakes.

18.6 Summit Trailhead.

5 Summit Lake

A backpack from deep pine and fir forests to the land above the trees and back again. Along the way are lots of lakes, wildflower gardens, and the opportunity to bag an easy peak.

Start: Summit Trailhead.
Total distance: 27.0 miles.
Difficulty: Strenuous as a two-day outing, moderate for a longer trip.
Total climbing: 3,830 feet.
Trail traffic: Light to medium.
Best months: Mid-June to October.
Maps: USGS Camp Nelson, Quinn Peak, Moses Mountain, and Camp Wishon quads; Forest Service Golden Trout and South Sierra Wilderness map.
Permits: A wilderness permit and a California campfire permit are both required and are issued at the Tule River Ranger Station in Springville.
Trailhead facilities: None. Nearest gas, phones, and groceries at Ponderosa, 2 miles south of Quaking Aspen on the Western Divide Highway.

Finding the trailhead: From the Tule River Ranger Station in Springville, 8 miles west of Porterville on California Highway 190, drive 27 miles to a junction where California Highway 190 becomes County Road M107, the Western Divide Highway. Turn left (north) onto Forest Road 21S50, North Road. A sign directs you to several trailheads, including SUMMIT, 11 MILES. In 4 miles the road splits and becomes unpaved, though it's fine for passenger cars. Turn left here and in 7 miles reach the road's end at the signed trailhead in a clearing.

The Hike

The trail descends gently to cross the south fork of Mountaineer Creek. As the path leaves the creek bed it traverses a windward-facing hillside until the route attains a ridgetop and rounds a little granite knob. At mile 3.0 is a junction marked by dilapidated signs where a trail heads west down to Camp Wishon. Keep going right, just beyond this lies Jacobsen Meadow. At Mowery Meadow (mile 4.0) another seldom-maintained trail coming from Grey Meadow joins this one on the right. Continue straight ahead (north) to Alpine Meadow. The path climbs moderate switchbacks until it meets the faint Griswold Trail (mile 5.3). Take the right fork and climb another mile to reach the top of a shoulder at about 9,300 feet. Here the trail swings left (west), then drops to cross a year-round creek. Just beyond, at mile 8.3 is a junction. Follow the left fork (west) toward Maggie Lakes. Lower Maggie Lake lies in a cirque beyond the final moraine at mile 9.3.

Leaving the north end of the lowest lake, cross over a little rise and descend westward through an open forest of red fir, lodgepole, and western white and foxtail pine to Frog Lakes—actually just one lake and one mud puddle connected by

Summit Lake offers good camping, fishing, and lots of wildflowers.

a log-choked gulch. Beyond the lake(s) the Summit Trail loses some elevation then begins to climb again along a fabulously flowery little watercourse to reach grassy Twin Lakes. There is camping nearby, but conscientious visitors will use a site 100 feet from the water, avoiding the disgraceful packer camp tucked between the two lakes, full of trash and much too near the shore. Beyond Twin Lakes the trail continues to climb, passing the junction (not shown on the Golden Trout Wilderness map) with the north end of the Pecks Canyon Trail at mile 11.3. Keep left (north) and climb steadily to the shoulder of Sheep Mountain at the border of Sequoia National Park (mile 12.3). If you are traveling with firearms or pets, you must turn around here. This is the highest point on the trail at 9,850 feet. Don't miss the opportunity to bag Sheep Mountain while you are here. Just follow the ridge on your left southward to the top. It's an easy walk of about 0.5 mile round trip (not included in this trip's mileage or total-climbing figures) with sensational views from its 10,000-foot summit of most of the western half of the Golden Trout Wilderness and the Great Western Divide.

After returning to the Summit Trail, drop down off the ridge to the west and keep left at an unsigned but obvious path that cuts off to the right (northeast) at mile

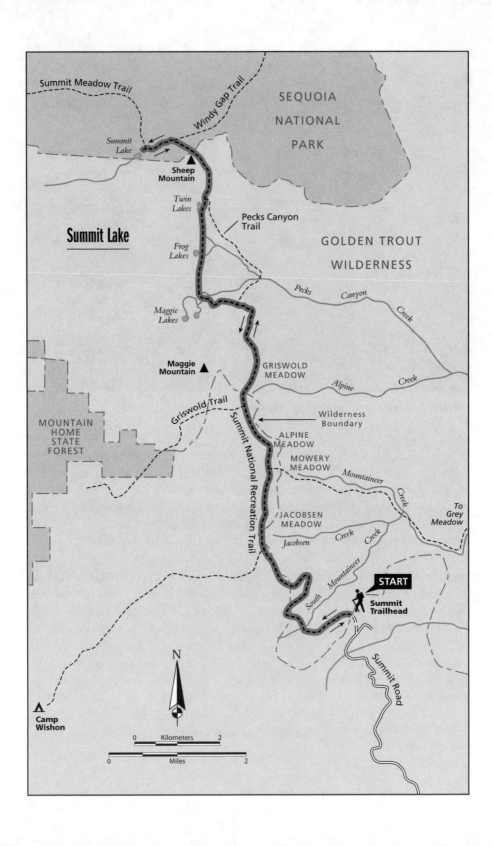

Summit Lake

Summit Meadow Trail

Windy Gap Trail

SEQUOIA
NATIONAL
PARK

*Summit
Lake*

**Sheep
Mountain**

*Twin
Lakes*

Pecks Canyon
Trail

*Frog
Lakes*

GOLDEN TROUT

WILDERNESS

Pecks   *Canyon*   *Creek*

*Maggie
Lakes*

**Maggie
Mountain**

GRISWOLD
MEADOW

Alpine   *Creek*

Griswold Trail

Wilderness
Boundary

MOUNTAIN
HOME
STATE
FOREST

ALPINE
MEADOW

MOWERY
MEADOW

Summit National Recreation Trail

Mountaineer

Creek

*To
Grey
Meadow*

JACOBSEN
MEADOW

Jacobsen   *Creek*   *Creek*

START

**Summit
Trailhead**

South   Mountaineer

N

Summit Road

**Camp
Wishon**

0   Kilometers   2

0   Miles   2

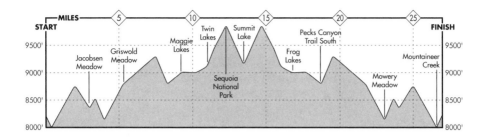

12.6. Descend through forest and more flowery meadows fed by dozens of little seeps and trickles. Soon Summit Lake appears below, and a short spur trail on the right at mile 13.5 cuts back northeast just a few yards to its shore. This pretty spot sparkles with a kaleidoscopic mixture of flowers: shooting stars, penstemon, fireweed, Labrador tea, lupines, asters, heather, daisies, and countless others. There are plenty of campsites and a hitching rail for horses. When you must, retrace your steps to the trailhead.

Key Points

0.0 Summit Trailhead.
3.0 Jacobsen Meadow.
4.0 Mowery Meadow and trail from Grey Meadow, continue straight (north).
5.3 Griswold Trail, continue straight (north).
8.3 Pecks Canyon Trail, south end, turn left (west).
9.3 Maggie Lakes.
11.3 Pecks Canyon Trail, keep left (north).
12.3 Sequoia National Park border.
12.6 Windy Gap connector trail, keep left.
13.5 Summit Lake.
27.0 Summit Trailhead.

6 Summit Lake Loop

A lollipop loop through a wide range of elevations and habitats from giant sequoia forests to timberline, as well as a series of inviting lakes.

Start: Summit Trailhead.
Total distance: 30.3 miles.
Difficulty: Strenuous.
Total climbing: 5,050 feet.
Trail traffic: Light.
Best months: Mid-June through October, but stream crossings may be impossible at the height of spring snowmelt. Check with rangers before setting out.
Maps: USGS Camp Nelson, Quinn Peak, Moses Mountain, and Camp Wishon quads;

Forest Service Golden Trout and South Sierra Wilderness map; Mountain Home State Forest map.
Permits: Required and available at the Tule River Ranger Station in Springville. A California campfire permit, valid for a full year, is also required and may be issued here.
Trailhead facilities: None. Nearest gas, phone, and groceries at Ponderosa, 2 miles south of Quaking Aspen on the Western Divide Highway.

Finding the trailhead: From the Tule River Ranger Station in Springville, 8 miles west of Porterville on California Highway 190, drive 27 miles to a junction where CA 190 becomes County Road M107, the Western Divide Highway. Turn left (north) onto Forest Service 21S50, North Road. A sign directs you to several trailheads, including SUMMIT, 11 MILES. In 4 miles the road splits and becomes unpaved, though it's fine for passenger cars. Turn left here and in 7 miles reach the road's end at the signed trailhead in a clearing.

The Hike

The trail descends gently to cross the south fork of Mountaineer Creek. As the path leaves the creek bed it traverses a windward-facing hillside to a ridgetop where it rounds a little granite knob. At mile 3.0 is a junction marked by dilapidated signs where a trail heads west down to Camp Wishon. Stay right to Jacobsen Meadow and Mowery Meadow where another seldom-maintained trail from Grey Meadow joins from the right. Continue straight ahead (north) to Alpine Meadow. The path climbs moderate switchbacks until it meets the faint Griswold Trail (mile 5.3). Take the right fork and climb another mile to reach the top of a shoulder at about 9,300 feet. Here the trail swings left (west), then drops to cross a year-round creek. Just beyond, at mile 8.3 is a junction. Follow the left fork (west) toward Maggie Lakes. Leaving the north end of the lowest lake, cross over a little rise and descend westward to Frog Lakes. The trail loses some elevation then begins to climb along a little watercourse to reach grassy Twin Lakes. The trail continues to climb, passing the junction (not shown on the Golden Trout Wilderness map) with the north end of the Pecks Canyon Trail at mile 11.3. Keep left (north) and climb steadily to the shoulder of Sheep Mountain at the border of Sequoia National Park (mile 12.3). Drop down off

Peaks of the Great Western Divide from Sheep Peak above Summit Lake

the ridge to the west and keep left at an unsigned but obvious path that cuts off to the right (northeast) at mile 12.6. Descend to a short spur trail to Summit Lake on the right at mile 13.5.

Leave the lakeshore on the little spur near the outlet stream that will become the Middle Fork of the Tule River. Pick up Summit Trail again, cross the outlet, and descend, sometimes quite steeply, through open brushy country, enjoying wide views of Sheep Mountain to the east and Moses Mountain to the southwest. Recross the creek, descend into forest, and drop relentlessly to meet and cross another tributary stream where there is a campsite, then pass the Tuohy Gap Trail in a clearing at mile 16.0. The east fork of the nascent Tule River coming from Summit Lake is almost lost as it winds its puny way among boulders in a huge rocky gorge much too big for such a small volume of water. Continue south on the Long Meadow Trail, paralleling the river for a time, then cross to the east side, wading carefully. Pass some fine campsites between the river and the trail, near which numerous seeps and runnels nourish a riot of exuberantly blooming flowers of all kinds and colors. Not far beyond the last of these, the shade deepens and you enter the magical stillness of the giant sequoia forest. The size of the trees should make the atmosphere of these groves intimidating, but somehow they seem to welcome rather than threaten the traveler.

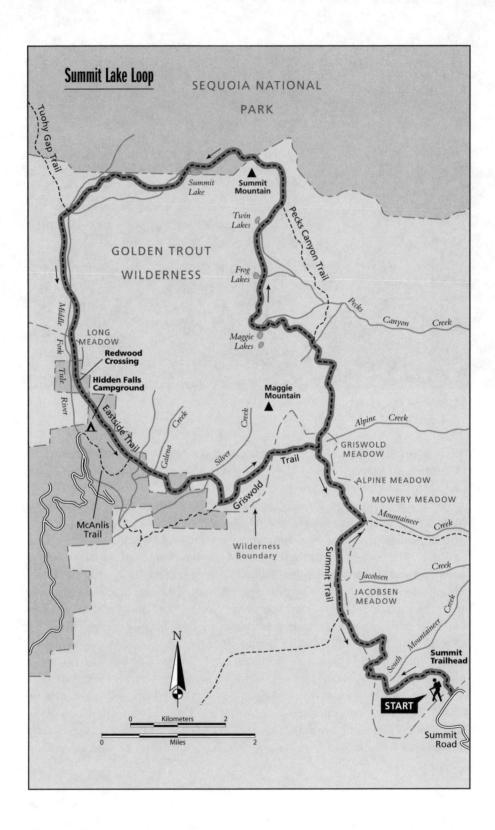

Summit Lake Loop

SEQUOIA NATIONAL PARK

Tuohy Gap Trail

Summit Lake

Summit Mountain ▲

Twin Lakes

Pecks Canyon Trail

GOLDEN TROUT WILDERNESS

Frog Lakes

Middle Fork Tule River

Pecks Canyon Creek

LONG MEADOW

Redwood Crossing

Hidden Falls Campground

Maggie Lakes

Eastside Trail

Galena Creek

Silver Creek

Maggie Mountain ▲

Alpine Creek

GRISWOLD MEADOW

McAnlis Trail

Griswold Trail

ALPINE MEADOW

MOWERY MEADOW

Mountaineer Creek

Wilderness Boundary

Summit Trail

Creek

Jacobsen Creek

JACOBSEN MEADOW

South Mountaineer Creek

Summit Trailhead

N

START

Summit Road

0 — Kilometers — 2

0 — Miles — 2

This may be because they are widely spaced enough to allow patches of sunlight through to permit understory ferns and flowers on a more human scale to flourish. The noisy chickarees (Douglas squirrels) scolding overhead aren't cowed, either. In fact, they help ensure the survival of the grove. (See Life in the Southern Sierra in this book's introduction.)

At mile 18.8, meet a junction with the Eastside Trail (not shown on the USGS or Forest Service maps). The left fork goes to Redwood Crossing, while your path continues straight ahead (southeast). The big trees thin out as you leave the moister river bottom, giving way to black oak, white fir, incense cedar, and sugar and ponderosa pine. The trail bobs up and down for a time, then drops into a rocky creekbed and disappears, but picks up again on the far side of the gully behind a fallen log. It negotiates several more little creeks sliding over metamorphic rocks that are treacherously slippery when wet. Watch your step.

At mile 20.0 the McAnlis Trail, a shortcut down to the road and campgrounds of Mountain Home State Forest, joins this one on the right. There is a sign here, but it only mentions the Griswold Trail ahead and Redwood Crossing behind. Climb another hump and descend to ford a little branch of Galena Creek blooming with a dazzling display of flowers including fragrant leopard lilies and mints, their aromas colliding with those of pungent wild onions. Pick your way down a gravelly, slippery slope to cross the main fork of Galena Creek where it tumbles over more or less regular granite steps in a pleasing series of little waterfalls. If it is early in the season and if the water is high and swift, this crossing is extremely dangerous. Better to retrace your steps to the McAnlis Trail, make your way back to one of the campgrounds in Mountain Home State Forest, and hitch a ride back to your car than to risk your life. If it is safe to cross, head up out of this drainage and pass over a hump that has not been cleared of fallen timber for some time, then descend steeply, sliding and kicking up dust, into the canyon of Silver Creek. Like most watercourses in this area, Silver Creek is lined with hazelnut bushes whose delicious nuts are a late summer treat for hikers and other animals.

At mile 22.6 reach the Griswold Trail junction and turn left (southeast), heading uphill. The junction is clear, though there is no sign. Toil uphill to reach a ridgetop and follow it, still climbing steeply. As you approach a bench, the grade becomes less

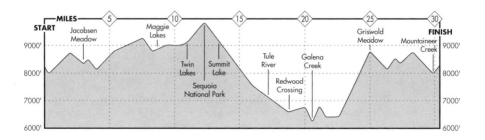

severe, and the path at last meets the Summit Trail at mile 25.0 just south of Griswold Meadow. Turn right (south) and retrace your steps on the Summit Trail to the trailhead.

Key Points

0.0 Summit Trailhead.

3.0 Jacobsen Meadow.

4.0 Mowery Meadow and trail from Grey Meadow, continue straight (north).

5.3 Griswold Trail, continue straight (north).

8.3 Peck's Canyon Trail, south end, turn left (west).

9.3 Maggie Lakes.

11.3 Pecks Canyon Trail, keep left (north).

12.3 Sequioa National Park border.

12.6 Windy Gap connector trail, keep left.

13.5 Summit Lake.

16.0 Tuohy Gap Trail, continue south on the Long Meadow Trail.

18.8 Redwood Crossing.

18.9 Eastside Trail, continue straight (southeast).

20.0 McAnlis Trail.

22.6 Griswold Trail, turn left (southeast).

25.0 Griswold Meadow junction with Summit Trail, turn right (south).

26.3 Mowery Meadow.

27.3 Jacobsen Meadow.

30.3 Summit Trailhead.

7 Grey Meadow Loop

A fine early- or late-season low-elevation day hike or weekend backpack.

Start: Jerkey Meadow Trailhead.
Total distance: 13.6 miles.
Difficulty: Moderately strenuous as a day hike. Easy as a backpack.
Total climbing: 1,860 feet.
Trail traffic: Light.
Best months: Accessible spring through fall; July through August can be hot.
Maps: USGS Camp Nelson and Hockett Peak quads; Golden Trout and South Sierra Wilderness map.

Permits: None for a day hike. Required for an overnight, and available at either the Kernville Ranger Station or the Tule River Ranger Station in Springville. There are no trailhead quotas in effect. A California fire permit is also required, available at any USDA Forest Service office.
Trailhead facilities: Camping, toilets, and water. Nearest gas, phones, and groceries are at Ponderosa, 2 miles south of Quaking Aspen on the Western Divide Highway, or at Road's End Resort on County Road M99.

Finding the trailhead: From the Tule River Ranger Station in Springville, 8 miles west of Porterville on California Highway 190, drive 27 miles to Quaking Aspen Camp where California Highway 190 becomes County Road M107, the Western Divide Highway. Continue south for 10 miles to Forest Service Road 22S02. Turn left (east). Drive 4 miles to Forest Road 22S82, Lloyd Meadows Road, and turn left (north). Continue 19 miles to the end of the road at Jerkey Meadow Trailhead.

From Kernville at the north end of Lake Isabella, drive 25 miles north on County Road M99 following alongside the Kern River to FR 22S82, Lloyd Meadows Road, just north of Johnsondale. Keep right and drive 24 miles to the end of the road.

The Hike

The Jerkey Meadow Trail begins at a series of signs with a wilderness skills quiz and a Leave No Trace Challenge, the answers to which can sometimes be found in a box labeled WILDERNESS SKILLS. Do not rely on the distances on the trailhead sign, since the trail has been rerouted. Begin walking northward through dappled sunlight beneath some truly magnificent old incense cedars and black oaks over a ground cover of lacy, white-flowered kit-kit-dizze. At mile 0.4 the trail intersects an older one that is shorter, but much steeper and badly eroded. Follow the MAIN TRAIL sign for an easier, more enjoyable hike. (The Golden Trout Wilderness map shows only the newer, longer trail, but the topo shows both.)

Climb gradually at first, then more steeply toward the ridgetop where the Jerkey Meadow Trail meets the Lewis Camp Trail at mile 2.2, the highest point on this hike at 6,900 feet. Walk straight ahead (northeast), enjoying glimpses of the peaks of the Great Western Divide across the canyon of the Little Kern River, then dip into a

The Forest Service cabin at Grey Meadow

shady gully to meet Fish Creek at mile 4.9. There is soft, sandy camping nearby where you'll be serenaded by warblers from the streamside willows. Once across the creek a trail sign directs you left (northwest) toward Grey Meadow. Another sign points toward Trout Meadows to the right, but that trail is long gone and is shown on neither the topo nor the Golden Trout map. Now begin a shadeless climb through manzanita over a ridge and down a usually dry creekbed to meet fenced Grey Meadow. Just beyond at mile 5.9 is Grey Meadow Cow Camp and Ranger Station, still in use but not always staffed. The main camping area, complete with outhouses and picnic tables, lies toward the lower end of the meadow. You might have to share it with a few cows.

To complete the loop return to a junction between the ranger station and cow camp cabin and follow the MAIN TRAIL sign eastward across the little spring-fed creek. The path rounds a curve over a sandy knoll, then resumes its eastward course toward the Little Kern, passing a seldom used trail at mile 6.8 that heads north toward Round Meadow. Continue straight ahead, descending gently through forest, and crossing Fish Creek again beside a small campsite. If you plan to visit the Little Kern at the bridge, ignore the shortcut trail to the right (south) at mile 8.6 and go on to the river at mile 9.0, where there are plenty of campsites and flat rocks for

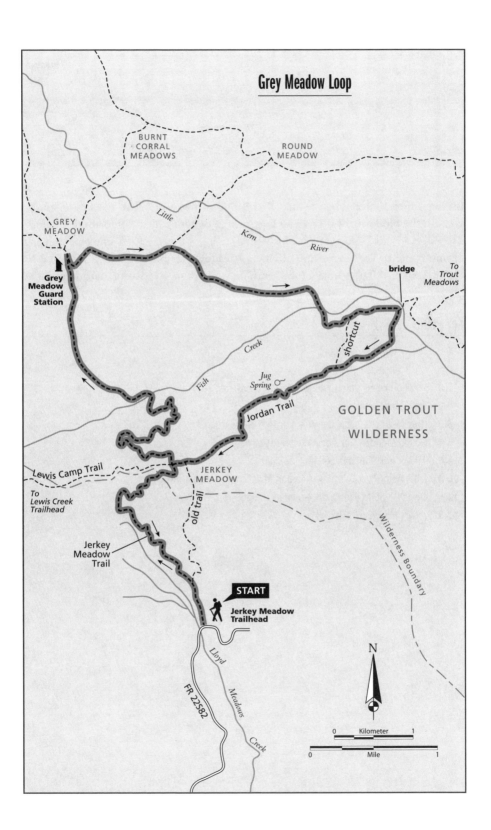

Grey Meadow Loop

BURNT CORRAL MEADOWS

ROUND MEADOW

GREY MEADOW

Little

Kern

River

bridge

To Trout Meadows

Grey Meadow Guard Station

shortcut

Creek

Fish

Jug Spring

Jordan Trail

GOLDEN TROUT

WILDERNESS

Lewis Camp Trail

To Lewis Creek Trailhead

JERKEY MEADOW

old trail

Jerkey Meadow Trail

START

Jerkey Meadow Trailhead

Wilderness Boundary

Lloyd

Meadows

Creek

FR 22S82

N

0 — Kilometer — 1

0 — Mile — 1

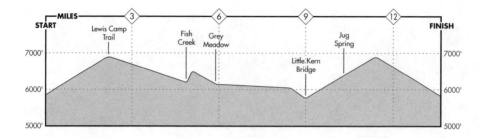

loafing. Enjoy the cool breeze and the rushing of the water, then head back south-west on the old Jordan Trail passing Jug Spring—where you will find another camp-site and a *very* old sign that says this would be a good place for a smoke! From Jug Spring climb to tiny, easily missed Jerkey Meadow, just beyond which is the Lewis Camp Trail crossing at mile 11.4. Continue straight ahead to your starting point at the Jerkey Meadow Trailhead.

Key Points

0.0 Jerkey Meadow Trailhead.

0.4 Old trail crossing.

2.2 Junction Lewis Camp Trail, go straight (northeast).

4.9 Fish Creek junction.

5.9 Grey Meadow, follow the MAIN TRAIL sign eastward.

6.8 Round Meadow junction, continue straight.

8.6 Jordan Trail shortcut, continue straight.

9.0 Little Kern River Bridge and Jordan Trail, turn right (southwest).

11.4 Lewis Camp Trail junction, continue straight.

13.6 Jerkey Meadow Trailhead.

8 Jerkey Meadow Trailhead to the Little Kern River

An out-and-back hike to the Little Kern River.

Start: Jerkey Meadow Trailhead.
Total distance: 9.2 miles.
Difficulty: Moderate.
Total climbing: 1,100 feet.
Trail traffic: Medium.
Best months: Accessible May through October, whenever the roads are open, but finest before mid-July.
Maps: USGS Hockett Peak and Camp Nelson quads; Forest Service Golden Trout and South Sierra Wilderness map.

Permits: None for a day hike. Wilderness permits and California campfire permits are required and are available at the Tule River Ranger Station in Springville for overnights.
Trailhead facilities: Camping, toilets, and water. Nearest gas, phones, and groceries are at Ponderosa, 2 miles south of Quaking Aspen on the Western Divide Highway, or at Road's End Resort on County Road M99.

Finding the trailhead: From the west, begin at the Tule River Ranger Station in Springville, 8 miles west of Porterville on California Highway 190. Drive 27 miles to a junction where CA 190 becomes County Road M107, the Western Divide Highway. Continue on CR M107 south for 10 miles to a dirt road (Forest Road 22S02). Turn left (east). Drive 4 miles to Forest Road 22S82, Lloyd Meadows Road, and turn left (north). Continue for 19 miles to the end of the road.

From the south, begin at the Kernville at the north end of Lake Isabella. Drive 25 miles north on CR M99 following alongside the Kern River to FR 22S82, Lloyd Meadows Road, just north of Johnsondale. Keep right and drive 24 miles to the end of the road.

The Hike

The Jerkey Meadow Trailhead is actually at (or near) Lloyd Meadows. This is an alternate route to the Little Kern Bridge from Hike 9, Lewis Camp Trail to the Little Kern. The hike begins at a series of signs with a WILDERNESS SKILLS quiz and a Leave No Trace Challenge, the answers to which can sometimes be found in a box labeled WILDERNESS SKILLS. Do not rely on the distances on the sign at the trailhead, since the Jerkey Meadow Trail has been rerouted and they are no longer accurate. Begin walking northward through dappled sunlight beneath some truly magnificent old incense cedars and black oaks over a ground cover of lacy, white-flowered kit-kit-dizze. At mile 0.4 the trail intersects an older one that offers a more direct route to the ridgeline, but is much steeper and badly eroded. Follow the MAIN TRAIL sign for an easier, more enjoyable hike. (The Golden Trout Wilderness map shows only the newer, longer trail, but the topo shows both.)

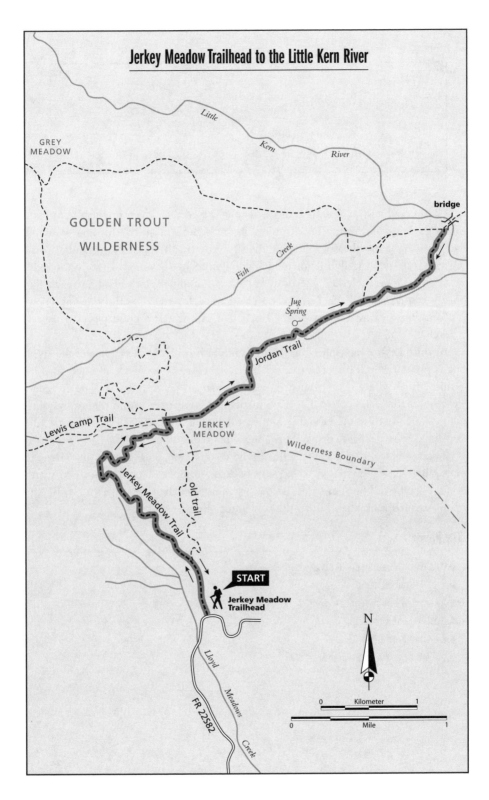

Jerkey Meadow Trailhead to the Little Kern River

Little Kern River

GREY
MEADOW

GOLDEN TROUT
WILDERNESS

bridge

Fish Creek

Jug
Spring

Jordan Trail

Lewis Camp Trail

JERKEY
MEADOW

Wilderness Boundary

Jerkey Meadow Trail

old trail

START
Jerkey Meadow
Trailhead

N

Lloyd Meadows Creek

FR 22S82

0 — Kilometer — 1

0 — Mile — 1

◀ *A bridge over the Little Kern River, one of only two bridges over this fork*

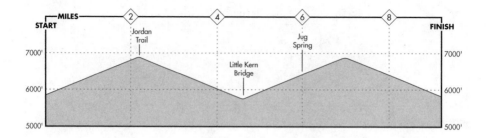

Climb gradually at first, then more steeply toward the ridgetop where your path meets the historic Jordan Trail at mile 2.2, the highest point on this hike at 6,900 feet. Turn right (northeast), following the signs toward the Little Kern Bridge, passing a CATTLE DRIVE trail junction, which you ignore. Just beyond this, off to the right is tiny, easy-to-miss Jerkey Meadow. Follow alongside the creekbed to reach Jug Spring, a small but reliable seep near a patch of willows alive with birdsong. There is a campsite nearby and a worn old sign that says this is a good place to have a smoke!

At mile 4.0 the trail splits, but the forks rejoin just before the river, and the right one is prettier. You'll hear the roar of the river before you can see it. Drop into its granite gorge where it is spanned by a substantial bridge at mile 4.6. The riverside elevation is about 5,800 feet. There are plenty of heavily used campsites nearby, some much too close to the river's edge. Some of the campfire rings are littered with foil. Foil-lined food packages do *not* burn; please pack them out.

There is a wonderful assortment of wildflowers here, especially in June: slender pink gilias, big yellow daisylike balsamroot, fuzzy milkweed, tall lupines, and wonderful big blue lollipops of nama. Enjoy the thunder of the river, bask for a while on a sun-warmed rock, then return the way you came.

Key Points

0.0   Jerkey Meadow Trailhead at Lloyd Meadows.

0.4   Old trail crossing.

2.2   Jordan Trail junction, turn right (northeast).

4.0   Unmarked trail split.

4.6   Little Kern River Bridge.

9.2   Jerkey Meadow Trailhead.

9 Lewis Camp Trail to the Little Kern River

An upside-down hike to the Little Kern River gorge on a historic trans-Sierra trail.

Start: Lewis Camp Trailhead.
Total distance: 9.2 miles.
Difficulty: Easy to moderate as a backpack, moderate as a day hike.
Total climbing: 1,900 feet.
Trail traffic: Medium.
Best months: May through October, whenever the roads are open, but finest before mid-July.
Maps: USGS Camp Nelson and Hockett Peak quads; Forest Service Golden Trout and South Sierra Wilderness map.

Permits: None needed for a day hike; required and available at the Tule River Ranger Station in Springville or from the Golden Trout Pack Station just next to the trailhead for overnight. A California campfire permit is also required and available here.
Trailhead facilities: Camping, picnic tables, and pit toilets, but no water. Nearest gas, phones, and groceries are at Ponderosa, 2 miles south of Quaking Aspen on the Western Divide Highway.

Finding the trailhead: From the west, begin at the Tule River Ranger Station in Springville, 8 miles west of Porterville on California Highway 190. Drive 27 miles to a junction where CA 190 becomes County Road M107, the Western Divide Highway. Turn left (north) onto Forest Road 21S50, North Road. A sign directs you to several trailheads, including LEWIS CAMP, 7 MILES. In about 4 miles the road splits. Turn right (northeast) onto Forest Road 20S79. The pavement ends here but the dirt road is fine for passenger cars. In less than a mile, the road splits again. Keep right on FR 20S79. Soon you will pass Golden Trout Pack Station, and just beyond that, in a wide area with picnic tables, is the Lewis Camp Trailhead.

The Hike

This is an upside-down hike, so the return trip will take longer than the outbound leg. Be sure to allow enough time and water to return to the trailhead.

The Lewis Camp Trailhead is not *at* Lewis Camp. It goes (or went) *to* Lewis Camp, formerly located at the Sequoia National Park border where the Kern Canyon Ranger Station is now. Begin at either of two trailheads a few yards apart. The more obvious one to the right is marked by a sign labeled LEWIS CAMP TRAIL 33E01. It is the steeper of the two and usually used by equestrians. The trailhead to the left is marked by a sign announcing that Sequoia National Park lies ahead and that no dogs or guns are allowed. Hikers usually take the left fork.

The route winds around a shoulder beneath Jeffrey pines, white firs, and incense cedars, with a good view to the left of a beautifully rounded classic Sierra granite dome. At mile 0.2 the two trailheads rejoin at a sign that says MAIN TRAIL. Continue downhill among scattered cabin-sized boulders, catching glimpses of the Little Kern River below and the Great Western Divide beyond to the north. As you descend,

These neatly spaced series of holes are drilled by red breasted sapsuckers, a kind of woodpecker that eats both the sugary pine sap and the insects stuck in it.

notice the enormous cones of the sugar pine scattered here and there. These are the longest pinecones in the world, sometimes measuring up to 24 inches.

You might also notice on the trunks of the incense cedars several series of perfectly regular horizontal rows of what appear to be nail holes. These are the work of the sapsucker, a kind of woodpecker that pecks a line of holes through the bark out of which sweet sap wells. The birds not only enjoy the sap but also return to the holes later to pick off a dessert of insects, which have also been attracted to the stuff and gotten themselves stuck in it.

At about mile 1.8 a path cuts off to the left (north) toward Grey Meadow. This trail is not shown on either the topo or the Golden Trout Wilderness map and is used to bring cattle into and out of the wilderness. Ignore it. Beyond, another sign says that you are now treading the historic Jordan Trail, built in 1861. (See History in this book's introduction.) At mile 2.0 find the Lloyd Meadows junction. The Golden Trout Wilderness map is more accurate and less confusing about this junction than the topo. There has been much trail reconstruction and relocation since the area became a wilderness, and the topo is not quite up to date. Go straight ahead (east) toward the Little Kern Bridge, passing another CATTLE DRIVE trail sign. Just

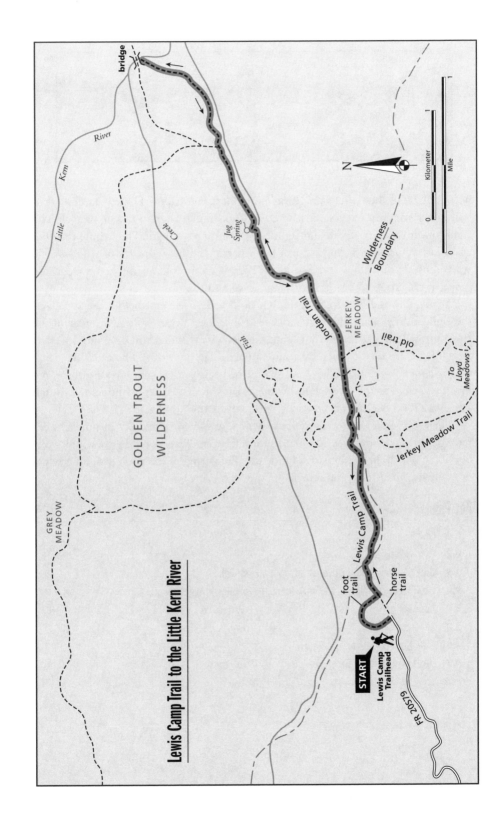

Lewis Camp Trail to the Little Kern River

GOLDEN TROUT WILDERNESS

GREY MEADOW

Little Kern River

Creek

Fish

Jug Spring

bridge

Jordan Trail

JERKEY MEADOW

Wilderness Boundary

old trail

To Lloyd Meadows

Jerkey Meadow Trail

Lewis Camp Trail

foot trail

horse trail

START

Lewis Camp Trailhead

FR 20S70

N

Kilometer

Mile

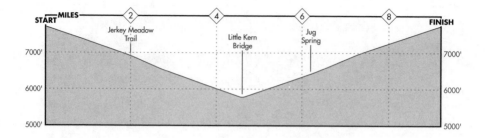

beyond it, off to the right, is tiny, easily missed Jerkey Meadow. There is an unmarked trail split just beyond at mile 2.1. The two forks rejoin later, so take your pick. The right fork follows the creek and is probably the more pleasant. They come together again just before Jug Spring, a small but reliable seep near a patch of willows alive with birdsong mornings and evenings. There is a campsite nearby and a worn old sign that tells you this is a good place to have a smoke!

At mile 3.6 the trail splits again, but both forks meet just before the river, and the right fork is, again, the better one. You will soon begin to hear the roar of the river, but will not catch sight of it until the last minute when you drop into its granite gorge where it is spanned by a substantial bridge (mile 4.6). The riverside elevation is about 5,800 feet. There are plenty of heavily used campsites nearby, some much too close to the river's edge. Some of the campfire rings are littered with foil. Foil-lined food packages do *not* burn; please pack them out.

There is a wonderful assortment of wildflowers here, especially in June: slender pink gilias, big yellow daisylike balsamroot, fuzzy milkweed, tall lupines, and wonderful big blue lollipops of nama. Enjoy the thundering of the river, bask for a while on a sun-warmed rock, and return the way you came.

Key Points

0.0 Lewis Camp Trailhead.

0.2 MAIN TRAIL sign.

1.8 Grey Meadow Cattle Drive cutoff, continue straight.

2.0 Lloyd Meadows/Jerkey Meadow junction, continue straight (east).

3.0 Jug Spring.

3.6 Second trail split.

4.6 Little Kern Bridge, turn around.

9.2 Lewis Camp Trailhead.

10 Trout and Willow Meadows

A great early-season lollipop-loop backpack to two pretty meadows.

Start: Lewis Camp Trailhead
Total distance: 17.5 miles.
Difficulty: Moderate.
Total climbing: 1,900 feet.
Trail traffic: Moderate.
Best months: Accessible June through October, but hot and dry by August.
Maps: USGS Camp Nelson and Hockett Peak quads; Forest Service Golden Trout and South Sierra Wilderness map.

Permits: Required for overnight; available at the Tule River Ranger Station in Springville or from the Golden Trout Pack Station just next to the trailhead.
Trailhead facilities: Camping, picnic tables, and pit toilets, but no water. Nearest gas, phones, and groceries are at Ponderosa, 2 miles south of Quaking Aspen on the Western Divide Highway.

Finding the trailhead: From the west, start at the Tule River Ranger Station in Springville, 8 miles west of Porterville on California Highway 190. Drive 27 miles to a junction where California Highway 190 becomes County Road M107, the Western Divide Highway. Turn left (north) onto Forest Service 21S50, North Road. A sign directs you to several trailheads, including LEWIS CAMP, 7 MILES. In about 4 miles the road splits. Turn right (northeast) onto Forest Road 20S79. The pavement ends here but the dirt road is fine for passenger cars. In less than a mile the road splits again. Keep right on FR 20S79. Soon you will pass Golden Trout Pack Station; just beyond that, in a wide area with picnic tables, is the Lewis Camp Trailhead.

The Hike

Begin at either of two trailheads a few yards apart. The more obvious one to the right is marked by a sign labeled LEWIS CAMP TRAIL 33E01. It is the steeper of the two and is usually used by horsemen. The trailhead to the left is marked by a sign announcing that Sequoia National Park lies ahead and that no dogs or guns are allowed. Hikers usually take the left fork. At mile 0.2 the two trailheads rejoin at a sign that says MAIN TRAIL. Continue downhill. At about mile 1.8 a path cuts off to the left (north) toward Grey Meadow. At mile 2.0 find the Lloyds Meadow junction. Go straight ahead (east) toward the Little Kern Bridge, passing another CATTLE DRIVE trail sign, to an unmarked trail split at mile 2.1. The two forks rejoin later, so take your pick. The right fork follows the creek and is probably the more pleasant. They come together again just before Jug Spring. At mile 3.6 the trail splits again, but both forks meet just before the river, and the right fork is, again, the better one.

After crossing the bridge over the Little Kern River at mile 4.6, the Jordan Trail curves to negotiate a stream gully, then splits at mile 4.9. This is the beginning of the lollipop part of the hike. You can proceed in either direction—both trails end up at

Trout Meadows is a popular weekend destination for backpackers.

Willow Meadows—but it will be described here counterclockwise, beginning on the southern (right) fork, returning on the northern (left) fork. The right-fork trail at first runs parallel to the Little Kern. As it climbs out of the river canyon, notice how the rock changes from light salt-and-pepper granite to darker lava, full of little pockmarks and airholes where gases escaped while the lava was still molten. This is the Little Kern Lava Flow, one of the oldest basalt flows (3.5 million years) in the Golden Trout Wilderness.

The Trout Meadows Trail winds its way generally southeast, gently rising and falling through forest, then makes an abrupt left to reveal the refreshing green grasses of Trout Meadows ahead. The trail remains on the left side of the fence enclosing the meadow and reaches the Trout Meadows Ranger Station at mile 7.6. The elevation here is about 6,200 feet. There is plenty of camping all around the meadow, though the water that feeds it is seldom more than a trickle. There are also his-and-hers outhouses near the ranger station, which is usually staffed on summer weekends. A nearby sign points left (northwest) to Burnt Corral Meadows, but you continue straight ahead toward Willow Meadows, passing the stone foundations of an old cabin and, beyond that, a stock gate. Be sure to close it behind you.

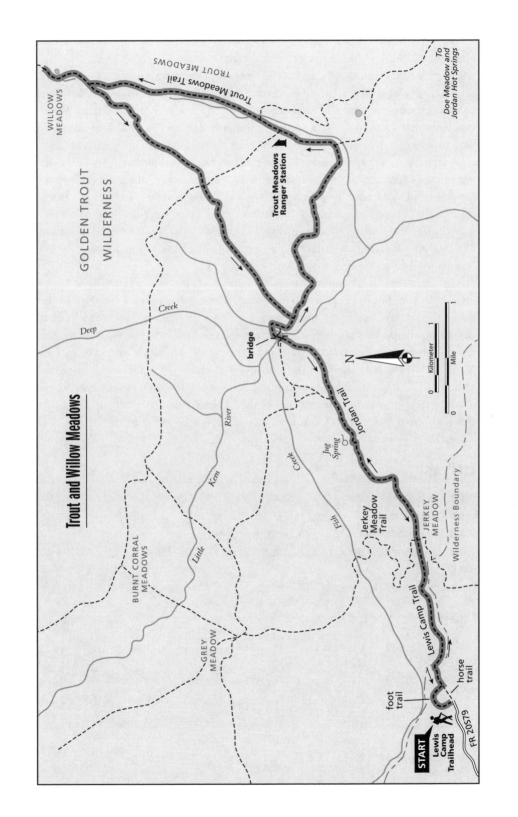

Trout and Willow Meadows

GOLDEN TROUT WILDERNESS

WILLOW MEADOWS

TROUT MEADOWS

Trout Meadows Trail

To Doe Meadow and Jordan Hot Springs

Trout Meadows Ranger Station

Deep

Creek

bridge

N

Jordan Trail

Jug Spring

River

Kem

Creek

Fish

Little

BURNT CORRAL MEADOWS

Jerkey Meadow Trail

JERKEY MEADOW

Wilderness Boundary

GREY MEADOW

Lewis Camp Trail

horse trail

foot trail

FR 20579

START
Lewis Camp Trailhead

Kilometer

Mile

Shortly beyond the gate, reach a well-marked junction with the trail to Jordan Hot Springs. Willow Meadows is 2 miles straight ahead (north). The trail through Jeffrey pine forest is unusually flat for the Sierra for almost a mile, then climbs almost imperceptibly as it passes Trout Meadows Spring bubbling up among willows and wild geraniums. Pass through another gate to reach the lower end of Willow Meadows. The topo actually shows a shallow pond at the south end of this meadow, but there is water in it only in the wettest of years. At the northern end of the meadow are several big packer campsites and a rather obscure unsigned junction at mile 9.6, the beginning of your return route. Note that Willow Meadows is not named at all on the Golden Trout Wilderness map, though there is a little horse icon indicating a public pasture. The best camping is near the junction, where a pipe has been installed to catch springwater. A few more minutes' hiking will take you to a series of meadows strung together, one after another along the valley, one of which has a more substantial creek flowing in early season than the others.

To complete this triangular-shaped "loop," pick up the unmarked Willow Meadows/Little Kern Shortcut that heads back southwest at a sharp angle from the sign that announces WILLOW MEADOWS near the pipe spring. Climb at once on switchbacks to the top of a hump, pass through another gate, and tread more level ground as the path flattens out and reaches another junction at mile 11.1. The right fork goes to Lion Meadows; the left, back down to Trout Meadows. Continue straight ahead toward the Little Kern Bridge. Toward the bottom, the trail splits, but both forks rapidly descend into the river gorge and rejoin at the bridge. This is where the lollipop section of the loop began (mile 12.9). From here, retrace your steps uphill to the Lewis Camp Trailhead.

Key Points

0.0 Lewis Camp Trailhead.

0.2 MAIN TRAIL sign.

1.8 Grey Meadow Cattle Drive cutoff, continue straight.

2.0 Lloyd Meadows/Jerkey Meadows junction, continue straight (east).

3.0 Jug Spring.

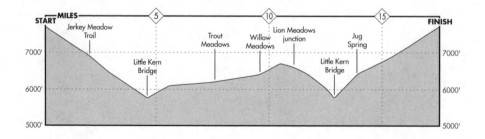

3.6   Second trail split.

4.6   Little Kern Bridge.

4.9   Willow Meadows Trail split. Loop begins. Turn right (south).

7.6   Trout Meadows Ranger Station.

9.6   Willow Meadows. Turn left (southwest) on the Willow Meadows/Little Kern Shortcut.

11.1   Lion Meadows junction, continue straight.

12.9   Little Kern River. Loop ends.

17.5   Lewis Camp Trailhead.

11 Lion Meadows Loop

A relatively low- to middle-elevation exploration of numerous tributaries of the Little Kern River, perfect in autumn for solitude and fall color.

Start: Second Clicks Creek Trailhead.
Total distance: 23.8 miles.
Difficulty: Moderate.
Total climbing: 4,430 feet.
Trail traffic: Light to medium.
Best months: Mid-July through October, at its finest in fall. Spring and early summer are beautiful, but the Little Kern crossing can be hazardous until midsummer.
Maps: USGS Camp Nelson, Hockett Peak,
Quinn Peak, and Kern Lake quads; Forest Service Golden Trout and South Sierra Wilderness map.
Permits: A wilderness permit and a California campfire permit are required and are available at the Tule River Ranger Station in Springville.
Trailhead facilities: Outhouses only. No water. Nearest gas, phones, and groceries at Ponderosa, 2 miles south of Quaking Aspen on the Western Divide Highway.

Finding the trailhead: From the Tule River Ranger Station in Springville, 8 miles west of Porterville on California Highway 190, drive 27 miles to a junction where CA 190 becomes County Road M107, the Western Divide Highway. Turn left (north) onto Forest Road 21S50, North Road. A sign directs you to several trailheads, including Clicks Creek. In 4 miles the road splits again and becomes unpaved, though it's fine for passenger cars. Turn left at the split and in 2 miles pass the first Clicks Creek Trailhead on the right, where there is no place to park. Drive a few yards farther to the second, newer, Clicks Creek Trailhead, also on the right. There is parking across the road near a yurt and some pit toilets.

The Hike

This is an especially fine hike in fall when the air is cool and crisp. The water level in the Little Kern is low enough to make the two crossings easy. Cattle, with their associated bawling, flies, and aroma, have been driven back down to lower elevations. Aspens, black oaks, willows, and dogwoods glow with warm reds, yellows, and golds, and there are plenty of juicy ripe berries.

Cross the road from the large parking area to the well-marked Clicks Creek Trailhead and descend very gently to hop a tributary of Clicks Creek, then pick up the main branch of the stream—still tiny at this point—and drop more steeply to a fenced meadow. Keep to the left of the fence on a path neatly outlined with logs, ignoring a path that cuts off to bisect the meadow to the right. At mile 1.0 an unmarked trail cuts back southeast to the Lewis Camp Trailhead. At the top of a little rise, a sign marks the entrance to the wilderness, then the path descends alongside the creek as it tumbles down a boulder-filled gorge lined with aspens. Where the grade becomes more gradual and the ground less rocky, occasional cow paths

The Great Western Divide from the Lion Meadows Trail

meander back and forth across the trail and disappear into the trees. It's easy to wander away from the main route if you're daydreaming. The forest is interrupted in several places by willowy gardens blooming with larkspurs and lilies in summer, golden with bracken and berry bushes in fall. The trail then drops quite steeply on switchbacks into lower-elevation habitats where Jeffrey pines, incense cedars, and black oaks mingle with, then replace lodgepole pines and white firs.

At mile 4.3 cross to the north side of Clicks Creek and reach a junction. There are signs, but some have fallen down; you'll have to look for them. Take the left fork northwest toward Mountaineer Creek and Lion Meadows; the right fork goes to Grey Meadow and is the way you will be returning. Stroll through gently rolling, fairly open sandy forest, passing another, fainter trail to Mountaineer Creek and Grey Meadow at mile 5.0, then a third trail to Grey Meadow at mile 5.3 before making the final descent to meet the Little Kern River.

Walk upstream for about 100 yards along the pebbly floodplain and reenter the forest on a trail neatly outlined with rocks that leads to a tidy junction at mile 5.8. One path goes left to a campsite; another, straight ahead to a FIRE SAFE area and points west. Your trail fords the Little Kern to the right (northeast) toward Rifle Creek and Lion Meadows. The river is wide and shallow here above its confluence

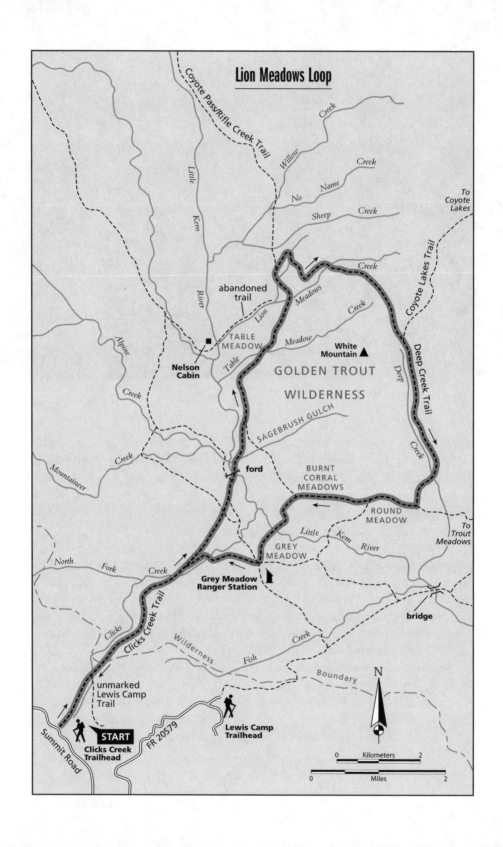

Lion Meadows Loop

Coyote Pass/Rifle Creek Trail

Willow Creek

No Name Creek

Sheep Creek

To Coyote Lakes

Little Kern River

Alpine

Creek

Creek

Mountaineer

Creek

North Fork

Clicks Creek

Clicks Creek Trail

Clicks

Summit Road

unmarked Lewis Camp Trail

START
Clicks Creek Trailhead

FR 20579

Lewis Camp Trailhead

Wilderness

Fish Creek

Boundary

abandoned trail

Lion Meadows

Meadow

Creek

Creek

TABLE MEADOW

Nelson Cabin

Table

GOLDEN TROUT

White Mountain ▲

Deep

WILDERNESS

Deep Creek Trail

Coyote Lakes Trail

SAGEBRUSH GULCH

Creek

ford

BURNT CORRAL MEADOWS

ROUND MEADOW

To Trout Meadows

Little Kern River

GREY MEADOW

Grey Meadow Ranger Station

bridge

N

0 — Kilometers — 2

0 — Miles — 2

with Mountaineer Creek, but wade with care, then climb steeply out of the gorge on the far side. The grade soon becomes more gradual. Just after crossing a pretty little stream that slides sensuously down a gully over granite slabs, reach a signed junction at mile 6.8. The right fork turns off toward Round Meadow. Your route, the left one, continues northward, ascends a ridge topped with a stand of black oaks, and drops to cross Table Meadow Creek as it gurgles through a tangle of wild rosebushes. On the far side, at the edge of sometimes slushy Table Meadow, is a pleasant campsite. Skirt the right side of the meadow, then climb over another ridge lined with more black oaks to find Lion Meadows at mile 8.9. The fenced meadow and enclosed buildings are the property of Pyle's Camp, where disadvantaged boys can participate in a remote outdoor experience and help maintain the wilderness. Keep to the left of the fence and skirt the meadow, hopping a couple of branches of Lion Creek. There is an inconspicuous unmarked junction with a shortcut route to the left that follows Lion Creek back down to the Little Kern and across it to the Nelson Cabin site. Ignore this (if you notice it at all). Where the fence turns a corner to the right, the Lion Creek Trail continues on ahead, curving slightly to the right as well, and meets a junction at mile 9.1. A sign on a Jeffrey pine that you'll miss if you're not looking for it points right (northeast) to Coyote Lakes. The left (unmarked) fork continues on to the north toward Coyote Pass and the headwaters of the Little Kern.

The Lion Creek Trail heads upstream along a slender branch of Lion Creek, becoming steeper as it goes. There are lots of fallen trees to negotiate in this section, but it is fairly easy to stay on track as long as you pay attention. The forest becomes eerily dark and quiet as you ascend a narrow gully, but in about a mile you swing right (southeast) and switchback up to where the deep shade is broken by more open spots of manzanita and ceanothus to gain a ridgetop. Continue to climb along the ridge. Lion Creek can be heard crashing down its gorge to the right, and to the left stretches an exhilarating vista up the canyon of the Little Kern to Farewell Gap at the head of the Great Western Divide. Pass a small campsite tucked between Lion Creek and the trail and shortly thereafter cross the creek.

Wind your way uphill, at first past a grassy seep, later through fir forest to the top of another ridge where there are a few broad, flat, but dry campsites. This is the highest point of the hike at 8,270 feet. A battered, tottering sign marked 32E06 indicates the Deep Creek Trail (mile 11.5). Hikers bound for Coyote Lakes turn left (north). Your route drops over the saddle and into the canyon of Deep Creek, near the head of which lies a meadow and a campsite. The trail fades in the grasses and sedges, but is easy to pick up again where the creek leaves the meadow. The canyon steepens and narrows to a tight "waist," then gradually opens out again, and the grade becomes less extreme.

Near the mouth of the canyon, the trail crosses Deep Creek and swings westward, then southward again to meet the Round Meadow/Trout Meadows junction at mile 15.1. Keep right (west) reach Round Meadow at mile 16.0. The footing becomes soft and sandy from the passage of countless sheep, cattle, horses, and humans wandering over the years between Burnt Corral Meadows, Round Meadow, and the Little Kern. An old trail heads south to cross the river here, but you should keep right and continue on toward Burnt Corral Meadows. The trail is better maintained and the river is easier to ford there. Cross a spring-fed creek, then reach another of those junctions marked by a single sign in a tree that is easy to miss unless you're watching for it. This one, at mile 17.3, just says MAIN TRAIL. It directs you southwest to the edge of Burnt Corral Meadows, a large open tract laced with little runnels of water from several inconspicuous springs, churned to mush by livestock. There are occasional campfire rings around the edge of the meadow, but unless you are here late in the season after the cattle have been moved back down to the valley, you will probably have plenty of bovine company. Whether the cattle are in residence or not, the innumerable meadow muffins they leave behind make camping here unappetizing. If you really must stop for the night soon, continue another 0.5 to the ford across the Little Kern and use the cozy campsite on the far side.

From here, climb up the slope out of the river valley and slog through deep sandy soil until Grey Meadow appears on the left. In a few minutes arrive at a campsite with a piped spring and picnic tables; just beyond, find a tree bristling with signs at mile 18.5. If you want to explore Grey Meadow Ranger Station, still used by the Forest Service, or the cow camp, still used by cowboys, or to use a toilet, keep straight ahead. To return your car at the Clicks Creek Trailhead, turn right (west) at the junction tree with all the signs. Hop a little creekbed and veer generally west over a little rise down to cross Clicks Creek at a pretty round pool, then meet the Clicks Creek Trail at mile 19.5. Turn left and retrace your steps up the hill to the parking area at the yurt.

Key Points

0.0   Clicks Creek Trailhead.

1.0   Lewis Camp Trail.

4.3   Grey Meadow junction, take left fork (northwest). This is the beginning of the loop.

5.0   Mountaineer Creek/Grey Meadow junction, continue straight.

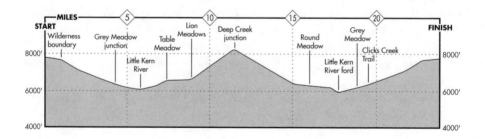

5.3 Yet another Grey Meadow junction, continue straight.

5.8 Mountaineer Creek/Little Kern crossing, turn right across river (northwest).

6.8 Round Meadow junction, turn left (north).

8.9 Lion Meadows.

9.1 Coyote Lakes junction, turn right (northeast).

11.5 Deep Creek junction, turn right (northeast).

15.1 Round Meadow Trail, turn right (west).

16.0 Round Meadow.

17.3 Burnt Corral Meadows, turn left (southwest).

18.5 Grey Meadow, turn right (west).

19.5 Clicks Creek Trail, turn left. This is the end of the loop.

23.8 Clicks Creek Trailhead.

12 Silver Knapsack Trail

A Boy Scout favorite, with plenty of variety and lots of ups and downs. Can be done as a shuttle or a slightly longer loop. This is not a hike for beginners.

Start: Summit Trailhead.
Total distance: 36.2 miles.
Difficulty: Moderately strenuous.
Total climbing: 4,300 feet.
Trail traffic: Medium to Maggie Lakes, light elsewhere.
Best months: July through October.
Maps: USGS Camp Nelson and Quinn Peak quads; Golden Trout and South Sierra Wilderness map.

Permits: A wilderness permit and a California campfire permit are required and are available at the Tule River Ranger Station in Springville.
Trailhead facilities: None at Summit, toilets only at Clicks Creek. Nearest gas, phone, and groceries are at Ponderosa, 2 miles south of Quaking Aspen on the Western Divide Highway.

Finding the trailhead: From the Tule River Ranger Station in Springville, 8 miles west of Porterville on California Highway 190, drive 27 miles to a junction where California Highway 190 becomes County Road M107, the Western Divide Highway. Turn left (north) onto Forest Road 21S50, North Road. A sign points to several trailheads, including SUMMIT, 11 MILES and CLICKS CREEK, 6 MILES. In 4 miles the road splits and becomes unpaved, though it's fine for passenger cars. Turn left here and in 2 miles reach the first Clicks Creek Trailhead. Pass this one and continue a few yards to a second trailhead, where there is more parking beside a yurt and some outhouses. If you are doing a shuttle, leave one car here. If not, drive another 5 miles to the road's end in a clearing at the signed Summit Trailhead.

The Hike

The Forest Service has a handout describing this trail, but do not rely on it for accurate mileage figures. From the Summit Trailhead, the trail descends gently to cross the south fork of Mountaineer Creek. As the path leaves the creek bed it traverses a windward-facing hillside until the route attains a ridgetop and rounds a little granite knob. At mile 3.0 is a junction marked by dilapidated signs where a trail heads west down to Camp Wishon. Keep going right to Jacobsen Meadow. At Mowery Meadow (mile 4.0) another seldom-maintained trail coming from Grey Meadow joins this one on the right. Continue straight ahead (north) to Alpine Meadow. The path climbs moderate switchbacks until it meets the faint Griswold Trail (mile 5.3). Take the right fork and climb another mile to reach the top of a shoulder at about 9,300 feet. Here the trail swings left (west), then drops to cross a year-round creek.

Extravagant gardens bloom along the Silver Knapsack Trail.

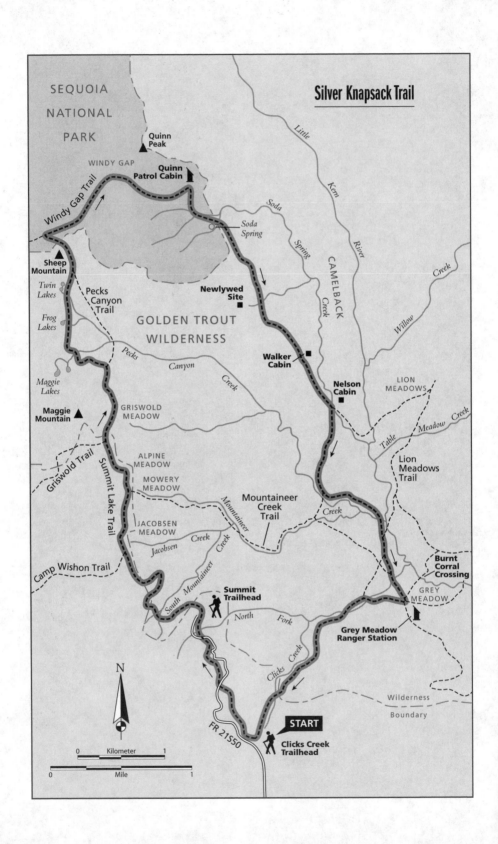

Just beyond, at mile 8.3 is a junction. Follow the left fork (west) toward Maggie Lakes. Lower Maggie Lake lies in a cirque beyond the final moraine at mile 9.3.

Leaving the shore, cross over a little rise and descend moderately through an open forest of red fir, lodgepole, and western white and foxtail pine to Frog Lakes—really just one lake and one mud puddle connected by a log-choked gulch. Beyond the lake(s) the Summit Trail loses some elevation, then begins to climb along a fabulously flowery little creek to reach grassy Twin Lakes. There is camping nearby, but please do not use the disgraceful packer site tucked between the two lakes, full of trash and much too near the shores. Beyond Twin Lakes the trail continues to climb, passing the junction (not shown on the Golden Trout Wilderness map) with the north end of the Pecks Canyon Trail at mile 11.3. Keep left (north) here and climb steadily to the shoulder of Sheep Mountain at the border of Sequoia National Park at mile 12.3. If you have firearms or pets, you must turn around here. This is the highest point on the loop at 9,850 feet.

Don't miss the opportunity to bag Sheep Mountain while you are here. Just follow the ridge on your left southward to the top. It's an easy walk of about 0.5 mile round trip (not included in this trip's mileage or total-climbing figures) with sensational views from its 10,000-foot summit. You can see most of the western half of the Golden Trout Wilderness and the Great Western Divide, culminating in Florence Peak, the highest point on the divide at 12,432 feet.

After returning to the main Summit Trail, drop down off the ridge to the left (west) and watch for an unsigned but obvious trail that cuts off to the right (northeast) toward Windy Gap at Mile 12.6. This trail is not shown on the 7.5-minute topo, but is on the Golden Trout Wilderness map. Follow this ridge northeast to Windy Gap on terrain that rises and falls for a short distance, then makes a few switchbacks down to meet the Windy Gap junction at mile 14.7. Turn right (south) on trail marked by blazes made of old license plates, pass through another blooming meadow, and descend to the Quinn Snow Survey Cabin (mile 16.5). A tiny creek runs by, and there are places to camp. The cabin, originally built by a sheepherder, is still in use by Forest Service personnel to measure winter snowpack. Turn right (south) here and follow the path curving around Soda Butte, then meet and wander along the north shore of Soda Creek through a stand of aspens. Cross to the south side of the creek on slippery rocks and logs, then watch for a spur trail heading left to Soda Spring, oddly not shown on either map (mile 17.7). The water is carbonated but doesn't taste very good, even with flavoring added. It probably should be purified before drinking, but by the time you have filtered it or waited for iodine to work, all the bubbles will be gone. There is some limited camping nearby. Return to the Silver Knapsack Trail and continue climbing southward out of the streambed. At the next creek crossing, leave Sequoia National Park and reenter the Golden Trout Wilderness.

This section of trail hasn't been cleared in years. For the next mile and more, you will have to pick your way over and around downed timber, keeping a sharp eye out to find the trail again after negotiating each obstacle. The route, such as it is, climbs over a shoulder then contours around a hillside, crossing several tributaries of Soda Spring Creek to reach a forest flat in an aspen grove. This spot is known as the New-lywed Site, where many years ago a local packer and his wife spent their wedding night. Presumably they did not have a June wedding, as the mosquitoes are numerous and voracious here in early season. The crossing of the next Soda Spring tributary beyond the Newlywed Site is marked by ducks to guide you through the shoulder-high thickets of willows. There is an especially fine wildflower garden here with tall lilies, lupines, larkspur, and orchids. The trail makes several short ups and downs as it traverses a rather steep hillside across a valley from the elongated ridge known as the Camelback, then turns abruptly east to descend very steeply along a tributary that flows down to Walker Cabin. The remains of the cabin, another relic of sheepherding days, stands at the head of a meadow at mile 20.8. The Boy Scouts have used this area for camping for generations and they, and perhaps sheepherders, too, have carved their initials on everything in sight.

Pick up the trail again just to the right of the meadow and continue descending through forest where sugar pine and incense cedar begin to replace the higher-elevation vegetation pines and white firs. Cross another pretty creek lined with horsetails, mints, and monkey flowers, climb out of its drainage, and descend again. When the terrain levels out and the forest opens a little, the trail rejoins Soda Spring Creek. A sign on a Jeffrey pine on your left points back to Newlywed and Wet Meadows. About 150 yards farther along in a grove of cottonwoods is a junction at mile 22.8. The left fork crosses the stream and heads east to Lion Meadows and Rifle Creek. Your route continues straight ahead (south). Just beyond the junction is the site of the Nelson Cabin. Don't look for the remains; construction of the cabin was barely begun before it was abandoned. From this point on, the trail gets more frequent maintenance, so you won't be wasting so much energy finding detours around forest debris. After crossing several low ridges, you reach a sandy opening where a sign on the ground marks another trail cutting back southwest to Parole Cabin and Mowery Meadow. A little farther on, Alpine Creek appears to your right just before it joins Mountaineer Creek, which in turn soon joins the Little Kern River. The trail drops to the riverside just before this confluence. Ducks will guide you to the easiest crossing (mile 26.1). This is the lowest point on the hike at about 6,050 feet. Now on the south side of the river, follow a neat rock-lined path downstream. Pass a sign and a campsite marked FIRE SAFE AREA on the left and, just beyond that, an orderly four-way junction. The right-hand path leads to a very pleasant campsite; the left goes back across the Little Kern toward Lion Meadows. Continue straight ahead, following the river downstream for a few yards before it curves southeast away from the trail.

At mile 26.6 hike past a turnoff to Mountaineer Creek and Mowery Meadow. Keep left, following signs toward Grey Meadow. At mile 30.0 pass a second Grey

Meadow junction in an open sandy flat and keep left again. At the next, more indistinct junction, watch for an inconspicuous sign on a Jeffrey pine that points left to Burnt Corral Crossing (of the Little Kern). Your route is directly ahead, though a big log has fallen across the path so that it is hard to see. Go around the log, dip through a shallow streambed, and just beyond discover an elaborate campsite with picnic tables and piped water at the edge of fenced Grey Meadow (mile 30.9). Just a few yards uphill from the campsite is a tree bristling with signs, one of which directs you to the toilets! In the same direction is Grey Meadow Cow Camp, still in use if you want to have a look at the real thing. The ranger station is next door and is occupied only now and then.

To continue your journey, return to the tree with the signs near the campsite and head west toward Clicks Creek. Cross the creek at a beautiful little pool, and just beyond the crossing meet another junction with the Lion Meadows Trail at mile 31.9. Continue upstream along the creek, crossing it again in about 0.5 mile. Switchback up through the forest, gradually leaving behind black oaks, incense cedars, and sugar pines to pick up white firs and, eventually, lodgepole pines. Pass a willowy glen full of larkspur, roses, dogwoods, ferns and berry bushes, then resume the stiff climb through forest, pausing to catch your breath at another willowy garden even more beautiful than the last. After a few more switchbacks, a cow path joins your trail from the left. Keep right and top a rise, just beyond which you leave the Golden Trout Wilderness at mile 34.9. Resume the climb alongside the creek as it cascades down through a rocky gulch lined with aspens. At the top is an unmarked junction (mile 35.2) with a trail that forks left to Junction Meadow and on to the Lewis Camp Trailhead. Climb more easily now to a meadow with a corral on the left. There is a clearly defined but unsigned intersection here, which you ignore. Cross a tributary of Clicks Creek and in minutes arrive at the trailhead and the official end of the Silver Knapsack Trail at mile 36.2.

If you have not left one car here to shuttle you back to the Summit parking area, cross the road and hike south about 0.2 mile to meet the junction with the trail to Summit Trailhead. This climbs up and down, crossing the road at several points to close the loop. This adds 4 miles to the hike, bringing the total to 40.2 miles.

Key Points

0.0 Summit Trailhead.

3.0 Jacobsen Meadow.

4.0 Mowery Meadow and trail from Grey Meadow, continue straight (north).

5.3 Griswold Trail, continue straight (north).

8.3 Pecks Canyon Trail, south end, turn left (west).

9.3 Maggie Lakes.

11.3 Pecks Canyon Trail, north end, keep left (north).

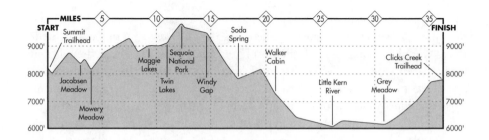

12.3 Sequoia National Park border.

12.6 Connector trail to Windy Gap, turn right (northeast).

14.7 Windy Gap, turn right (south).

16.5 Quinn Patrol Cabin, turn right (south).

17.7 Soda Spring.

20.8 Walker Cabin.

22.8 Nelson Cabin junction, continue straight (south).

24.3 Parole Cabin junction, turn left (east).

26.1 Mountaineer Creek/Little Kern River.

26.6 First Mowery Meadow junction, keep left toward Grey Meadow.

30.0 Second Mowery Meadow junction, keep left.

30.9 Grey Meadow, turn right (west).

31.9 Lion Meadows Trail junction.

35.2 Junction Meadow Trailhead junction.

36.2 Clicks Creek Trailhead, shuttle parking.

36.4 Junction with trail to Summit Trailhead.

40.2 Summit Trailhead.

The Kern River

The main fork of the Kern River flowing through this central section of the wilderness is officially called the North Fork, as distinguished from the South Fork, which is east of it, and the Little Kern, which is actually the west fork. Confused? A glance at the map or a moment at the riverside makes it clear that, whatever it is called, this is the defining and most exciting feature of this part of the range. The Kern is the longest river in the Southern Sierra, and since it follows a preexisting fault where the rock has been weakened and is more vulnerable to erosion, the gorge through which it races is thousands of feet deep in places, and truly spectacular. Born of ice and snow on the high Sierra Crest, the river rushes into the wilderness at the Sequoia National Park boundary at the Kern Canyon Ranger Station on an arrow-straight course. About halfway through the Golden Trout, it makes a wide curve, bending first east, then back to the west to leave the wilderness where it meets the Little Kern River at Forks of the Kern. Along the way, tributary streams fling themselves into the gorge in dozens of waterfalls. Lava has poured into the canyon at intervals, too, transforming the walls into beautiful sculptures and living, hands-on geology lessons. Rainbow trout thrive in the cold water, and birds and wildlife of all kinds frequent the banks.

There are only two widely spaced bridges over the Kern River within the wilderness, and unlike the Little Kern, it cannot be forded elsewhere, even late in the year. Many lives have been lost in attempts, including that of John Jordan who pioneered the Jordan Trail across the mountains. He drowned in 1862 attempting to cross the river on a raft. Therefore, all the hikes in this section begin and end on the west side of the Kern, though Hike 16 takes you across to the east side and back again. (See section 5 for east side approaches.)

The trailheads in this section, with one exception, are the same as those in section 2: Lloyd Meadows and Lewis Camp. There are no trailhead quotas in effect, and you can request your wilderness permit by mail if you like, but you're required to pick up your campfire permit in person (whether or not you plan to have a fire). California campfire permits are available at most Forest Service offices and are valid for a year. The Tule River Ranger Station in Springville, the Kernville Ranger Station, and the Lewis Camp Pack Station can issue wilderness permits.

See section 2 and individual hikes for driving and camping information.

13 Forks of the Kern

An out-and-back day hike to the confluence of the Kern River and the Little Kern.

Start: Forks of the Kern Trailhead.
Total distance: 4.4 miles.
Difficulty: Easy to moderate.
Total climbing: 2,200 feet.
Trail traffic: Medium to heavy on weekends, lighter on weekdays.
Best months: May through October, hot in midsummer.

Maps: USGS Hockett Peak quad; Forest Service Golden Trout and South Sierra Wilderness map.
Permits: None for a day hike.
Trailhead facilities: Camping and toilets. There is no water at the trailhead. Nearest groceries, gas, and phones are at Road's End Resort about 3 miles south of Johnsondale on County Road M99.

Finding the trailhead: From the west, begin at the Tule River Ranger Station in Springville, 8 miles west of Porterville on California Highway 190. Drive 27 miles to a junction where California Highway 190 becomes County Road M107, the Western Divide Highway. Continue south on CR M107 for 20 miles to Forest Road 22S02. Turn left (east) then drive 4 miles to Lloyd Meadows Road (Forest Road 22S82) and turn left (north). Continue for 22 miles to Forest Road 20S67, Forks of the Kern Road, and turn right. The parking area is 2 miles down the road.

From the south, starting in Kernville at the north end of Lake Isabella, drive 35 miles north on CR M99 following alongside the Kern River to FR 22S82, Lloyd Meadows Road, just north of Johnsondale. Keep right and drive 22 miles to FR 20S67, Forks of the Kern Road, and turn right. The parking area is 2 miles down the road.

The Hike

This is an upside-down hike and the trailhead elevation is less than 5,800 feet, so be sure to carry plenty of water for the return (uphill) trip. This trail is also used by whitewater rafters who put in at the Forks for the notorious Forks of the Kern run, Class III through V rapids all the way. Because hikers, rafters, and packers hauling rafts all share this route, the trail is wide and extremely well graded, probably one of the most painless ups and downs you are likely to encounter in the Sierra.

A set of WILDERNESS SKILLS interpretive panels near the trailhead along with a box containing booklets with "quiz" answers teaches safety and Leave No Trace principles. Rafters sign in at the trailhead, and anglers are encouraged to help with a trout study—all indications that this is a popular spot.

The Forks of the Kern Trail starts out on reddish volcanic dust instead of the more usual gray granite sand as it descends through the colorful Little Kern Lava Flow. This is a 3.5-million-year-old solidified outpouring of molten rock that has cooled into more or less regular columns similar to those at the Devil's Postpile in

The wild whitewater of the Kern River challenges the most experienced rafters.

the central Sierra. For contrast, glance back up over your right shoulder to the south-west at the pale pointed granite spires of The Needles, a more typical sight in the Sierra Nevada.

You descend through a wonderfully crazy mix of vegetation. Jeffrey pines, black oaks, live oaks, and gray pines, usually found only on the west side of the mountains, mingle with piñon pines, usually found only on the east. The most spectacular plant around is called flannelbush, a large shrub that almost explodes with big, furry, bright yellow flowers in May and June.

After a couple of long, easy switchbacks, the Forks of the Kern Trail swings north and the main fork of the Kern comes into view snaking its way off to the east. Just before you reach the bottom of the canyon, a little spring creates a muddy trickle that you must hop across just before you reach a grassy flat with campsites at mile 2.2. The river runs behind a screen of willows and alders, one of which bears a sign that says FORKS OF THE KERN. Peering through the foliage, you can see the Little Kern rushing past. If the water level is low enough to cross safely, the easiest spot to do it is about 50 yards upstream from the sign. From here you can follow the main fork of the Kern upstream for miles. Do not even consider crossing the main fork,

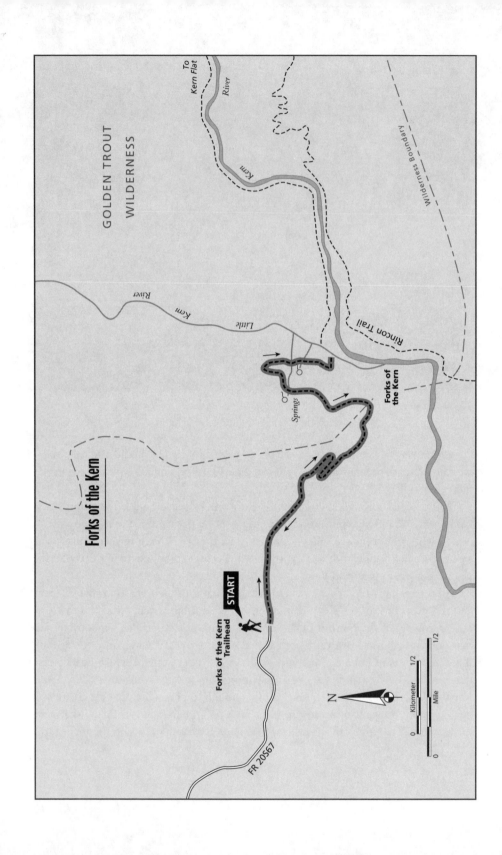

Forks of the Kern

GOLDEN TROUT
WILDERNESS

To
Kern Flat

Kern River

Kern

Wilderness Boundary

Kern River

Little

Rincon Trail

Springs

Forks of
the Kern

START

Forks of the Kern
Trailhead

FR 20S67

N

0   1/2   Kilometer

0   Mile   1/2

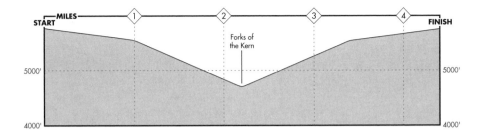

however; this river has claimed too many lives already. The first opportunity to get to the other side is over the bridge at Kern Flat 6 miles upstream. There are, however, plenty of safe spots to dangle your feet by the riverside and have a picnic. Return the way you came.

Key Points

0.0 Forks of the Kern Trailhead.

2.2 Forks of the Kern.

4.4 Forks of the Kern Trailhead.

14 Little Kern Lake

An out-and-back backpack beginning on the historic Jordan Trail, then following the Wild and Scenic Kern River to visit an unusual pair of lakes.

Start: Lewis Camp Trailhead.
Total distance: 34.4 miles.
Difficulty: Moderate.
Total climbing: 5,200 feet.
Trail traffic: Medium to light.
Best months: June through October.
Maps: USGS Camp Nelson, Hockett Peak, and Kern Lake quads; Forest Service Golden Trout and South Sierra Wilderness map.

Permits: Required and available at the Tule River Ranger Station in Springville and the Golden Trout Pack Station next door to the trailhead.
Trailhead facilities: Camping, picnic tables, and pit toilets, but no water and no trash pickup. Nearest gas, phone, and groceries are at Ponderosa, 2 miles south of Quaking Aspen on the Western Divide Highway.

Finding the trailhead: From the Tule River Ranger Station in Springville, 8 miles west of Porterville on California Highway 190, drive 27 miles to a junction where California Highway 190 becomes County Road M107, the Western Divide Highway. Turn left (north) onto Forest Road 21S50, North Road. A sign directs you to several trailheads, including LEWIS CAMP, 7 MILES. In about 4 miles the road splits. Turn right (northeast) onto Forest Road 20S79. The pavement ends here, but the dirt road is fine for passenger cars. In less than a mile, the road splits again. Keep right on FR 20S79. Soon you will pass Golden Trout Pack Station; just beyond that, in a wide area with picnic tables, is the Lewis Camp Trailhead.

The Hike

Like so many features of the Golden Trout Wilderness, Kern Lake and Little Kern Lake are anomalies, quiet ponds tucked into the gorge of an otherwise swiftly flowing river. While most of the lakes in the Sierra Nevada were gouged out by glaciers between several million and perhaps 20,000 years ago, these two came into being when a nineteenth-century landslide dammed up a section of the Kern River.

Begin at either of two trailheads a few yards apart. The more obvious one to the right is marked by a sign labeled LEWIS CAMP TRAIL 33E01. It is the steeper of the two and is usually used by horsemen. The trailhead to the left is marked by a sign announcing that Sequoia National Park lies ahead and that no dogs or guns are allowed. Hikers usually take the left fork. At mile 0.2 the two trailheads rejoin at a sign that says MAIN TRAIL. Continue downhill. At about mile 1.8 a path cuts off to the left (north) toward Grey Meadow. At mile 2.0 find the Lloyd Meadows junction. Go straight ahead (east) toward the Little Kern Bridge passing another CATTLE DRIVE trail sign to an unmarked trail split at mile 2.1. The two forks rejoin later. The right fork follows the creek and is probably the more pleasant. They come together again just before Jug Spring. At mile 3.6 the trail splits again, but both forks meet

Tranquil Little Kern Lake offers good camping.

just before the river, and the right fork is, again, the better one. The bridge over the Little Kern River is at mile 4.6.

After crossing the bridge the trail splits at mile 4.7. The right fork runs parallel to the Little Kern and then climbs out of the river canyon. The trail winds its way generally southeast, then makes an abrupt left at Trout Meadows. The trail remains on the left side of the fence and reaches the Trout Meadows Ranger Station at mile 7.6. A nearby sign points left (northwest) to Burnt Corral Meadows, but continue straight ahead toward Willow Meadows to a stock gate. Be sure to close it behind you. Shortly beyond the gate, reach a junction with the trail to Jordan Hot Springs. Continue straight ahead (north) 2 miles to Willow Meadows. Pass through another gate to reach the lower end of Willow Meadows. At the northern end of the meadow are several big packer campsites and a rather obscure unsigned junction at mile 9.6.

Head northward out of Willow Meadows, passing through a stock gate. Please close it behind you. The Lewis Camp Trail splits at the beginning of another meadow, but the two forks rejoin at the far side. Conscientious hikers will take the left fork around the western edge of the meadow: The right fork cuts through the center, leaving a scar across the fragile vegetation that should be allowed to heal. The route begins to climb gently along an arrow-straight gully moistened by occasional

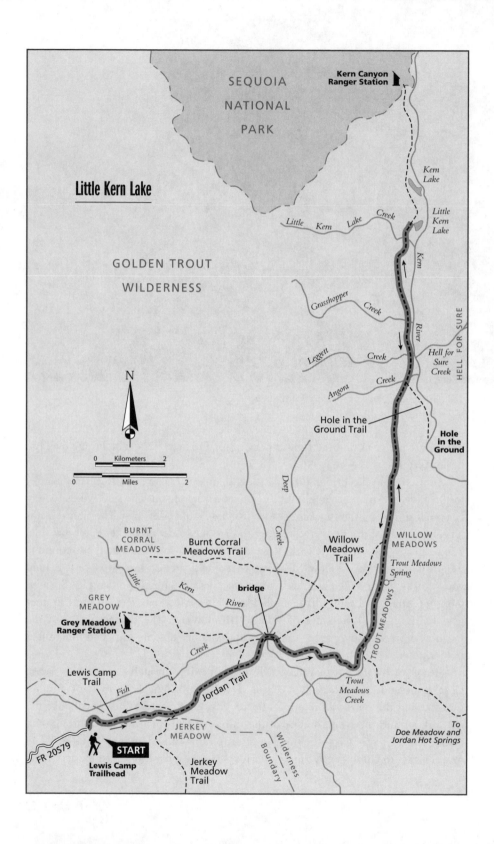

Little Kern Lake

SEQUOIA

NATIONAL

PARK

Kern Canyon Ranger Station

Kern Lake

Little Kern Lake

Little Kern Lake Creek

GOLDEN TROUT

WILDERNESS

Grasshopper Creek

Kern River

HELL FOR SURE

Leggett Creek

Hell for Sure Creek

N

Angora Creek

Hole in the Ground Trail

Hole in the Ground

0 Kilometers 2

0 Miles 2

Deep Creek

BURNT CORRAL MEADOWS

Burnt Corral Meadows Trail

Willow Meadows Trail

WILLOW MEADOWS

Little Kern River

Trout Meadows Spring

GREY MEADOW

bridge

Grey Meadow Ranger Station

TROUT MEADOWS

Lewis Camp Trail

Creek

Jordan Trail

Trout Meadows Creek

Fish

To Doe Meadow and Jordan Hot Springs

FR 20S79

START

JERKEY MEADOW

Wilderness Boundary

Lewis Camp Trailhead

Jerkey Meadow Trail

seeps and springs. Both the straight path and the springs are good hints that you are following a fault. Top out at about 6,900 feet and head downhill, gently at first, then more steeply, dropping into the gorge of the Kern River, which you will be able to hear long before you can see it. Follow the river upstream to a junction in a grove of black oaks at mile 13.8. Here a lateral trail cuts off to the right (southeast) to Hole in the Ground. Continue straight ahead and hop Angora Creek (probably dry by midsummer). Descend rather steeply and in minutes arrive at the riverside at 6,100 feet in a shady flat among huge old incense cedars and Jeffrey pines, fire-scarred at their bases. Immediately beyond a stock gate are a number of very fine large campsites. Walk upstream along the wide floodplain alongside the river, hop across Leggett Creek, also dry late in the season, then cross Grasshopper Creek at mile 15.8. This whole area is known as Grasshopper Flat. North of the creek are the remnants of a developed campground dating from the time before this was designated a wilderness area. In midsummer this low-elevation zone can be hot and the urge to splash in the river irresistible.

The floodplain becomes sunnier and more rocky beyond the campground, but the trail soon makes a turn to the left (northwest) and begins a steep but fortunately shady series of switchbacks away from the river. It rounds a hump, passes over a saddle, then descends, less precipitously than it rose, to a little, sometimes dry creek. This is the inlet to Little Kern Lake. Cross over it on a miniature bridge, then pass through another gate and follow the trail around the western edge of the lake to avoid a muddy pond, and reach the lakeshore at the northern end at mile 17.2. There is good camping here. It's a lovely tranquil spot for a layover day, fishing, or watching the ducks paddle among the reeds along the shore. You can take a short day hike upstream to shallow Kern Lake, or continue northward for 2 more miles to the Kern River Ranger Station and the border of Sequoia National Park. You also can scramble up the slope near the lake's outlet to get a look at the logjam and remains of the landslide that created the lake, then admire the crashing cascade of water where the Kern resumes its usual unobstructed course down the canyon.

Return the way you came.

Option: You can begin and end this hike at the Jerkey Meadow Trailhead if you prefer. Start at a series of signs with a wilderness skills quiz and a Leave No Trace Challenge. Do not rely on the distances on the sign at the trailhead since the trail has been rerouted and they are no longer accurate. Begin walking northward. At mile 0.4, follow the "Main Trail" sign. Climb toward the ridgetop where your path meets the Jordan Trail at mile 2.2, turn right (northeast) following the signs toward the Little Kern Bridge, passing a "Cattle Drive" trail junction, which you ignore. Follow the creekbed to reach Jug Spring. At mile 4.0 the trail splits, but the forks rejoin just before the river, and the right one is prettier. Drop into the granite gorge to the bridge at mile 4.6. Pick up the trail to Willow Meadows here. Continue from there.

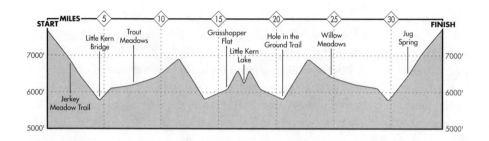

Key Points

0.0 Lewis Camp Trailhead.

0.2 MAIN TRAIL sign.

1.8 Grey Meadow Cattle Drive cutoff, continue straight.

2.0 Lloyd Meadows/Jerkey Meadow junction, continue straight (east).

3.0 Jug Spring.

3.6 Second trail split.

4.6 Little Kern Bridge.

4.7 Willow Meadows Trail split, turn right.

7.6 Trout Meadows Ranger Station.

9.6 Willow Meadows.

13.8 Hole in the Ground junction, continue straight.

15.8 Grasshopper Flat.

17.2 Little Kern Lake, turn around.

34.4 Lewis Camp Trailhead.

15 Doe Meadow and Kern Flat Loop

A flower-filled hike to the Kern River. It can be done with a short car shuttle, but if you don't mind another 4 miles of walking partly on a road, you can make a complete loop.

Start: Jerkey Meadow Trailhead.
Total distance: 22.8 miles as a shuttle, 26.8 as a loop.
Difficulty: Moderate.
Total climbing: 2,500 feet.
Trail traffic: Moderate.
Best months: July. This lower-elevation hike is cooler and more comfortable earlier in the year, but the Little Kern is too dangerous to cross during spring snowmelt. May and June are glorious months here, and the wildflowers are worth the effort if you are willing to make an out-and-back journey to Kern Flat, avoiding the river crossing, instead of a shuttle or loop.

Maps: USGS Hockett Peak and Casa Vieja Meadow quads; Forest Service Golden Trout and South Sierra Wilderness map.
Permits: Required and available at the Kernville Ranger Station or the Tule River Ranger Station in Springville.
Trailhead facilities: Camping and toilets at Forks of the Kern Trailhead, no water. Camping, toilets, and water at the Jerkey Meadow Trailhead. Nearest gas, phones, groceries at Ponderosa 2 miles south of Quaking Aspen on the Western Divide Highway.

Finding the trailhead: From the west, begin the Tule River Ranger Station in Springville, 8 miles west of Porterville on California Highway 190. Drive 27 miles to Quaking Aspen Camp where California Highway 190 becomes County Road M107, the Western Divide Highway. Continue south for 20 miles to Forest Road 22S02; turn left (east) and continue for about 4 miles to Lloyd Meadows Road (Forest Road 22S82), then turn left (north). Continue for 22 miles to Forest Road 20S67, Forks of the Kern Road, and turn right if you have two vehicles and plan a shuttle. The parking area is 2 miles down the road. Leave one vehicle here. Return 2 miles back to FR 22S82, turn right, and continue driving north for less than 2 miles to the end of Lloyd Meadows Road at Jerkey Meadows Trailhead.

From the south, from Kernville at the north end of Lake Isabella, drive 25 miles north on County Road M99 following the Kern River, then swinging left (west) to FR 22S82, Lloyd Meadows Road, just north of Johnsondale. Keep right and drive 24 miles to the end of the road, turning off 2 miles before the end to the Forks of the Kern Trailhead if you are shuttling cars.

The Hike

Check with local rangers to find out whether the Little Kern is safe to cross at the Forks before you begin. Begin walking northward from the wilderness skills quiz and Leave No Trace Challenge. At mile 0.4 follow the Main Trail sign for an easier more enjoyable hike. Climb gradually at first, then more steeply toward the ridgetop to the Jordan Trail at mile 2.2. Turn right (northeast) following the signs toward the Little Kern Bridge, passing a CATTLE DRIVE trail junction, which you ignore. Follow

the creekbed to Jug Spring. At mile 4.0 the trail splits, but the forks rejoin just before the river, and the right one is prettier. Drop into the granite gorge of the Little Kern River where it is spanned by a substantial bridge at mile 4.6.

After crossing the bridge, the Jordan Trail curves to negotiate a stream gully, then splits at mile 4.7. Keep to the right (south) fork. The trail runs parallel to the Little Kern at first. As you climb out of the river canyon, notice how the rock changes from light salt-and-pepper granite to darker lava, full of little pockmarks and holes where gases escaped when the lava was still molten. This is the Little Kern Lava Flow, one of the oldest basalt flows (3.5 million years) in the wilderness. The trail winds its way generally southeast, gently rising and falling through forest, then makes an abrupt left to reveal the refreshing green of Trout Meadows ahead. The path keeps to the left side of the fence enclosing the meadow and reaches the Trout Meadows Ranger Station at mile 7.6. (There is a fenced passageway through the meadow that makes a shortcut north to meet the Doe Meadow Trail on the other side, but if you want to drop by the ranger station, keep straight ahead.) There is plenty of camping all around the meadow, and there are outhouses near the ranger station, which is staffed on summer weekends.

At a signed junction at the edge of the meadow near the station, turn right (south again) onto the Jordan/Doe Meadow Trail skirting Trout Meadows on your right side, then walk southeast toward Kern Flat through forest. In about a mile a pipe delivers water from Cold Spring into a watering trough; a campsite lies beyond. The drop becomes steeper and rockier as you descend to Doe Meadow—which isn't a meadow at all, but a brushy basin that was burned over in 1975. Both evergreen and deciduous black oaks are making a strong comeback now. Cross and recross a tributary stream, and continue to follow the relentless switchbacks down to meet the river trail at the wide grass-lined floodplain of Kern Flat at mile 14.6. Turn right (south) near the riverside and enter the river gorge.

The hiking here can be hot, but you can dunk in the river almost anytime to cool off, and there are plenty of shady campsites. The scenery along the trail is dramatic. Osa Creek and Soda Creek crash one after another into the river from the opposite side. Deadman Canyon Creek, which you must ford, comes tumbling into the Kern next on your side of the river. The walls become steeper, and you must climb above the bottom of the gorge for a time. There is a good view here of Rattlesnake Creek plunging down into the river back on opposite side again. As you approach the confluence of the Kern and the Little Kern at the Forks, the rock changes from gray granite to more colorful metamorphics. Plod across a sandy floodplain, then ford at the widest spot you can find. From here, at mile 20.6, climb out of the canyon over a couple of long, easy switchbacks that head south, then

◀ *Early morning view of the Kern River near the Forks*

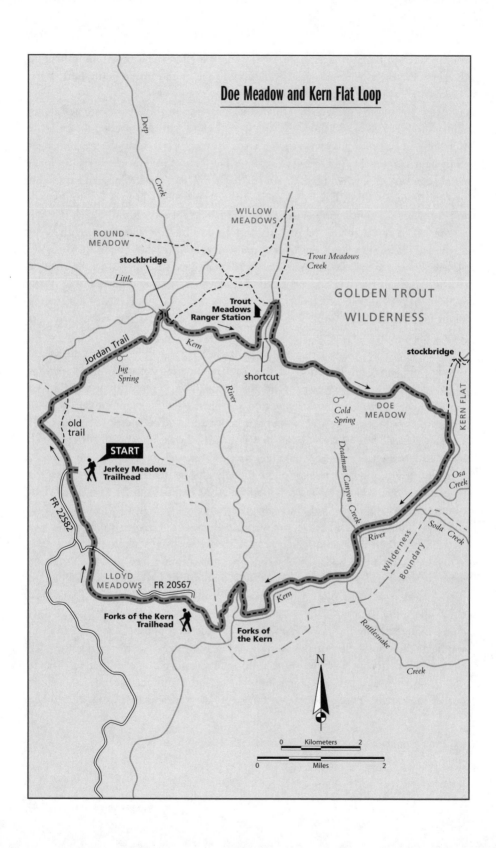

Doe Meadow and Kern Flat Loop

Deep

Creek

WILLOW
MEADOWS

ROUND
MEADOW

stockbridge

Little

*Trout Meadows
Creek*

**Trout
Meadows
Ranger Station**

GOLDEN TROUT

WILDERNESS

Jordan Trail

Kern

shortcut

stockbridge

*Jug
Spring*

*Cold
Spring*

DOE
MEADOW

KERN FLAT

old
trail

START

**Jerkey Meadow
Trailhead**

River

Deadman Canyon Creek

*Osa
Creek*

FR 22S82

Soda Creek

LLOYD
MEADOWS   FR 20S67

Wilderness

Boundary

**Forks of the Kern
Trailhead**

River

**Forks of
the Kern**

Kern

Rattlesnake

Creek

N

0   Kilometers   2

0   Miles   2

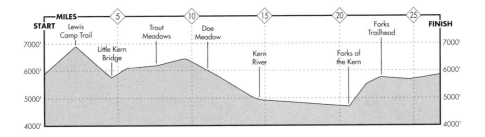

climb gradually toward The Needles and past the 3.5 million year-old Little Kern Volcanic flow to the Forks Trailhead. If you have left a vehicle there, this is the end of your journey. If not, follow the road leaving the campground and the trailhead westward for 2 miles until it joins Lloyd Meadows Road, or the trail that parallels it, and turn right (north) where you meet the Jerkey Meadow Trailhead in 2 more miles.

Key Points

0.0 Jerkey Meadow Trailhead.

0.4 Old trail crossing.

2.2 Jordan Trail junction, turn right (northeast).

4.0 Unmarked trail split.

4.6 Little Kern Bridge.

4.7 Willow Meadows Trail split, turn right.

7.6 Trout Meadows Ranger Station, turn right (south).

14.6 Kern Flat, turn right (south).

20.6 Forks of the Kern.

22.8 Forks Trailhead, shuttle parking.

24.8 Lloyd Meadows Road.

26.8 Jerkey Meadow Trailhead.

16 Central Wilderness Grand Tour

This route is one of the few that allow exploration of the wonderfully diverse country on both sides of the Kern River, making use of the only two bridges within the wilderness spanning the main fork of the Kern. It's a real expedition, with lots of altitude gain and loss.

Start: Jerkey Meadow Trailhead at Lloyd Meadows.
Total distance: 79.1 miles.
Difficulty: Strenuous.
Total climbing: 10,690 feet.
Trail traffic: Varies; moderate overall, heaviest near the Kern River Ranger Station and Jordan Hot Springs.
Best months: July through October.
Maps: USGS Hockett Peak, Kern Lake, Kern Peak, Templeton Mountain, Monache Meadow,
and Casa Vieja Meadow quads; Forest Service Golden Trout and South Sierra Wilderness map.
Permits: Required and available at the Kernville Ranger Station or the Tule River Ranger Station in Springville.
Trailhead facilities: Camping, toilets, and water. Nearest gas, phones, and groceries are at Ponderosa, 2 miles south of Quaking Aspen on the Western Divide Highway or at Road's End Resort on County Road M99.

Finding the trailhead: From the west, begin at the Tule River Ranger Station is Springville, 8 miles west of Porterville on California Highway 190. Drive 27 miles to a junction where CA 190 ends and the Western Divide Highway, County Road M107, begins, just before Quaking Aspen Camp. Drive south for 10 miles on the Western Divide Highway to a dirt road (Forest Road 22S02). Turn left (east), drive 4 miles to Lloyd Meadows Road, and turn left (north). Continue for 19 miles to the end of the road.

From the south, starting at Kernville at the north end of Lake Isabella, drive 25 miles north on County Road M99 following alongside the Kern River to Forest Road 22S82, Lloyd Meadows Road, just north of Johnsondale. Keep right and drive 24 miles to the end of the road.

The Hike

Check with rangers to make sure streams are safe to cross if you plan to begin this trip before early July. Begin walking northward from the wilderness skills quiz and Leave No Trace Challenge. At mile 0.4 follow the Main Trail sign for an easier, more enjoyable hike. Climb gradually at first, then more steeply toward the ridgetop to the Jordan Trail at mile 2.2. Turn right (northeast) following the signs toward the Little Kern Bridge, passing a CATTLE DRIVE trail junction, which you ignore. Follow the creekbed to Jug Spring. At mile 4.0 the trail splits, but the forks rejoin just before the river, and the right one is prettier. Drop into the granite gorge of the Little Kern River where it is spanned by a substantial bridge at mile 4.6.

After crossing the bridge, the Jordan Trail curves to negotiate a stream gully, ascends rapidly out of the river gorge, then splits at mile 4.7. Take the left fork

Columnar basalt is a striking volcanic feature near the Volcano Falls–Kern River confluence.

toward Willow Meadows and climb through forest to another junction at mile 6.5. Turn left (northwest); the right fork goes down to Trout Meadows Guard Station. Bob up and down over roller-coaster trail, hopping several tributaries feeding the Little Kern. Ford Deep Creek, the last of this series of streams, then cross a hump to reach the Deep Creek Trail heading right (north) at mile 8.7. In a few minutes you recross Deep Creek and follow its east bank upstream, climbing more and more steeply. At the final crossing back to the western shore, fill up with water again. You will be leaving the creek behind to tackle a long, dry climb ahead to an 8,276-foot saddle in open forest. There are a few large, flat, but dry campsites on top.

Here, at mile 12.4 is a junction marked by what is left of a sign propped up by rocks. It is marked simply 32E06. Your faint path turns right and climbs very steeply eastward through currant and snowberry bushes that are sometimes overgrown and scratchy. Now and then if you can spare the energy to look back over your shoulder, you can catch a glimpse of White Mountain to the south and, a bit later, Angora Mountain to the southeast. Cross a saddle and traverse a slope, lose some hard-won elevation, then climb over a second saddle. At last the Deep Creek Trail drops to meet the first of several very welcome packer campsites at the head of a tributary of Grasshopper Creek. Fill up with water again before you leave this spot for the next grueling climb. The route leaves the meadow heading north between a tributary

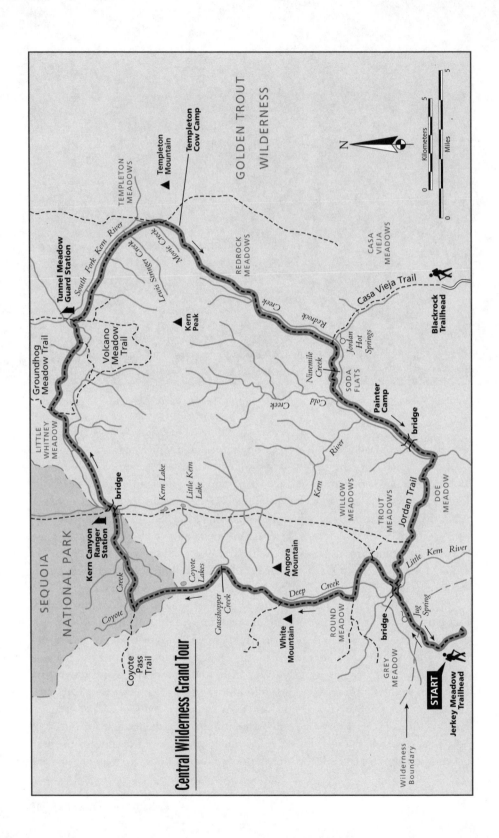

Central Wilderness Grand Tour

SEQUOIA NATIONAL PARK

GOLDEN TROUT WILDERNESS

Templeton Cow Camp

▲ Templeton Mountain

TEMPLETON MEADOWS

Tunnel Meadow Guard Station

South Fork Kern River

Lewis Stringer Creek

Movie Creek

Groundhog Meadow Trail

Volcano Meadow Trail

▲ Kern Peak

LITTLE WHITNEY MEADOW

REDROCK MEADOWS

Redrock Creek

Ninemile Creek

CASA VIEJA MEADOWS

Casa Vieja Trail

Jordan Hot Springs

Blackrock Trailhead

SODA FLATS

Painter Camp

bridge

Cold Creek

bridge

Kern Canyon Ranger Station

Kern Lake

Little Kern Lake

Kern River

WILLOW MEADOWS

TROUT MEADOWS

Jordan Trail

DOE MEADOW

Coyote Lakes

Coyote Creek

Grasshopper Creek

▲ Angora Mountain

Deep Creek

Little Kern River

Coyote Pass Trail

▲ White Mountain

ROUND MEADOW

bridge

Jug Spring

GREY MEADOW

START

Jerkey Meadow Trailhead

Wilderness Boundary

N

Kilometers 0 5

Miles 0 5

creek below and a jagged rocky spine above, then swings west and labors up more switchbacks to gain an open windswept ridge. Climb this to reach the high point of the tour at 10,850 feet. Below, at the base of the gravelly slope to the east, lie Coyote Lakes.

Descend to a junction at mile 18.3 in a timbered saddle marked by several signs in various stages of decrepitude. One faint trail heads left (west) down Willow Creek to Lion Meadows. The trail to Coyote Lakes heads right (east). After visiting the lakes you will return to this intersection and follow the trail to the north toward the Sequoia Park boundary. To make the detour to Coyote Lakes, descend eastward on switchbacks into the cirque to reach the lakeshore at mile 18.6. The trail runs along the northern edge of the larger of the two and leads to several campsites in a flat between this lake and the smaller one.

Fishing is great; wildflowers abound. It's a great spot for a layover, especially on a hike as long as this one.

When you are ready (or when you must) leave the lakes and retrace your steps to the junction at the saddle above them (mile 18.9). Turn right (north) and climb to the gap at the top of the ridge informally known as Coyote Lakes Pass at 10,250 feet. This marks the boundary of Sequoia National Park. From here you can look toward Coyote Pass in the northwest, with Vandever and Florence Peaks beyond. The panorama to the northeast extends all the way to the main Sierra Crest. Flounder down the other side of this pass through deep scree until you meet the beginning of a tributary of Coyote Creek, where the footing becomes firmer. Descend along the creek to reach a meadow twinkling with yellow monkey flowers and lavender shooting stars (and sometimes humming with mosquitoes). Beyond the meadow the trail rises and falls gently, crossing the often dry bed of Coyote Creek to meet the Coyote Pass Trail at mile 20.9. Turn right (east) at the sign pointing toward the Kern River.

The route hops back and forth over Coyote Creek, then begins to drop more steeply alongside the stream as it tumbles down the gorge toward the Kern River. At one point the trail leaves the riverside to negotiate a tributary flowing in from the northwest, then reaches and crosses Coyote Creek again on a big log to its south side. Shortly thereafter, a grand vista of the Kern Canyon opens wide enough to display the steep chasm on the opposite side where Golden Trout Creek plunges over Volcano Falls. Coyote Creek thunders down its own dramatic gorge right beside you to meet the Kern just downstream. The last 1,000-foot descent toward the Kern River is a real knee-knocker that ends at a shady flat under black oaks and Jeffrey pines. Here you make your last traverse of Coyote Creek, using downed logs. Ahead is the Kern Canyon Ranger Station, staffed in summer, on your left. Just beyond it, the trail splits at mile 25.9. The left fork follows the river upstream to Funston Meadow. You keep right, heading toward Golden Trout Creek, and descend toward the bridge. You have dropped clear down to 6,400 feet here. On the way a sign marks a side trail to Soda Springs, where fizzy but unappetizing water bubbles to the surface. There is a large but buggy and boring camping area. Continue on down to the river, where there are plenty of better, but more popular campsites near the bridge at mile 26.2.

From here cross a large manzanita-covered flat for about a mile then climb up a few steep rocky switchbacks to where a lava flow ran over the cliff to the Kern River. This lava flow is the most recent in the region, less than 5,000 years old and is known as Malpais (bad lands). The Swiss cheese texture of the rocks comes from gas bubbles in the lava while it was still molten. Look for the long, spectacular series of drops that make up Volcano Falls to your left about half way up your climb up and out of Golden Trout Creek. Cross the creek on a natural bridge made of travertine. Look at the falls below the crossing, which are more beautiful than those farther up. Continue to climb through a little meadow and then back into the forest to a lava boulder field. Stay on the south side of the creek until a three-way junction at mile 30.8 from which the southern fork goes along the Malpais lava flow, the right toward Volcano Meadow and the left along the fence that encloses the Little Whitney Meadow. At the other side of the meadow turn right and wade the stream at mile 31.2. Pass an inconspicuous sign on the left of the trail saying Kern River. The ridge to the north confines trail and creek to a narrow notch alongside the lava flow. Hop a little tributary of Golden Trout Creek and hike along its northern bank. Continue through the sandy forest passing southwest of little Groundhog Meadow to a junction at mile 34.1. Once you come out of the forest cross a willow thicket, then cross Golden Trout Creek again. You will meet a fence that turns left. Follow it to the Ramshaw Meadows junction just short of the Tunnel Meadow Guard Station at mile 35.0. Turn right (southeast) at this junction, climb a saddle between two red cinder cones, and pass through a gate. Wind your way down to the left to the head of broad Ramshaw Meadows, where the South Fork of the Kern flows away toward Olancha Peak on the skyline. The meadow has been grazed heavily and is somewhat barren, but among the clumps of sagebrush blooms a rare treasure, the Ramshaw abronia *(Abronia alpina)*. Look for a low, matted kind of sand verbena with slightly sticky foliage and clusters of small pale lavender flowers. It is an endangered species that is found in isolated patches in this region and nowhere else in the world! Follow along the strip of meadow between the river's edge and the forest, then hike over a forested saddle, hop Lewis Stringer, and meet vast Templeton Meadows clasping the base of Templeton Mountain, a round volcanic dome. It is easy to lose the actual trail here among the maze of cow paths in the sandy soil, so keep your topo handy to stay on course. As you draw even with Templeton Mountain, look for a vague junction in the meadow at mile 42.0 and keep right (south). Hop Movie Stringer Creek (a cabin farther upstream was the backdrop for a long-forgotten horse opera) and climb a gradual slope to reach Templeton Cow Camp at mile 42.7.

The trail begins climbing gradually, then becomes steeper and eroded after swinging left further up the canyon until you reach the high point at 10,250 feet.

Begin a long, steep, heavily eroded trail to a trail junction. Turn left (southwest) and go 0.1 mile to another junction in Redrock Meadows at mile 47.1. Continue straight then over a shoulder of Indian Head, a big red lump of metavolcanic rock. Descend a series of switchbacks to Redrock Creek. Descend along the eastern bank of the creek to a junction at mile 51.1. Turn left past a burned section of forest, then turn left again shortly before Jordan Hot Springs at mile 51.3. This is another great choice for a layover, or at least an extended rest and relaxing bath. From the Jordan camping area, cross Ninemile Creek and descend gradually westward through the forest. Pass by the trail that goes right (north) to Sidehill Meadow along Cold Meadow Creek. Soon reach the fenced meadow at Soda Flat, where a naturally carbonated spring discolors surrounding vegetation. This is private property; the well-kept cabin is still in use. Beyond the flat, the oak-shaded trail steepens and becomes rockier, finally arriving at another junction, not very well marked, at mile 60.6. The left fork is the more direct route to the Kern, but the right one toward Hells Hole is more scenic. Follow the right fork if the water level is low enough get across Ninemile Creek; otherwise, take the left.

The longer, scenic route to the right (west) passes through a gate and over the creek. As you climb out of the creekbed, you pass a wonderful rocky little gorge where Ninemile Creek makes a pretty fall. Drop to the Kern River to find the site of old Painter Camp—once a sawmill. One cabin and the remains of a second are all that's left. The junction along the river at mile 61.1 points upstream toward Hells Hole, but you head downstream to the left. At mile 61.4 meet the southern branch of the trail coming from Jordan Hot Springs (if you didn't go that way in the first place). Follow the relatively flat path along the river until you must climb over a saddle beside a rocky bump, then descend and continue on alongside the river to the bridge over the Kern just north of Grouse Creek (mile 63.6). Once across, ford Hockett Peak Creek and a couple of unnamed tributaries to reach wide grassy Kern Flat, the low point of the hike at less than 5,000 feet. Skirt the west side of the flat, then begin the climb away from the river to meet the junction with the Doe Meadow Trail at mile 64.8. Don't forget to fill up with water when you cross the first tributary on your mostly waterless climb up through Doe Meadow. From this point, follow hike 15 in reverse back to the Jerkey Meadow Trailhead.

Key Points

0.0 Jerkey Meadow Trailhead at Lloyd Meadows.

0.4 Old trail crossing.

2.2 Jordan Trail Junction, turn right (northeast).

4.0 Unmarked trail split.

4.6 Little Kern River Bridge.

4.7 Willow Meadows Trail Junction, turn left.

6.5 Willow Meadows/Trout Meadows junction, turn left (northwest).

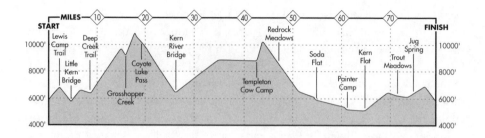

8.7 Deep Creek Trail.

12.4 Junction 32E06, turn right (east).

18.3 Coyote Lakes junction, turn right (east).

18.6 Coyote Lakes.

18.9 Coyote Lakes junction, turn right (north).

20.9 Coyote Pass Trail, turn right (east).

25.9 Kern Canyon Ranger Station, keep right.

26.2 Kern River Bridge.

30.8 Volcano Meadow junction, continue straight.

31.2 Little Whitney Meadow, turn right (east).

34.1 Groundhog Meadow junction, continue straight.

35.0 Ramshaw Meadows junction.

42.0 Templeton Mountain junction.

42.7 Templeton Cow Camp.

47.1 Redrock Meadows, turn left (southwest).

51.1 Kern River junction, turn left.

51.3 Jordan Hot Springs.

60.6 Painter Camp junction.

61.1 Kern River at Painter Camp.

61.4 Second junction.

63.6 Kern River Bridge.

64.8 Doe Meadow Trail junction.

79.1 Jerkey Meadow.

The Great Western Divide

Norrth of the Golden Trout Wilderness, the subrange of the Great Western Divide splits off from the main Sierra Crest and plunges like a dagger southward into the west-central portion of the wilderness, separating the drainage of the Little Kern from the North (main) Fork of the Kern River. It defines the boundary between Sequoia National Park and the Golden Trout from the Mineral King region to Coyote Lakes. Here is wild alpine scenery at its finest, crowned by 12,432-foot Florence Peak, second highest point in the wilderness. There are giddy views of pointed peaks and clear glacial lakes beneath skies at one moment impossibly blue, roiling with thunderclouds the next. Whistling pikas and marmots scurry among rock piles above patches of green meadows and intimate gardens of belly flowers.

The nearest and most practical access to this high country is over Farewell Gap from Mineral King in Sequoia National Park. Wilderness permits are required, but there are no quotas in place as long as you are headed directly over Farewell Gap and do not plan to spend the night within the park. If you do, you will have lots of competition for permits on weekends. You can contact the park service at www.nps.gov/seki, or phone the wilderness office at (559) 565–3764 for more information. Pick up your permit at the Mineral King Ranger Station near Cold Springs Campground. It's open 7:00 A.M. to 3:30 P.M. June through early September. At other times you can self-register on one of the forms available outside the ranger station.

It is possible to enter Golden Trout Wilderness via Franklin and Shotgun Passes, or via Wet Meadows and Hockett Meadows from the Atwell Mill Trailhead, but only the Farewell Gap route is described here. The others involve so much travel inside the park that they are outside our scope.

The trailheads in the Mineral King Valley begin at about 7,800 feet. Anyplace you go is up! If you are sensitive to rapid elevation gain, camping overnight near the trailhead is a good idea. Unfortunately, there are only two small campgrounds nearby, Atwell Mill and Cold Springs. Both cost $8.00 and are first come, first served. (This is in addition to the $10 fee you already paid to enter the park.)

The trails are well maintained in the park, of course, but the farther into the wilderness you travel, the more obscure they become. Still, none is especially difficult to follow if you pay attention and carry a map.

Important! The marmots that live at Mineral King have developed a taste for the minerals found in antifreeze and will chew through your radiator hose to get them. You are many miles from help in Three Rivers if your car becomes disabled at the trailhead. Apparently the rodents' cravings are strongest when they first emerge from hibernation in spring, so early-season hikers, or their vehicles, are most at risk. You can rent a portable marmot-proof fence at Silver City to erect around your car, but since marmots do burrow, these may not be very effective. If you plan an extended backpack from Mineral King before mid-July, remember to check under your hood for damage (or for furry stowaways) before you start back down the road. A spare radiator hose might be a good idea too.

17 Bullfrog Lakes

A vigorous climb through some of the Sierra's finest wildflower gardens to a pair of high alpine lakes.

Start: Farewell Gap Trailhead.
Total distance: 17 miles.
Difficulty: Moderately strenuous.
Total climbing: 4,020 feet.
Trail traffic: Medium.
Best months: July to October.
Maps: USGS Mineral King quad; Forest Service Golden Trout and South Sierra Wilderness map.

Permits: Available in advance through Sequoia National Park or at the Mineral King Ranger Station near Cold Springs Campground on the Mineral King Road.
Trailhead facilities: None. Water and toilets are available at nearby campgrounds; phones, food, and showers, at Silver City about 4 miles back down the road. The nearest reliable source of gas is 25 miles away in Three Rivers.

Finding the trailhead: Drive through the town of Three Rivers on California Highway 198, and when the buildings begin to thin out at the far end, watch for the Mineral King turnoff to the right (east). In about 10 miles enter Sequoia National Park at a kiosk, where you pay an entrance fee of $10 per car, good for seven days. Follow the steep, winding, and very narrow road for 25 miles to its end and park in a lot near a cluster of cabins. Walk back down the driveway from the parking area, cross over a bridge, and turn right onto the dirt road heading to the pack station. The trail begins near the stables.
   Note: Marmot alert! Be sure to read the introduction to this section.

The Hike

The Mineral King Valley must be one of the most sublimely beautiful places in the world. Its sharp peaks and silvery waterfalls are reminiscent of the Swiss Alps, but infinitely wilder. No placid milk cows or tidy farmhouses here, just brilliant red and white rocks, splashes of wildflower color over the green, green meadows, rustling cottonwood groves, and windblown clusters of foxtail pines on the high, lonely ridges. Your journey into this paradise begins at the signed trailhead on the way to the pack station. A second sign, this one with trail mileages, appears at mile 0.2. Marmots scatter in all directions as you hike up the east side of the valley, heading south toward Farewell Gap, the obvious low point between Vandever Mountain on the right and the ridge culminating in Florence Peak on the left. The climb to the pass begins as an almost imperceptible ascent at first, then continues on a series of well-graded switchbacks. It crosses runoff streams from numerous springs and snow patches, including the outlet creeks of Crystal and Franklin Lakes. All this water nourishes such an extravagant show of wildflowers that it's difficult to make any forward progress. The variety is so rich—a new species at every step. Among these

Yellow-bellied marmots at Mineral King have developed a taste for antifreeze.

are some especially brilliant and beautiful gentians, with deep, cuplike corollas of the purest, brightest, most electric royal blue.

The Farewell Gap Trail contours along a hillside for a while then begins a second set of switchbacks, at the top of which the Franklin Pass Trail cuts off to the left (northeast) at mile 3.8. Your route continues on toward Farewell Gap in a dense and aromatic patch of Bigelow sneezeweed, wild onions, and corn lilies. The view back down the valley becomes more spectacular the farther you climb. At last you reach the top of barren, windy Farewell Gap at mile 6.4 (10,587 feet); a sign welcomes travelers to the Golden Trout Wilderness.

From here descend on clinking, jingling metamorphic rock chips toward the floor of Farewell Canyon for more than a mile on rather tedious switchbacks. Just past the final switchback is an obscure junction. Some hikers take the upper (left) fork to avoid a short stretch of steep climbing, but do not use this route in the early season—it forces you to wade the outlet creek from the lakes above on some very slick rock at the top of a long, scary drop. The water flows too fast and deep to cross safely. Take the other, right-hand fork, which crosses the outlet creek at an easier, safer spot, even though it's slightly longer, at least until midseason. Just beyond the forks, turn sharply left (northeast) at a duck (mile 7.5). There is no sign here, either. The Bullfrog Lakes Trail begins to climb very steeply, and in about another 0.2 mile

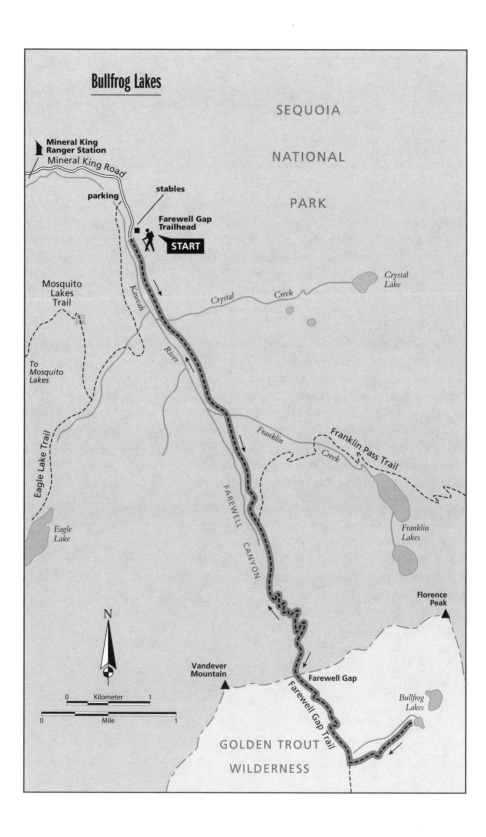

Bullfrog Lakes

Mineral King Ranger Station

Mineral King Road

parking

stables

Farewell Gap Trailhead

START

SEQUOIA

NATIONAL

PARK

Crystal Lake

Crystal Creek

Kaweah

River

Mosquito Lakes Trail

To Mosquito Lakes

Franklin

Franklin Pass Trail

Creek

Eagle Lake Trail

FAREWELL CANYON

Eagle Lake

Franklin Lakes

Florence Peak

N

Vandever Mountain

Farewell Gap

Bullfrog Lakes

Farewell Gap Trail

0   Kilometer   1

0   Mile   1

GOLDEN TROUT

WILDERNESS

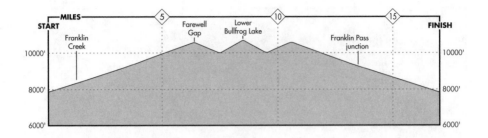

reaches a fallen-down signpost and a faint junction where the other, more hazardous fork of the trail rejoins. Keep right, following along the east side of the creek. The climb to the lakes is rough, but the scenery provides plenty of excuses to stop to catch your breath and look around. The long, narrow, silvery creek from the Bullfrog Lakes snakes down a mountainside of multicolored rocks, dotted with picturesque groupings of foxtail pines. Behind, across the canyon of the headwaters of the Little Kern, is another stunning panorama of Vandever Mountain and surrounding peaks.

Finally the route leaves the last tree behind and, at mile 8.5, finds the lower of the Bullfrog Lakes at 10,700 feet nestled in a classic glacial cirque. The upper lake is just above this one, out of sight, but it's fairly easy to reach by a short scramble. Notice the interesting change in the nature of the rock surrounding the lakes: Chunky white granite on the left abruptly gives way to much older red metamorphic material on the right. There are a few flat, not-too-rocky campsites at the lake's west end. Bears aren't especially common here but there are plenty of marmots, and no trees at all for hanging food. A bear canister and/or extreme vigilance are recommended. Return the way you came.

Key Points

0.0 Farewell Gap Trailhead.

0.2 Stables.

3.8 Franklin Pass junction, continue straight.

6.4 Farewell Gap.

7.5 Bullfrog Lakes turnoff, turn left (northeast).

8.5 Lower Bullfrog Lake.

17.0 Farewell Gap Trailhead.

18 Silver Lake

An out-and-back hike to a high alpine lake on the Great Western Divide.

Start: Farewell Gap Trailhead.
Total distance: 26.6 miles.
Difficulty: Moderately strenuous.
Total climbing: 5,160 feet.
Trail traffic: Medium.
Best months: July to October.
Maps: USGS Mineral King and Quinn Peak quads; Forest Service Golden Trout and South Sierra Wilderness map.

Permits: Available in advance through Sequoia National Park or at the Mineral King Ranger Station on the Mineral King Road near Cold Springs Campground.
Trailhead facilities: None. Water and toilets are available at nearby campgrounds; phones, food, and showers, at Silver City, about 4 miles back down the road. The nearest reliable source of gas is 25 miles away in Three Rivers.

Finding the trailhead: Drive through the town of Three Rivers on California Highway 198, and when the buildings begin to thin out at the far end, watch for the Mineral King turnoff to the right (east). In about 10 miles enter Sequoia National Park at a kiosk, where you pay an entrance fee of $10 per car, good for seven days. Follow the steep, winding, and very narrow road for 25 miles to its end and park in a lot near a cluster of cabins. Walk back down the driveway from the parking area, cross over a bridge, and turn right onto the dirt road heading to the pack station. The trail begins near the stables.

Note: Marmot alert! Be sure to read the introduction to this section.

The Hike

Begin your journey into the sublimely beautiful Mineral King Valley from the signed trailhead on the way to the pack station. A second sign, appears at mile 0.2. The climb to the pass begins almost imperceptibly, then continues on a series of well-graded switchbacks. The trail contours along a hillside for a while then begins a second set of switchbacks, at the top of which the Franklin Pass trail cuts off to the left (northeast) at mile 3.8. Your route continues on toward Farewell Gap at mile 6.4 (10,587 feet) where a sign welcomes travelers to the Golden Trout Wilderness. Descend toward the floor of Farewell Canyon for more than a mile on rather tedious switchbacks. Just past the final switchback is an obscure junction. Some hikers take the upper (left) fork to avoid a short stretch of steep climbing, but do not use this route in early season. It forces you to wade the outlet creek from the lakes above on some very slick rock at the top of a long drop. Take the right-hand fork, which crosses the outlet creek at an easier, safer spot, even though it's slightly longer, at least until mid-season. Just beyond the forks, come to the Bullfrog Lakes turnoff at a duck (mile 7.5).

If you do not plan to visit the lakes, continue straight ahead southeast along the left (east) side of the creek, stirring up a delicious fragrance of pennyroyal with your

Silver Lake, jewel of the Great Western Divide

passage. This pale lavender member of the mint family makes an excellent tea. There is a large pleasant campsite across the stream in a grove of foxtail pines just before the path becomes steeper and the creek drops over a ledge. The creek and canyon floor drop away to the right, but the trail stays high along the mountainside, now and then making a switchback through flower gardens so dense they sometimes obscure the path.

At mile 9.8 the trail splits. There is no sign. The right fork initially cuts back northwest, then drops down to cross the nascent Little Kern River and continues on to Wet Meadows. Your narrow, rocky route continues straight ahead and, at mile 10.6, just before you hop a plunging creek, reaches a second unmarked shortcut down to the Little Kern. This one is not shown on the Golden Trout Wilderness map. Contour around the base of a granitic knob. (The GTW map incorrectly shows the trail going over the top of it. Then, on the far side of the knob, the *topo* incorrectly shows two parallel trails heading east, while the GTW map shows only one. There were two trails at one time, but only the upper one still exists.) At mile 11.8, tucked back in a notch, is the signed Silver Lake Trail to the left (north), and just beyond it, Shotgun Creek. Note that the Golden Trout Wilderness map shows the trail to Silver Lake beginning on the east side of Shotgun Creek and recrossing the

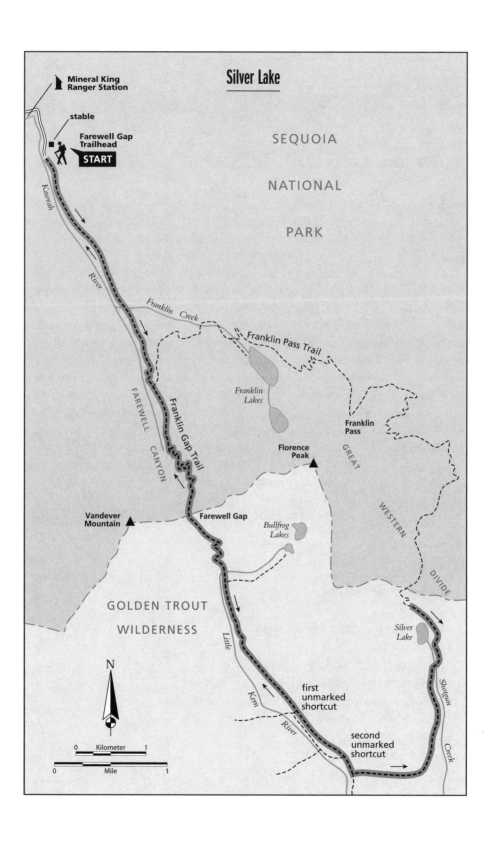

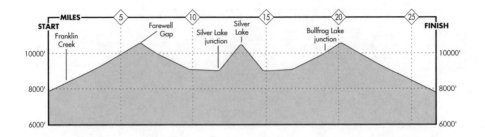

creek about a 0.5 mile up. In fact, the trail begins on the west side and does not come close to the stream until it reaches the lake. If you have less than a quart of water, walk a few yards farther to the creek and fill up before you tackle the steep pull ahead.

Heading north, the trail to the lake starts in shady forest that shortly gives way to more open, pebbly country among patches of chinquapin. The sandy flats beside the trail are spangled with tiny yellow and magenta monkey flowers and delicate white popcorn flowers. After topping a rise, the route passes a willow-choked meadow, then proceeds up an open slope before switching back toward the outlet creek in a riot of wildflowers to find Silver Lake (10,520 feet) at mile 13.3. It lies in a classic High Sierra setting at the base of a rocky, barren glacial cirque, surrounded by willows and red mountain heather. There is good camping on the southeast side of the lake, across the outlet in a grove of foxtail pines alive with squawking Clark's nutcrackers.

Option: You can camp at the lake and return the way you came, or you can make an extensive high-altitude loop back to Mineral King. The loop trail is not shown on the Golden Trout Wilderness map, but it is on the topo and in this book. It heads eastward around the lake, then climbs steeply out of the cirque at its upper end, over Shotgun Pass, where it reenters Sequoia National Park, then heads back to Farewell Gap via Franklin Pass and Franklin Lakes.

Key Points

0.0   Farewell Gap Trailhead.

0.2   Stables.

3.8   Franklin Pass junction, continue straight.

6.4   Farewell Gap.

7.5   Bullfrog Lakes turnoff, continue straight.

9.8   First unmarked Wet Meadows junction, continue straight.

10.6   Second unmarked Wet Meadows junction, continue straight.

11.8   Silver Lake turnoff, turn left (north).

13.3   Silver Lake, turn around.

26.6   Farewell Gap Trailhead.

19 Coyote Lakes

A spectacular out-and-back tour into the high country along the Great Western Divide.

Start: Farewell Gap Trailhead.
Total distance: 39.2 miles.
Difficulty: Moderate to strenuous, depending on how fast you travel.
Total climbing: 6,750 feet.
Trail traffic: Medium to Farewell Gap, fairly light beyond.
Best months: July to October.
Maps: USGS Mineral King, Quinn Peak, and Kern Lake quads; Forest Service Golden Trout and South Sierra Wilderness map.

Permits: Available in advance through Sequoia National Park or at the Mineral King Ranger Station on the Mineral King Road near Cold Springs Campground.
Trailhead facilities: None. Water and toilets are available at nearby campgrounds; phones, food, and showers at Silver City about 4 miles back down the road. The nearest reliable source of gas is 25 miles away in Three Rivers.

Finding the trailhead: Drive through the town of Three Rivers on California Highway 198, and when the buildings begin to thin out at the far end, watch for the Mineral King turnoff to the right (east). In about 10 miles enter Sequoia National Park at a kiosk, where you pay an entrance fee of $10 per car, good for seven days. Follow the steep, winding, and very narrow road for 25 miles to its end and park in a lot near a cluster of cabins. Walk back down the driveway from the parking area, cross over a bridge, and turn right onto the dirt road heading to the pack station. The trail begins near the stables.

Note: Marmot alert! Be sure to read the introduction to this section.

The Hike

Begin your journey into the sublimely beautiful Mineral King Valley from the signed trailhead on the way to the pack station. A second sign appears at mile 0.2. The climb to the pass begins almost imperceptibly, then continues on a series of well-graded switchbacks. The trail contours along a hillside for a while then begins a second set of switchbacks, at the top of which the Franklin Pass trail cuts off to the left (northeast) at mile 3.8. Your route continues on toward Farewell Gap at mile 6.4 (10,587 feet) where a sign welcomes travelers to the Golden Trout Wilderness. Descend toward the floor of Farewell Canyon for more than a mile on rather tedious switchbacks. Just past the final switchback is an obscure junction. Some hikers take the upper (left) fork to avoid a short stretch of steep climbing, but do not use this route in early season. It forces you to wade the outlet creek from the lakes above on some very slick rock at the top of a long drop. Take the right-hand fork, which crosses the outlet creek at an easier, safer spot, even though it's slightly longer, at least until mid-season. Just beyond the forks, come to the Bullfrog Lakes turnoff at mile 7.5.

Headwaters of the Little Kern River below Farewell Gap

If you do not plan to visit the lakes, continue straight ahead southeast along the left (east) side of the creek, stirring up a delicious fragrance of pennyroyal with your passage. This pale lavender member of the mint family makes an excellent tea. There is a large pleasant campsite across the stream in a grove of foxtail pines just before the path becomes steeper and the creek drops over a ledge. The creek and canyon floor drop away to the right, but the trail stays high along the mountainside, now and then making a switchback through flower gardens so dense they sometimes obscure the route.

At mile 9.8 the trail splits. There is no sign. The right fork initially cuts back northwest, then drops down to cross the nascent Little Kern River and continues on to Wet Meadows. Your narrow, rocky route continues straight ahead and, at mile 10.6, just before you hop a plunging creek, reaches a second unmarked shortcut down to the Little Kern. This one is not shown on the Golden Trout Wilderness map. Contour around the base of a granite knob. (The GTW map mistakenly shows the trail going over the top of it. Then, on the far side of the knob, the *topo* incorrectly shows two parallel trails heading east, while the GTW map shows only one. There were two trails at one time, but only the upper one still exists.)

At mile 11.8, tucked back in a notch, is the signed Silver Lake Trail and, just beyond it, Shotgun Creek. (The topo shows two parallel trails here, but only the

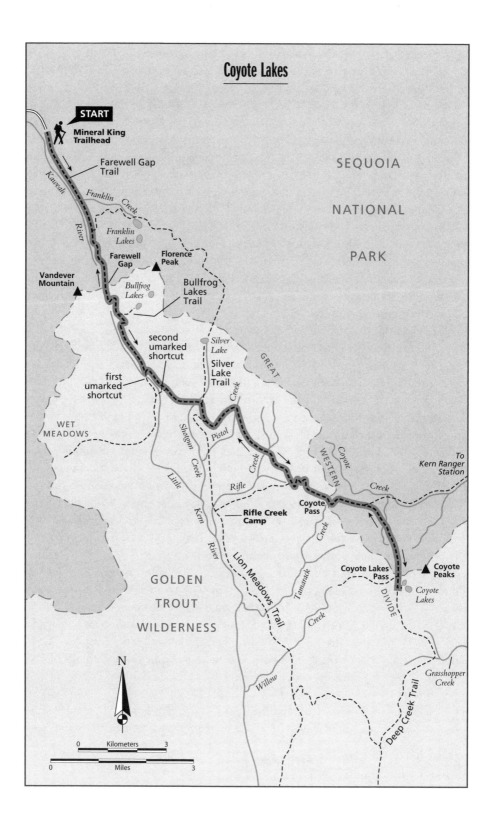

Coyote Lakes

START
Mineral King
Trailhead

Farewell Gap
Trail

Kaweah

Franklin Creek

SEQUOIA

NATIONAL

PARK

*Franklin
Lakes*

**Farewell
Gap**

▲ **Florence
Peak**

**Vandever
Mountain** ▲

*Bullfrog
Lakes*

**Bullfrog
Lakes
Trail**

River

second
umarked
shortcut

*Silver
Lake*

**Silver
Lake Trail**

GREAT

first
umarked
shortcut

Creek

WET
MEADOWS

Shotgun Creek

Pistol Creek

WESTERN

Coyote

To
Kern Ranger
Station

Little

Rifle

Creek

**Rifle Creek
Camp**

**Coyote
Pass**

Kern

**Coyote Lakes
Pass**

▲ **Coyote
Peaks**

GOLDEN

TROUT

WILDERNESS

River

Lion Meadows Trail

Tamarack Creek

DIVIDE

*Coyote
Lakes*

N

Willow

Deep Creek Trail

*Grasshopper
Creek*

| 0 | Kilometers | 3 |

| 0 | Miles | 3 |

upper one is still in use.) Cross the creek and at mile 12.1 meet the junction to Rifle Creek Camp and Coyote Pass. Keep left (southeast) toward Coyote Pass. Your route makes a big arc around a ridge presenting a grand vista down the Little Kern Canyon to the main fork of the Kern River. Look for The Needles in the distance to the south on the right side of the basin. Beneath them, the Little Kern and the "Big" Kern meet at Forks of the Kern. To the south and east looms the crest of the Great Western Divide studded with sharp little granite teeth. The trail curves around the mountainside and crosses Pistol Creek. Fill up here with water. It can be a hot, dry walk to the next reliable source. The sandy trail toils up over a saddle under sparse foxtails and silver pines. It dips a bit to cross Rifle Creek, then climbs again, higher and higher above the Little Kern River gorge. A final series of switchbacks, thankfully mostly shaded, takes you over a saddle at 10,350 feet, actually higher than Coyote Pass itself. Drop into a gully to cross a little seep, the origin of a tributary of Tamarack Creek. There is camping nearby. Now climb to 10,160-foot Coyote Pass among monster granite boulders and scraggly foxtail pines. Here you reenter Sequoia National Park at mile 16.1.

Descend from the pass on a sandy, but moderate grade amid the science-fiction-like city of rocks. Where the trail makes a swing to the left, the headwaters of Coyote Creek seep to the surface, flow quietly for a few hundred yards, disappear underground for another few hundred yards, then reappear aboveground for good. There are a few campsites on the far side. At mile 17.1 meet the clearly marked Coyote Lakes junction, where your route turns right (southeast) and crosses the creekbed. The path rises and falls gently, skirts the edge of a meadow twinkling with yellow monkey flowers and lavender shooting stars (and sometimes humming with mosquitoes), then turns right to follow alongside a tributary of Coyote Creek. The grade gradually steepens, and by the last few switchbacks before the top, you are floundering through deep scree. This 10,250-foot gap at mile 19.1 between the Coyote Peaks is known informally as Coyote Lakes Pass. Coyote Pass is almost visible to the northwest, with Vandever and Florence Peaks beyond it. The panorama to the northeast extends all the way to the main Sierra Crest.

Drop down the other side of the gap and reach a junction at mile 19.3 marked by several signs in various stages of decrepitude. The trail to the right (west) goes down to Willow Creek and Lion Meadows and is seldom maintained, though there are a few ducks. The route straight ahead (south) goes on to Grasshopper Creek and thence to Deep Creek (see Hike 20). Your trail turns left and drops steeply to Coyote Lakes, nestled in a cirque and separated from one another by an isthmus of glacial till. There is plenty of camping around the shore and lots wildflowers and hungry trout.

You can return the way you came, using the trail description in Hike 20, Northern Golden Trout Tour to make a loop, or explore other parts of the wilderness from here.

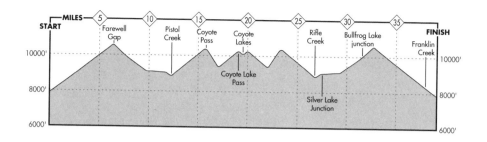

Key Points

0.0   Farewell Gap Trailhead.

0.2   Stables.

3.8   Frankin Pass junction, continue straight.

6.4   Farewell Gap.

7.5   Bullfrog Lakes turnoff.

9.8   First unmarked Wet Meadows junction, continue straight.

10.6   Second unmarked Wet Meadows junction, continue straight.

11.8   Silver Lake turnoff, continue straight.

12.1   Rifle Creek Camp/Coyote Pass junction, keep left (southeast).

16.1   Coyote Pass.

17.1   Coyote Lakes junction, turn right (southeast).

19.1   Coyote Lakes Pass.

19.3   Lakes junction, turn left.

19.6   Coyote Lakes.

39.2   Farewell Gap Trailhead.

20 Northern Golden Trout Tour

A wide-ranging lollipop loop around the northwest quadrant of the wilderness with lots of elevation change and scenic variety.

Start: Farewell Gap Trailhead.
Total distance: 49.1 miles.
Difficulty: Strenuous.
Total climbing: 10,080 feet.
Trail traffic: Varying from medium to light.
Best months: July to October.
Maps: USGS Mineral King, Quinn Peak, and Kern Lake quads; Forest Service Golden Trout and South Sierra Wilderness map.
Permits: Available in advance through Sequoia National Park or at the Mineral King Ranger Station on the Mineral King Road near Cold Springs Campground.
Trailhead facilities: None. Water and toilets are available at nearby campgrounds. Phones, food, and showers at Silver City.

Finding the trailhead: Drive northeast through the town of Three Rivers on California Highway 198, and when the buildings begin to thin out at the far (north) end, watch for the Mineral King turnoff to the right (east). After about 10 miles enter Sequoia National Park at a kiosk, where you pay an entrance fee of $10 per car, good for seven days. Follow the steep, winding, and very narrow road for 25 miles to its end and park in a lot near a cluster of private cabins. Walk back down the driveway from the parking area, cross over a bridge, and turn right onto the dirt road heading to the pack station. The trail begins near the stables about 4 miles back down the road. The nearest reliable source of gas is 25 miles away in Three Rivers.

Note: Marmot alert! Be sure to read the introduction to this section.

The Hike

The loop part of the hike can be followed in either direction, but is described counterclockwise here. Begin from the signed trailhead on the way to the pack station. A second sign appears at mile 0.2. The climb to the pass begins gradually, then continues on a series of well-graded switchbacks. The trail contours along a hillside for a while then begins a second set of switchbacks, at the top of which the Franklin Pass trail cuts off to the left (northeast) at mile 3.8. Your route continues on toward Farewell Gap at mile 6.4 (10,587 feet) where a sign welcomes travelers to the Golden Trout Wilderness. Descend toward the floor of Farewell Canyon for more than a mile on rather tedious switchbacks. Just past the final switchback is an obscure junction. Some hikers take the upper (left) fork to avoid a short stretch of steep climbing, but do not use this route in early season. It forces you to wade the outlet creek from the lakes above on some very slick rock at the top of a long drop. Take

Afternoon sun lights up a snag on Coyote Pass.

the right-hand fork, which crosses the outlet creek at an easier, safer spot, even though it's slightly longer, at least until mid-season. Just beyond the forks, come to the Bullfrog Lakes turnoff at mile 7.5.

After visiting the lakes (adding 2 miles for the round trip), return to the main trail and continue southeast along the left (east) side of the creek, stirring up a delicious fragrance of pennyroyal with your passage. This pale lavender member of the mint family makes an excellent tea. There is a large pleasant campsite across the stream in a grove of foxtail pines just before the path becomes steeper and the creek drops over a ledge. The creek and canyon floor drop away to the right, but the trail stays high along the mountainside, now and then making a switchback through tangles of wildflowers so dense they sometimes obscure the path.

At mile 9.8 the trail splits. There is no sign. The right fork initially cuts back northwest then drops down to cross the nascent Little Kern River and continues on to Wet Meadows. Your narrow, rocky route continues straight ahead, and at mile 10.6, just before you hop a plunging creek, reaches a second unmarked shortcut down to the Little Kern. This one is not shown on the Golden Trout Wilderness map. Contour around the base of a granitic knob. (The GTW map incorrectly shows the trail going over the top of it. Then, on the far side of the knob, the *topo* incorrectly shows two parallel trails heading east, while the GTW map shows only one. There were two trails in former, prewilderness days, but only the upper one remains.) At mile 11.8 look for the signed Silver Lake Trail tucked back in a notch on the left. A visit to the lake involves a steep, but worthwhile, 3-mile round-trip detour.

To continue on the main trail, cross Shotgun Creek just a few yards beyond the Silver Lake turnoff and, at mile 12.1, meet the junction to Rifle Creek Camp and Coyote Pass. Turn sharply right (northwest). In a few yards the trail will switch back to the southeast again, but it is easy to miss this turn. Stay alert for an old sign nailed high on a fir on the right side of the trail and, just beyond that, an equally inconspicuous line of rocks. As soon as you make this acute-angled turn, you will have to crawl over a fallen tree to find the trail again. Continue down the slope through dense ceanothus, manzanita, and chinquapin (long pants recommended). In the places where forest replaces scrub, there are lots of fallen logs that make this section of the route slow and tedious. Hop or ford Pistol Creek, climb over a saddle, then cross Rifle Creek, the last of the firearms, but not of the fords. There is a shortcut trail here heading east along the south side of Rifle Creek toward Coyote Pass that is still shown on the Golden Trout Wilderness map, but it is quite overgrown. The topo map does not show this eastbound route, but *does* show another one heading northwest toward the Little Kern. This one is even more obscure than the last; you probably won't notice it at all. At mile 15.1 the trees part to reveal Rifle Creek Camp in a meadow where you will find several large packer campsites, complete with tables, grills, a piped spring, corrals, and even an outhouse. Ignore the sign on the

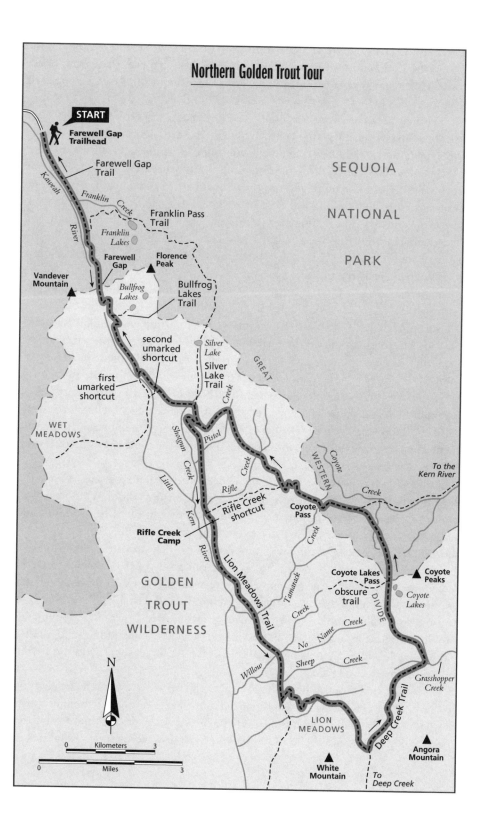

Northern Golden Trout Tour

START
Farewell Gap
Trailhead

Farewell Gap
Trail

Kaweah

Franklin Creek

Franklin Pass
Trail

Franklin
Lakes

River

Farewell
Gap

Florence
Peak

Vandever
Mountain

Bullfrog
Lakes

Bullfrog
Lakes
Trail

SEQUOIA

NATIONAL

PARK

second
umarked
shortcut

Silver
Lake

Silver
Lake
Trail

first
umarked
shortcut

GREAT

WET
MEADOWS

Pistol

Shotgun

Creek

Creek

Coyote

WESTERN

To the
Kern River

Creek

Little

Rifle

Rifle Creek
shortcut

Coyote
Pass

Kern

Rifle Creek
Camp

River

Creek

DIVIDE

Coyote Lakes
Pass

Coyote
Peaks

obscure
trail

Coyote
Lakes

GOLDEN

Lion Meadows Trail

Tamarack

Creek

No Name

Creek

TROUT

Creek

WILDERNESS

Sheep

Creek

N

Willow

Grasshopper
Creek

LION
MEADOWS

Deep Creek Trail

0   Kilometers   3

0   Miles   3

White
Mountain

Angora
Mountain

To Deep Creek

tree near the first campsite and corral pointing to Lion Meadows even though this is your destination. Instead, cross the meadow and pick up a path that begins beside a second campsite, where you turn left and keep an eye out for blazes. The trail will soon become obvious.

The trail now climbs over a hump then descends southward, sometimes quite steeply, alongside an often dry gully. Eventually the Little Kern becomes audible, then visible, to the right (west), and you walk alongside it through its narrow gorge, continuing to descend. As the grade lessens, the route veers away from the river and begins a series of rolling dips and rises in alternating forest and brush, crossing two smaller streams, then fording flowery Tamarack Creek. At mile 18.8 it reaches Willow Creek crossing and a three-way junction, though the signs point in only two directions. The third (northeast) path is the abandoned Willow Meadows Trail, a shortcut route to Coyote Lakes not shown on the Golden Trout Wilderness map. Ford Willow Creek, then smaller No Name Creek, and finally Sheep Creek, still on rolling terrain. At mile 20.0, at the head of a little meadow, watch for an inconspicuous sign tacked to a tree on the left indicating the Coyote Lakes cutoff.

Turn sharply left (northeast). If you find yourself skirting fenced Lion Meadows on your left, you have missed the turn. Follow a little tributary of Lion Creek on a gradually steepening grade, scrambling over an occasional downed tree. The way through the forest is eerily dark and quiet for the next mile before the route turns right and switchbacks up a slope, where the shade is broken by sunny patches of manzanita and ceanothus. The slope, tops out on a ridge along which you continue to ascend. Lion Creek can be heard crashing down its gorge to the right. To the left, framed by trees, are exhilarating vistas of the canyon of the Little Kern and the Great Western Divide.

Leave the ridge, pass a small campsite and soon thereafter cross Lion Creek. Be sure to tank up here; you have a long, hard, waterless climb ahead. Wind your way uphill, passing a grassy seep, then ascend through mostly fir forest to a more or less sunny shoulder. There are a few flat, big, but dry campsites on top. At mile 22.6 is a junction where what is left of a sign, propped up by rocks to your right, is marked simply 32E06. This trail drops south down the other side of the shoulder to Deep Creek. Your faint path turns left and climbs very steeply eastward through currant and snowberry bushes that are sometimes overgrown and scratchy. Now and then if you can spare the energy to look back over your shoulder, you can catch glimpses of White Mountain to the south and, a bit later, Angora Mountain to the southeast. Cross a saddle and traverse a slope, first losing, then regaining some elevation as you trudge across a second saddle.

At last the trail drops to meet the first of several very welcome packer campsites at the head of a tributary of Grasshopper Creek. There is more camping farther down the meadow. Fill up with water again before you leave this spot since you have another long climb ahead. The route leaves the meadow heading north through a notch between the creek below and a jagged rocky spine above, then swings west and labors up more switchbacks to gain an open, windswept ridge. Climb this ridge to reach the high point of this tour at 10,850 feet. Below, at the base of the gravelly slope to the east, lie Coyote Lakes. Descend to a junction at mile 28.6, marked by several signs in various stages of decrepitude. The trail to the left (west) goes down to Willow Creek and Lion Meadows and is seldom maintained, although there are a few ducks. To visit the Coyote Lakes, turn right (east) and drop steeply into the cirque containing upper Coyote Lake at mile 28.9. The upper lake is separated from the lower one by an isthmus of glacial till. There is plenty of camping around the shore, and lots of wildflowers and hungry trout.

To continue the tour, climb back up to the junction with the tumbledown signs at mile 29.2 and turn right (north) to climb to the 10,250 foot gap between Coyote Peaks, informally known as Coyote Lakes Pass at mile 29.3. Vandever and Florence Peaks are visible to the northwest and the panorama to the northeast extends all the way to the main Sierra crest. Coyote Pass itself isn't quite visible from here, but is in a direct line to Vandever and Florence Peaks from where you stand. Now the Coyote Lakes trail flounders downhill on steep, sandy switchbacks. The footing gradually becomes firmer and the slope gentler, and the path turns left to follow alongside a tributary of Coyote Creek, skirting a meadow twinkling with yellow monkey flowers and lavender shooting stars and sometimes humming with mosquitoes. The path rises and falls gently, passes a couple of campsites, then crosses the creek bed of the headwaters of Coyote Creek where it meets the clearly marked Coyote Pass junction at mile 31.3.

Turn left (west) and ascend the moderate sandy hillside through a science fiction-like city of rocks and some scraggly foxtail pines to reach 10,160 foot Coyote Pass where you leave Sequoia National Park and return to the Golden Trout Wilderness at mile 32.3. Drop into a gully watered by a little seep where there is a good campsite, then climb again to reach an unnamed shaded saddle at 10,350 feet, actually higher than Coyote Pass itself. Now begin a long series of switchbacks, sometimes hot and treeless, high above the Little Kern River gorge. Cross the main branch of Rifle Creek then contour along the slope, making a few minor ups and downs to Pistol Creek. Hop this one too and follow the trail as it describes a wide arc around another ridge. A look southward back down the Little Kern Canyon allows a glimpse of The Needles in the distance on the right side of the basin. Just below these lies the confluence of the Little Kern and the main fork of the Kern River.

At mile 36.3, meet the junction to Rifle Creek Camp, where you began the loop section of this tour. Now retrace your steps back up over Farewell Gap to your trailhead at Mineral King at mile 48.5. Don't forget to check for marmots under the hood before you start your car.

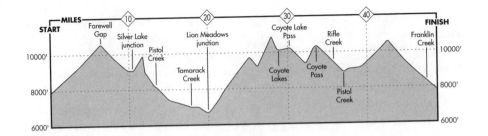

Key Points

0.0 Farewell Gap Trailhead.

0.2 Stables.

3.8 Franklin Pass junction, continue straight.

6.4 Farewell Gap.

7.5 Bullfrog Lakes turnoff.

9.8 First unmarked Wet Meadows junction, continue straight.

10.6 Second unmarked Wet Meadows junction, continue straight.

11.8 Silver Lake turnoff, continue straight.

12.1 Rifle Creek Camp junction, turn right (northwest).

15.1 Rifle Creek Camp.

18.8 Willow Creek junction.

20.0 Coyote Lakes/Lion Meadows junction, turn left (northeast).

22.6 Deep Creek cutoff.

28.6 Coyote Lakes junction.

28.9 Coyote Lakes.

33.4 Coyote Pass.

42.7 Farewell Gap.

49.1 Farewell Gap Trailhead.

Heart of the Wilderness

This is a land of great scenic beauty as well as historical and geologic interest. There is good fishing for golden and rainbow trout and wonderful displays of wildflowers. Wildlife is abundant, but not troublesome.

The Blackrock Ranger Station and the nearby trailhead from which all the journeys in this part of the wilderness begin is tucked into the center of the Southern Sierra at the end of a fairly long slow stint of mountain driving from any direction. It is accessible by road only from the south on Forest Road 21S03, off Forest Road 22S05, Sherman Pass Road. You can reach Sherman Pass Road from Kernville in the south, Kennedy Meadows from the east, or Porterville from the west.

This is a very popular trailhead for several reasons. The first is that it is the gateway to Jordan Hot Springs. For most of the last century, the site was an important social center and vacation destination for locals and tourists. A small seasonal community made up of cabins, lodge, dining room, corral, bathhouse, store, and sawmill, complete with mail delivery and a phone line, was operated commercially until the area became a wilderness. The buildings are still privately owned and are maintained as a historical landmark. Hikers and equestrians nowadays enjoy relaxing in the warm pools along Ninemile Creek, exploring the old resort and camping in the forest nearby.

The Blackrock Trailhead also allows the quickest access to the main fork of the Kern River from the east, and to the South Fork of the Kern and the Kern Plateau from the west (at least for ordinary passenger cars). It draws anglers and day hikers from the nearby pack station and campground as well. Since all of the trails begin at 8,900 feet, hikers are not faced with any extreme elevation gain the first day out; in fact, all hikes start out downhill.

Despite all these attractions, there is plenty of solitude to be had in this part of the wilderness for those willing to hike beyond the hot springs.

This part of the Golden Trout Wilderness is administered by the Inyo National Forest, which does not require a campfire permit in addition to a wilderness permit. You can pick up your wilderness permit at the Blackrock Ranger Station—closed Tuesday and Wednesday—or in advance by mail. There are no quotas. For further information, contact the Mount Whitney Ranger District, Inyo National Forest Wilderness Permit Office, 873 North Main Street, Bishop, CA 93514; (760) 873–2485; www.fs.fed.us/r5/inyo.

21 Casa Vieja Meadows

A short upside-down day hike.

Start: Blackrock Trailhead.
Total distance: 3.8 miles.
Difficulty: Easy.
Total climbing: 740 feet.
Trail traffic: Moderate.
Best months: Mid-June through October.
Maps: USGS Casa Vieja Meadows quad; Forest Service Golden Trout and South Sierra Wilderness map.

Permits: None for a day hike. Available from the Blackrock Ranger Station (closed Tuesday and Wednesday) for overnights.
Trailhead facilities: Camping, water, toilets. Nearest gas, groceries, and telephone at Kennedy Meadows.

Finding the trailhead: From Interstate 395 north of Pearsonville, turn west onto Ninemile Canyon Road. At the Chimney Peak Fire Station, it turns into Kennedy Meadows Road, Forest Road 22S05. Pass the Kennedy Meadows Store and continue 13 miles to a four-way junction. Turn right (north) onto Forest Road 21S03. The ranger station is just ahead on the right. From the station drive 8 miles north to the end of the road.

The Hike

The trail begins in white and red fir, lodgepole, and silver pine forest. It descends gently, passing a wildly blooming and sometimes buggy little meadow. The spring-fed creek that arises here gurgles beside you between lupine-lined banks all the way down to Casa Vieja Meadows. Beyond a fence, the meadow glows vivid green early in the season and is interlaced with a network of little creeks inhabited by beautiful golden trout. Around its edges the forest floor is strewn with tiny but exquisitely flavorful wild strawberries in midsummer.

The trail skirts the left (west) side of the meadow and passes the eponymous *casa vieja* or "old house," an unprepossessing wooden cabin. Out in the center on a little rise is the ranger station, still occasionally used by the Forest Service but not regularly staffed. Trails fan out from here in all directions. One heads southwest to Osa

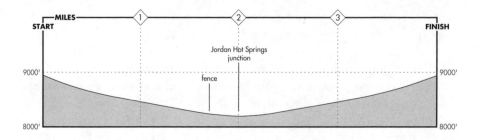

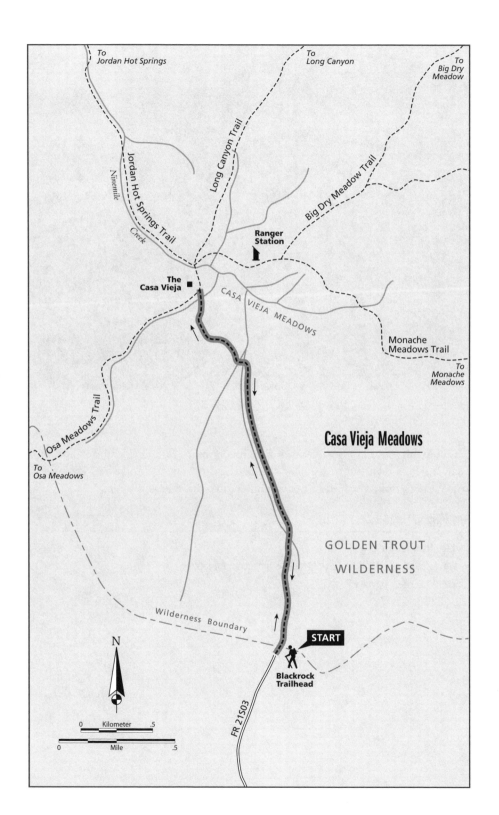

To
Jordan Hot Springs

To
Long Canyon

To
Big Dry
Meadow

Long Canyon Trail

Jordan Hot Springs Trail

Ninemile

Creek

Big Dry Meadow Trail

Ranger
Station

The
Casa Vieja

CASA VIEJA MEADOWS

Monache
Meadows Trail

To
Monache
Meadows

Osa Meadows Trail

To
Osa Meadows

Casa Vieja Meadows

GOLDEN TROUT

WILDERNESS

Wilderness Boundary

N

START

**Blackrock
Trailhead**

FR 21S03

0   Kilometer   .5

0   Mile   .5

Unmanned Forest Service Ranger Station at Casa Vieja Meadows

Meadows, the next northwest to Jordan Hot Springs, the third northeast up Long Canyon, the fourth east to Big Dry Meadow, and the last to Monache Meadows. If you are not bound for further destinations, return the way you came.

Key Points

- **0.0** Blackrock Trailhead.
- **1.9** Casa Vieja Meadows/Osa Meadows junction, turn around.
- **3.8** Blackrock Trailhead.

22 Jordan Hot Springs

An upside-down hike to a historic site and a soak in a natural hot spring.

Start: Blackrock Trailhead.
Total distance: 12 miles.
Difficulty: Strenuous as a day hike, moderate as a backpack.
Total climbing: 2,400 feet.
Trail traffic: Medium.
Best months: Mid-June through October.
Maps: USGS Casa Vieja Meadows quad; Forest Service Golden Trout and South Sierra Wilderness map.

Permits: None for a day hike. Available at Blackrock Ranger Station (closed Tuesday and Wednesday) for overnights, or at the Kernville Ranger Station.
Trailhead facilities: Camping, water, toilets. Nearest gas, groceries, and telephones at Kennedy Meadows.

Finding the trailhead: From Interstate 395 north of Pearsonville, turn west onto Ninemile Canyon Road. At the Chimney Peak Fire Station, this turns into Kennedy Meadows Road, Forest Road 22S05. Pass the Kennedy Meadows Store and continue 13 miles to a four-way junction. Turn right (north) onto Forest Road 21S03. The Blackrock Ranger Station is just ahead on the right. From here drive 8 miles north to the end of the road.

From Kernville at the north end of Lake Isabella, drive 28 miles north on County Road M99 following alongside the Kern River to the Sherman Pass Road, Forest Road 22S05, just before the Johnsondale Bridge. Turn right and follow this narrow, winding road for 32 miles to the Blackrock Ranger Station, then on to the trailhead 8 miles north at the end of the road. If it is early in the season, check with the Forest Service first to make sure the pass is open and clear of snow.

The Hike

In 1861 John Jordan built a trail across the Sierra Nevada from Visalia to Olancha (See History in this book's introduction). Near where the route crosses Ninemile Creek, hot mineral waters gurgle out of the earth in several spots to mingle with the cool stream water in pools perfect for bathing. By the early twentieth century, the area had become a social and communications center connected by phone line with the many scattered summer cow camps via the Tunnel Meadow Guard Station. Cattlemen, sheepherders, miners, and inevitably tourists gathered to "take the waters" in an idyllic setting of forest and meadow. Tubs were built for bathing, a sawmill was constructed, and cabins, corrals, a store, a dining hall, and even a dance floor were added. It was operated as a commercial resort until the wilderness was established and is now in the National Register of Historic Places.

This is an upside-down hike. You lose, then regain 2,400 feet, an important consideration if your plan is to do it as a day hike. If you linger too long in the hot pools, you may find yourself overtaken by darkness before you can get back to the trailhead.

Soaking trail-weary bones in Jordan Hot Springs

Follow the trail from Black Rock Trailhead to Casa Vieja Meadows, passing the first signed junction to Osa Meadows at mile 1.9. Turn left (northwest) at the second one, the Jordan Trail, at mile 2.0, descending along Ninemile Creek beside a continuously unrolling multicolored ribbon of wildflowers. Just a sampling of these includes lilies, larkspur, columbines, lupines, senecio, ranger's buttons, goldenrod, fireweed, cinquefoil, cow parsnips, asters, pennyroyal, buckwheat, and rein orchis. As you descend, the overhead vegetation changes, too, from red and white fir and lodgepole pine to Jeffrey pine and Douglas fir. The Jordan Trail crosses back and forth over the creek, where the water is swift and strong early in the season but later on diminishes to expose rocks that are slick and slimy. Watch your step. The grade eventually lessens, and magnificent old incense cedars, sugar pines, and black oaks appear. A spur trail cuts off toward a public pasture and the old resort. You can explore, but don't camp here. The main trail keeps right to pass a tumbledown cabin. Beyond this, it crosses Ninemile Creek on fallen logs and reaches a Y intersection. The right fork leads north up Redrock Creek; the left goes to the hot springs and beyond to the Kern River. Mounds of a pale-colored rock called travertine have been deposited by the evaporation of the mineral-rich water along Ninemile Creek. When the air is still and cool, steam from the springs reveals their whereabouts.

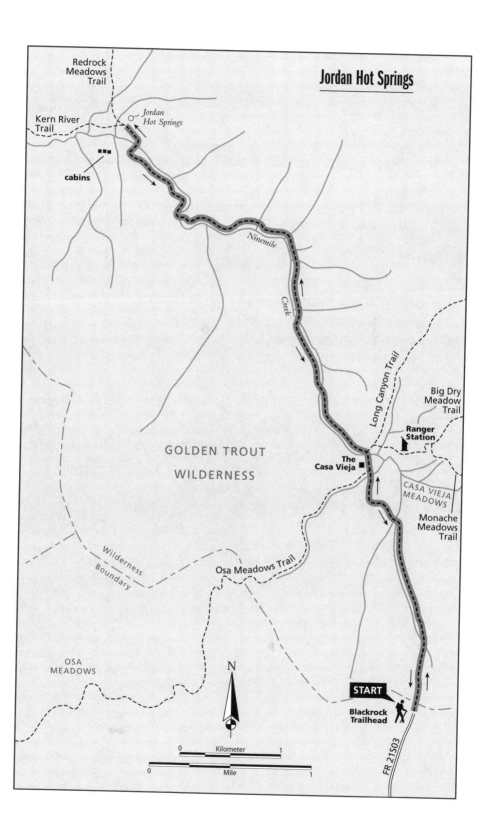

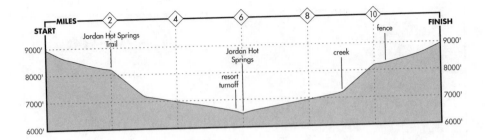

There is good camping in the trees surrounding the open meadow through which the creek flows and plenty to see and do before returning the way you came.

Key Points

0.0 Blackrock Trailhead.

1.9 Casa Vieja Meadows/Osa Meadows junction, turn left (northwest).

2.0 Ninemile Creek/Jordan Trail junction, turn left (northwest).

6.0 Jordan Hot Springs, turn around.

12.0 Blackrock Trailhead.

23 Redrock Meadows/Templeton Mountain Loop

A hike packed with variety: hot springs, a taste of the Old West, interesting geology, and lots of flowers.

Start: Blackrock Trailhead.
Total distance: 26.3 miles.
Difficulty: Moderately strenuous.
Total climbing: 5,350 feet.
Trail traffic: Moderate to Jordan Hot Springs, light beyond.
Best months: Mid-June through October.
Maps: USGS Casa Vieja, Kern Peak, Templeton Mountain, and Monache Mountain quads;

Forest Service Golden Trout and South Sierra Wilderness map.
Permits: Available at the Blackrock Ranger Station (closed Tuesday and Wednesday) or at the Kernville Ranger Station.
Trailhead facilities: Camping, water, toilets. Nearest gas, groceries and phones at Kennedy Meadows.

Finding the trailhead: From Interstate 395 south of Pearsonville, turn west onto Ninemile Canyon Road. At the Chimney Peak Fire Station, this turns into Kennedy Meadows Road, Forest Road 22S05. Pass the Kennedy Meadows Store and continue 13 miles to a four-way junction. Turn right (north) onto Forest Road 21S03. The Blackrock Ranger Station is just ahead on the right. From here drive 8 miles north to the end of the road.

From Kernville at the north end of Lake Isabella, drive 28 miles north on County Road M99 following alongside the Kern River to Sherman Pass Road, FR 22S05, just before the Johnson-dale Bridge. Turn right and follow this narrow, winding road for 32 miles to the Blackrock Ranger Station, then on to the trailhead 8 miles north at the end of the road. (If it is early or late in the season, check with the Forest Service first to make sure the road is open over Sherman Pass.)

The Hike

Follow the trail from Black Rock Trailhead to Casa Vieja Meadows passing the first signed junction to Osa Meadows at mile 1.9. Turn left (northwest) at the second one, the Jordan Trail, at mile 2.0, descending along Ninemile Creek. A spur trail cuts off toward a public pasture and the old resort. The main trail keeps right to pass a tumbledown cabin. Beyond this, it crosses Ninemile Creek on fallen logs and reaches a Y intersection. The right fork leads north up Redrock Creek, the left goes to Jordan Hot Springs at mile 6.0, the lowest point on this hike at 6,500 feet. From the signed junction just northeast of the hot springs and the nearby camping area, keep right (northeast). Pass a small area blackened in a fire that occurred in 2000, wade Redrock Creek, and keep right (north) again at another junction at mile 6.2; the left fork goes back toward the Kern River. Hike upward along the east bank of Redrock Creek as it tumbles over little waterfalls into tempting pools surrounded by wild-flowers. Eventually you cross the creek again and wade through an open boggy area

fed by several springs, dense with water-loving sedges, rushes, horsetails, and monkey flowers. Now ascend a series of switchbacks beginning in bracken fern that gives way to chaparral as the ground becomes drier and sandier. Top out on a shoulder at the "back" of Indian Head, a big red lump of metavolcanic rock, topped with a nubbin of marble that rears up out of a sea of gray granite and granitic sand. If it weren't for the forest cover, the contrast between Indian Head and its surroundings would be even more striking than it is. The trail drops down from the shoulder of the peak, dips into Redrock Meadows, and disappears in another mass of spring-watered foliage, but there are signs posted to keep you on track. At mile 10.2 reach a signed junction in lodgepole forest. The left fork, seldom maintained and not shown on the Golden Trout Wilderness map, heads northeast to Cold Meadow. Your route continues straight ahead (northeast). There are some good campsites between two branches of the creek not far from the remains of an old cabin. Beyond this, at mile 10.3, another sign directs you right (northeast again) toward Templeton Meadows.

Cattle have almost completely obliterated the trail in the sandy soil, so you might have to do a bit of scouting to find the place where it reappears. It becomes visible for only a short stretch before disappearing again among meadow grasses, but is not hard to regain if you pause to spot the blazes on the other side before rushing out into the middle. Begin the long, steep, waterless upward grind on heavily eroded trail that tops out at 10,250 feet, the highest point on the loop. You get no view for your efforts, but do reach a beautiful stand of foxtail pines. The way down the canyon on the other side is equally steep, eroded, and dry at first, but becomes gentler as it swings right (northeast) and approaches Templeton Meadows. It levels out alongside Templeton Cow Camp, a real, working piece of the Old West at mile 14.5. Follow the fence line around the property, turning right (east) when the fence does. There are no signs here, and this turn is not shown on the topo, but it does appear on the Golden Trout map. Soon the meadow opens before you with the volcanic cone of Templeton Mountain squatting in the middle. Olancha Peak appears in the distance to the east, and a glance back over your shoulder to the north reveals Mount Langley, Cirque Peak, and the Sierra Crest.

Reenter the forest to find flat, sandy, but sometimes dry campsites on both sides of the trail. The path skirts the base of Templeton Mountain and, when nearly halfway past it, meets a broken signpost marking an older trail heading north (mile 15.4). Keep straight ahead (east) to reach another junction at mile 16.1, where you turn right (south) toward Fat Cow Meadow. Hop a tributary of Strawberry Creek. Next, cross a little stringer of Fat Cow Meadow and climb a low rise to reach the Long Canyon/Monache Meadows junction marked by a sign that is little more than splinters at mile 17.0. Continue right (southwest) toward Long Canyon, hump up

◀ *A family backpacking in the Golden Trout Wilderness*

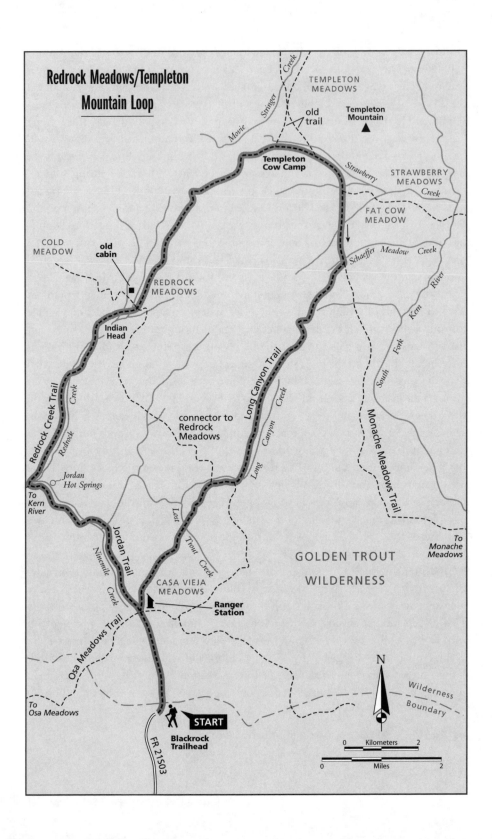

Redrock Meadows/Templeton Mountain Loop

TEMPLETON MEADOWS

old trail

Templeton Mountain ▲

Movie Stringer Creek

Templeton Cow Camp

Strawberry

STRAWBERRY MEADOWS

Creek

FAT COW MEADOW

Schaeffer Meadow Creek

COLD MEADOW

old cabin

REDROCK MEADOWS

Indian Head

South Fork Kern River

Redrock Creek Trail

Redrock Creek

connector to Redrock Meadows

Long Canyon Trail

Long Canyon Creek

Monache Meadows Trail

Jordan Hot Springs

To Kern River

Jordan Trail

Lost Trout Creek

To Monache Meadows

Ninemile Creek

CASA VIEJA MEADOWS

GOLDEN TROUT

WILDERNESS

Ranger Station

Osa Meadows Trail

N

To Osa Meadows

Wilderness Boundary

🚶 START Blackrock Trailhead

FR 21S03

0   Kilometers   2

0   Miles   2

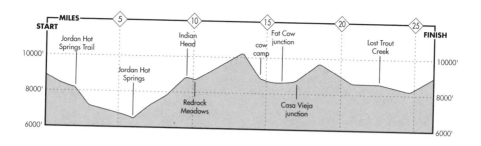

and over a saddle, then descend to cross a sandy flat and skirt a willowy meadow. Again, cattle have churned up the trail, but a sign directs you through the worst part. Follow the obvious straight fault line of Long Canyon, lined with pleasant meadows but unsuitable for camping because of the presence of cattle and associated flies and cowpies.

Another almost-gone sign out in the middle of one of these meadows marks a faint trail heading back northwest to Redrock Meadows (mile 20.8). Hike a short distance past this and ford Long Canyon Creek to find a newer sign at mile 21.8 directing you onward toward Casa Vieja Meadows. Now traversing rolling, forested country, cross Lost Trout Creek to pick up a northern finger of Casa Vieja Meadows, which you follow back to the Jordan Hot Springs Trail junction at mile 24.3. From here ascend the final 2 miles back to the Blackrock Trailhead.

Key Points

0.0 Blackrock Trailhead.

1.9 Casa Vieja Meadows.

2.0 Ninemile Creek/Jordan Trail junction, turn left (northwest).

6.0 Jordan Hot Springs, keep right (northeast).

6.2 Kern River junction, keep right (north).

10.2 Redrock Meadows, continue straight (northeast).

10.3 Templeton Meadows junction, turn right (northeast).

14.5 Templeton Cow Camp, turn right (east) when fence does.

15.4 Abandoned connector trail, continue straight (east).

16.1 Fat Cow junction, turn right (south).

17.0 Long Canyon/Monache Meadow junction, continue right (southwest).

20.8 Connector to Redrock Meadows, continue straight (west).

21.8 Casa Vieja Meadows junction, turn left (southwest).

24.3 Casa Vieja Meadows, and Jordan Hot Springs Trail junction, continue straight (south).

26.3 Blackrock Trailhead.

The Sierra Crest and the Kern Plateau

All the hikes in this section begin at Horseshoe Meadow, one of the very few trailhead locations so close to the Sierra Crest. By the time you get out of your car, you are already on the Kern Plateau at an elevation of 10,000 feet. Convenient as this is, hikers who hit the trail at once after gaining thousands of feet from the floor of the Owens Valley in less than an hour may find themselves incapacitated by altitude sickness. At least one good night's sleep at the trailhead and an unhurried pace the first day out will help.

This is perfect hiking country, with trails to suit everybody's taste and ability. There are lots of day hikes as well as opportunities for extended expeditions of a week or more. You can travel from the Sierra Crest all the way across the plateau to the northwestern border of the wilderness where the main fork of the Kern River comes in from Sequoia National Park. Or you can explore the high country southward to the border of the South Sierra Wilderness and beyond.

The dominant feature of this region is the South Fork of the Kern, which a glance at the map will tell you is actually the east fork. The South Fork is not the impassable barrier to travel that the main fork is. It is spanned by only one bridge within the wilderness, but by midseason the water level is usually low enough to wade (carefully) in a few wide, shallow places. The river wanders through a land of forests and enormous meadows not at all typical of the Sierra Nevada, some still green, many now in sagebrush. Occasional cowboys, clusters of cattle, and isolated tumbledown herders' cabins provide picturesque atmosphere or constitute a blight on the landscape depending upon your point of view. Rounded volcanic domes such as Templeton Mountain and a scattering of startling red cinder cones squat in the meadows. Some of these have poured out rivers of lava that have turned the surrounding country into moonscape. The most conspicuous features of this region, apart from the river itself, are Kern Peak (11,510 feet) and Olancha Peak (12,123 feet), one or the other of which can usually be spotted from all over the wilderness. The higher elevations up to timberline support stands of foxtail pines, tough and windblown and found almost nowhere but the Southern Sierra. Also occurring naturally here and nowhere else in the world are the beautiful golden trout that can be spotted in almost every stream, an attraction whether you are an angler or simply an admirer.

Because the location is so convenient and the country so grand, and because these trailheads are also used by those heading into Sequoia Park and lands to the north, this is the most popular entrance into the wilderness, and the only place where trailhead quotas are in effect. These apply only to Cottonwood Pass, however; other routes leaving Horseshoe Meadow, such as Trail and Mulkey Passes, have no quotas.

As you would expect, the trails nearest the trailhead get the most maintenance since they are most heavily used. Some of those to the south—especially Mulkey Pass, the usual route for moving cattle into the high country—have been trampled into oblivion, and the footing is heavy and slow. In fact, wherever trails pass through meadows where cattle graze, you'll need to keep your map handy and stay alert.

Bear canisters are not required in this region, but are strongly recommended. Food storage boxes are available at trailheads. Do not leave food in your car. Remember that you are required by law to keep your food out of the reach of bears. If you lose it, it's your fault.

24 Cottonwood Pass

A scenic and convenient route to the Pacific Crest Trail (PCT) and the Kern Plateau as well as a pleasant out-and-back day hike.

Start: Cottonwood Pass Trailhead.
Total distance: 5.8 miles.
Difficulty: Moderate.
Total climbing: 1,350 feet.
Trail traffic: Moderate.
Best months: Mid-June through mid-October.
Maps: USGS Cirque Peak quad; Forest Service Golden Trout and South Sierra Wilderness map.
Permits: None for a day hike; required and available in advance or at the Mount Whitney

Ranger Station in Lone Pine for overnight trips. Note that his is the only trailhead in the Golden Trout Wilderness for which trailhead quotas have been set. If you plan to begin your backpack on a summer weekend, be sure to apply for your permit in advance, or arrive at the ranger station very early.
Trailhead facilities: Camping, toilets, water. Nearest gas, groceries, and phones in Lone Pine.

Finding the trailhead: From Lone Pine on Interstate 395, drive west on Whitney Portal Road (the only traffic signal in town) for 3 miles to Horseshoe Meadow Road. Turn left (south) and climb the dizzying, hairpin-turning road for 20 miles to a signed junction. Go straight ahead just past the junction to the campground and trailhead parking area.

The Hike

The Cottonwood Pass Trail begins at a set of big interpretive signs near the toilets. Just beyond, another sign reminds travelers that the national park boundary is 8 miles ahead and that no pets or firearms are permitted beyond that point. The path is sandy and flat at first, lined with yellow tufts of sulfur-flower buckwheat and pale blue lupines in a mixed forest of lodgepole and foxtail pines. At mile 0.3 it meets a junction at which you continue straight ahead (west); the right-hand fork leads back northeast to the pack station and the Cottonwood Lakes Trailhead, while the left (south) fork goes to Trail Pass. Skirt the north side of Horseshoe Meadow and ignore a second Trail Pass cutoff to the south. The topo map shows another trail joining yours from the north from Golden Trout Camp about 0.5 mile from the last junction, but this is no longer in use and has been obliterated.

At the upper end of the meadow, a little spur trail cuts left (southwest) for a few yards to an old rancher's cabin with a beautiful view out across the open land to the east. There are good campsites nearby, but camping is prohibited near the cabin itself. Back on the main Cottonwood Pass Trail, rock-hop a flowery little creek, climb a short distance, then rock-hop the creek back to the other side again. The grade

Cottonwood Pass lies above the open meadow on the Tunnel Meadow Trail.

increases gradually on sandy footing until it begins some fairly steep switchbacks under an almost pure stand of foxtail pines. Please heed the signs that remind hikers not to shortcut these switchbacks. The resulting erosion would eventually wash out the trail and damage the surrounding vegetation. The delicious aroma at your feet is produced by the little bunches of light purple pennyroyal, a member of the mint family that makes excellent tea.

As you gain elevation, the horseshoe shape of the eponymous meadow below is revealed. Cross an ephemeral creek in an open willow-choked gully blooming with senecio, ranger's buttons, fireweed, and numerous other species, return to the forest, and pant up the last few switchbacks to the pass at mile 2.9. It is a breezy spot at 11,200 feet with picturesque wind-flagged foxtail pines clinging stubbornly to scoured rocky pinnacles. The view to the east extends beyond the Owens Valley all the way to Telescope Peak in the Panamint Mountains, beyond which lies Death Valley. Just to the west of the pass, at the head of a meadow, the Cottonwood Pass Trail meets a signed junction with the Pacific Crest Trail. Unless your plans take you farther, retrace your steps to the trailhead.

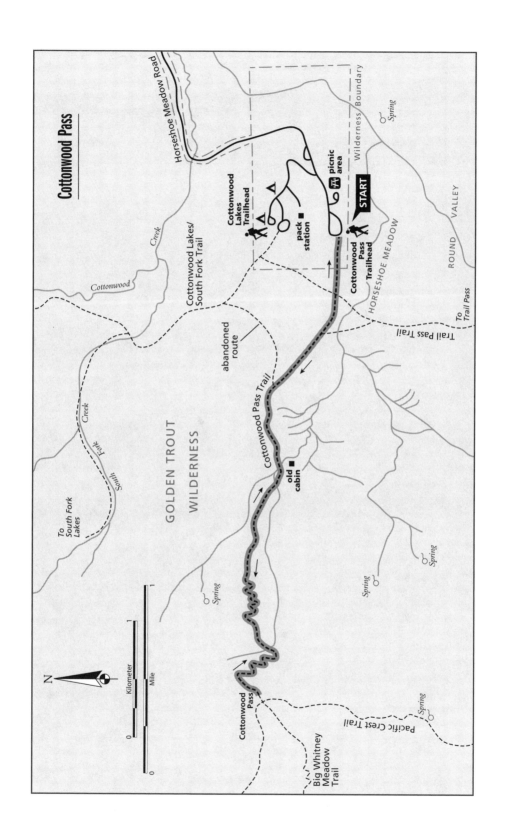

Cottonwood Pass

N

Kilometer

Mile

Horseshoe Meadow Road

Creek

Cottonwood

Cottonwood Lakes Trailhead

pack station

Cottonwood Lakes/
South Fork Trail

abandoned
route

picnic
area

START

Cottonwood
Pass Trailhead

Wilderness Boundary

HORSESHOE MEADOW

ROUND VALLEY

To Trail Pass

Trail Pass Trail

Cottonwood Pass Trail

GOLDEN TROUT
WILDERNESS

South Fork Creek

To
South Fork
Lakes

old
cabin

Spring

Spring

Spring

Spring

Cottonwood Pass

Big Whitney
Meadow Trail

Pacific Crest Trail

Spring

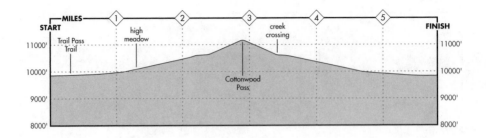

Key Points

0.0 Cottonwood Pass Trailhead.

0.3 Trail Pass/pack station junction, continue straight (west).

2.9 Cottonwood Pass.

5.8 Cottonwood Pass Trailhead.

25 Trail Pass

One of the shortest, easiest routes to the Pacific Crest Trail (PCT) and the back-country.

Start: Cottonwood Pass Trailhead.
Total distance: 5 miles.
Difficulty: Easy to moderate.
Total climbing: 600 feet.
Trail traffic: Light to moderate.
Best months: Mid-June through mid-October.
Maps: USGS Cirque Peak quad; Forest Service Golden Trout and South Sierra Wilderness map.

Permits: None for a day hike; required and available in advance or at the Mount Whitney Ranger Station in Lone Pine for overnight trips.
Trailhead facilities: Camping, toilets, water. Nearest gas, groceries, and phones in Lone Pine.

Finding the trailhead: From Lone Pine on Interstate 395, drive west on Whitney Portal Road (the only traffic signal in town) for 3 miles to Horseshoe Meadow Road. Turn left (south) and climb the dizzying, hairpin-turning road for 20 miles to a signed junction. Go straight ahead just past the junction to the campground and trailhead parking area.

The Hike

The Cottonwood Trail Pass begins at a set of big interpretive signs near the toilets. Just beyond, another sign reminds travelers that the national park boundary is 8 miles ahead and that no pets or firearms are permitted beyond that point. The path is sandy and flat at first, lined with yellow tufts of sulfur-flower buckwheat and pale blue lupines in a mixed forest of lodgepole and foxtail pines. At mile 0.3 it meets a junction. One path leads back northeast to the pack station and the Cottonwood Lakes Trailhead. Cottonwood Pass lies straight ahead. Your trail turns left (south) heading directly toward Trail Peak. It is forested about three-quarters of the way up, topped by a bare rubbly point. It cuts through a branch of Horseshoe Meadow, spangled with meadow penstemon, daisies, goldenrod, and little elephant-heads, then crosses the creek on a flattened log. The sandy stretch on the far side is carpeted with tiny but brilliant magenta monkey flowers early in the season. Beyond, the path begins an easy climb through lodgepole forest, crossing a flowery spring-fed creek that waters Round Valley just below.

At mile 1.8 the remnant of an old trail, seldom used or maintained, cuts off to the left (northeast) to skirt the other side of Round Valley. Your trail makes a switchback to the right (southwest) and begins a steeper ascent up the draw to Trail Pass (10,500 feet). Near the top, pass under the remains of an old telephone line and meet the Pacific Crest Trail at mile 2.5.

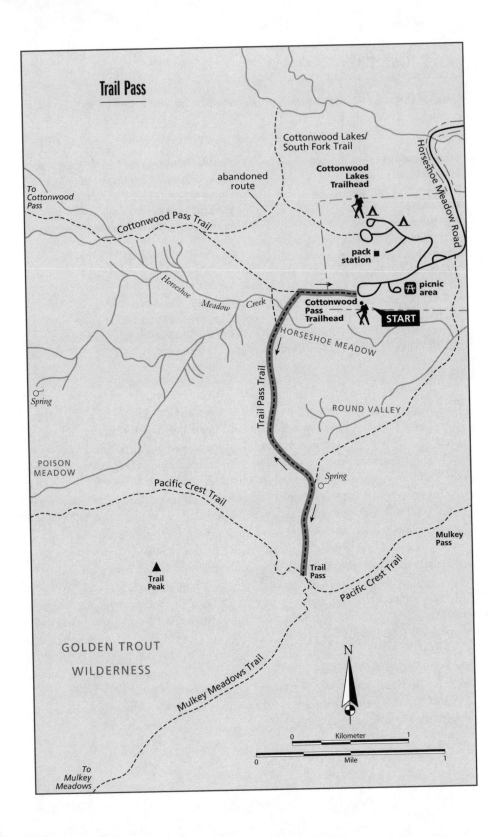

Trail Pass

Cottonwood Lakes/
South Fork Trail

abandoned
route

**Cottonwood
Lakes
Trailhead**

Horseshoe Meadow Road

*To
Cottonwood
Pass*

Cottonwood Pass Trail

**pack
station**

Horseshoe

Meadow Creek

**Cottonwood
Pass
Trailhead**

START

picnic
area

HORSESHOE MEADOW

Trail Pass Trail

ROUND VALLEY

Spring

POISON
MEADOW

Pacific Crest Trail

Spring

Mulkey
Pass

Trail
Pass

Pacific Crest Trail

▲
**Trail
Peak**

GOLDEN TROUT

WILDERNESS

Mulkey Meadows Trail

N

*To
Mulkey
Meadows*

0   Kilometer   1

0   Mile   1

Looking down on Horseshoe Meadow from Trail Pass

Key Points

0.0 Cottonwood Pass Trailhead.

0.3 Cottonwood Pass/Pack Station junction, turn left (south).

1.8 Unsigned junction with unmaintained trail.

2.5 Trail Pass.

5.0 Cottonwood Pass Trailhead.

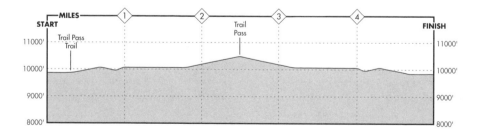

26 Mulkey Cow Camp

An out-and-back hike into the Old West.

Start: Cottonwood Pass picnic area.
Total distance: 6 miles.
Difficulty: Moderate only because of soft footing.
Total climbing: 950 feet.
Trail traffic: Light.
Best months: Mid-June through October.

Maps: USGS Cirque Peak quad; Forest Service Golden Trout and South Sierra Wilderness map.
Permits: None for a day hike; required and available in advance or at the Mount Whitney Ranger Station for overnight trips.
Trailhead facilities: Toilets and water. Camping nearby. Nearest gas, groceries, and phones in Lone Pine.

Finding the trailhead: From Lone Pine on Interstate 395, drive west on Whitney Portal Road (the only traffic signal in town) for 3 miles to Horseshoe Meadow Road. Turn left (south) and climb the dizzying, hairpin-turning road for 20 miles to a signed junction. Go straight ahead toward the Cottonwood Pass Trailhead and turn left at the next junction into the picnic area.

The Hike

The Mulkey Pass Trail is a short route to the Pacific Crest Trail (PCT), but is not much used by hikers because the trailhead is not marked and the footing is sandy and deep. Ranchers use the trail to drive cattle to and from the cow camp and beyond to other summer grazing allotments in the wilderness, so it is pretty thoroughly trampled and indistinct. Still, it's a chance to glimpse a traditional way of life rapidly disappearing from the West.

Begin on the south side of the picnic area on an unmarked trail and head out across Horseshoe Meadow, wading or jumping two branches of the creek, keeping to the east end of Round Valley. At mile 0.5 meet an unmarked junction and follow the left fork due south up into the forest; the right fork turns west to connect with the Trail Pass Trail. Flounder through the heavy footing to meet the Pacific Crest Trail at Mulkey Pass at mile 1.3, then descend the sandy winding route down the other side, passing a little spring-fed pocket meadow off to the left. The trail swings west around the base of a rocky ridge to arrive at a green and flowery meadow surrounded by a fence beside a beautifully weathered cabin (mile 2.9). The cow camp is in use in the summer. Please do not disturb. You can continue on down the trail toward Mulkey Meadows and camp near a little tributary stream, but you might have bovine company. Return the way you came.

A windblown foxtail pine on the ridge near Mulkey Pass

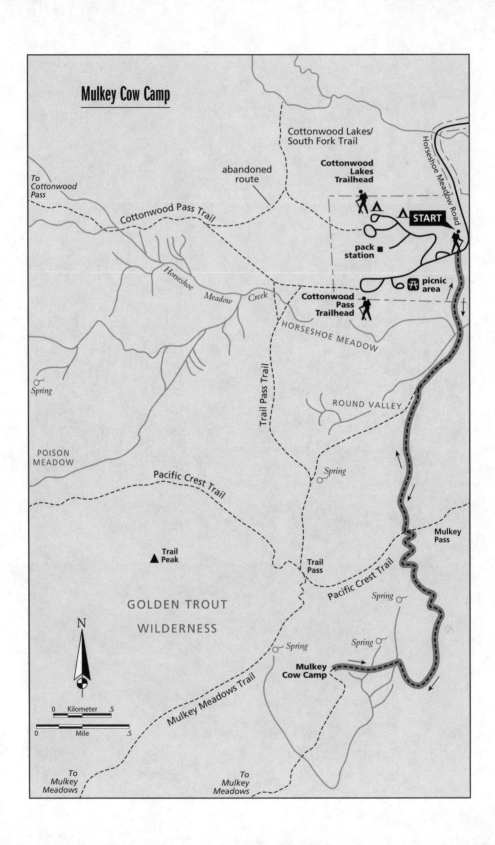

Mulkey Cow Camp

To Cottonwood Pass

Cottonwood Pass Trail

Cottonwood Lakes/ South Fork Trail

abandoned route

Cottonwood Lakes Trailhead

Horseshoe Meadow Road

START

pack station

picnic area

Cottonwood Pass Trailhead

Horseshoe Meadow Creek

HORSESHOE MEADOW

Trail Pass Trail

Spring

POISON MEADOW

ROUND VALLEY

Spring

Pacific Crest Trail

▲ **Trail Peak**

GOLDEN TROUT

WILDERNESS

Trail Pass

Mulkey Pass

Pacific Crest Trail

Spring

Spring

Spring

Mulkey Cow Camp

Mulkey Meadows Trail

N

0   Kilometer   .5

0   Mile   .5

To Mulkey Meadows

To Mulkey Meadows

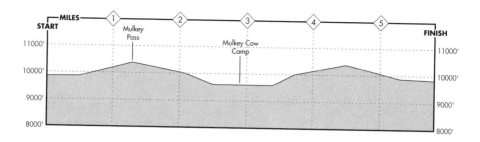

Key Points

0.0 Cottonwood Pass picnic area.

0.5 Unmarked trail junction, keep left (south).

1.3 Mulkey Pass/PCT, continue straight.

2.9 Mulkey Cow Camp, turn around.

6.0 Cottonwood Pass picnic area.

27 Trail Pass, Mulkey Pass, and the Pacific Crest Trail

A day-hike loop that includes a short section of the Pacific Crest Trail (PCT).

Start: Cottonwood Pass Trailhead.
Total distance: 5.7 miles.
Difficulty: Easy to moderate.
Total climbing: 600 feet.
Trail traffic: Light to medium.
Best months: June through October.

Maps: USGS Cirque Peak quad; Forest Service Golden Trout and South Sierra Wilderness map.
Permits: None.
Trailhead facilities: Camping, toilets, water. Nearest gas, groceries, and phones in Lone Pine.

Finding the trailhead: From Lone Pine on Interstate 395, drive west on Whitney Portal Road (the only traffic signal in town) for 3 miles to Horseshoe Meadow Road. Turn left (south) and climb the dizzying, hairpin-turning road for 20 miles to a signed junction. Go straight ahead just past the junction to the campground and trailhead parking area.

The Hike

The section of this loop between Trail Pass and the trailhead is on unmarked and unmaintained trail. Be sure to carry and consult your topo map. The trail begins at a set of big interpretive signs near the toilets. Just beyond, another sign reminds travelers that the National Park Boundary is 8 miles ahead and that no pets or firearms are permitted beyond that point. The path is sandy and flat at first. At mile 0.3 it meets a junction. One path leads back northeast to the pack station and the Cottonwood Lakes trailhead. Cottonwood Pass lies straight ahead. Your trail turns left (south) and heads directly toward Trail Peak. It cuts through a branch of Horseshoe Meadow. Beyond, the path begins an easy climb, crossing a spring-fed creek that waters Round Valley just below. At mile 1.8 the remains of an old trail cuts off to the left (northeast) to skirt the other side of Round Valley. The trail makes a switchback to the right (southwest) and begins a steeper ascent up the draw to Trail Pass (10,500 feet). Near the top, pass under the remains of an old telephone line and meet the Pacific Crest Trail at mile 2.5.

Turn left (east) and contour around the south side of a forested peak to meet the Mulkey Pass Trail junction at mile 3.4. Leave the PCT here and turn left (north). Descend the sandy, gravelly path alongside a little gully where a very small spring nourishes a tiny narrow garden. At first the trail runs along the right (west) side of the creek; then it crosses and descends along the east side.

At mile 4.4 where the terrain flattens and the forest opens onto Round Valley, the Mulkey Pass Trail begins to curve to the right (northeast). Leave the path here

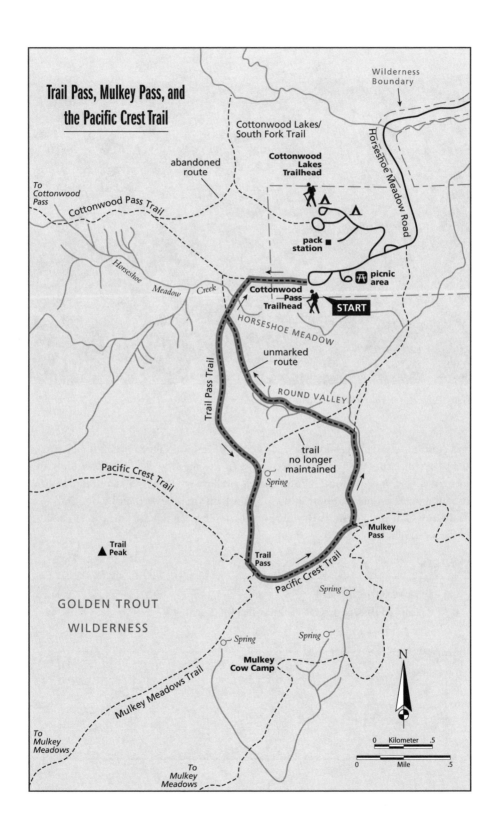

Trail Pass, Mulkey Pass, and the Pacific Crest Trail

Wilderness
Boundary

Cottonwood Lakes/
South Fork Trail

abandoned
route

**Cottonwood
Lakes
Trailhead**

Horseshoe Meadow Road

*To
Cottonwood
Pass*

Cottonwood Pass Trail

Horseshoe

Meadow Creek

**pack
station**

**picnic
area**

**Cottonwood
Pass
Trailhead**

START

HORSESHOE MEADOW

Trail Pass Trail

unmarked
route

ROUND VALLEY

Pacific Crest Trail

trail
no longer
maintained

Spring

▲ **Trail
Peak**

Trail Pass

**Mulkey
Pass**

Pacific Crest Trail

Spring

GOLDEN TROUT

WILDERNESS

Spring

Spring

**Mulkey
Cow Camp**

N

Mulkey Meadows Trail

*To
Mulkey
Meadows*

*To
Mulkey
Meadows*

0   Kilometer   .5

0   Mile   .5

Kern Peak on the ridgeline above Mulkey Meadows from Mulkey Pass

and continue straight ahead toward the center of Round Valley to pick up a less distinct path that runs along the western edge of the meadow. The meadow ends, the forest resumes, and the route climbs over a saddle where only intermittent sections of trail are still visible. At about mile 5.3, this faint trail meets the obvious Trail Pass Trail on which you began. Turn right (north) and retrace this back to the Horseshoe Meadow Trailhead.

Key Points

0.0   Cottonwood Pass Trailhead.

0.3   Cottonwood Pass/pack station junction, turn left (south).

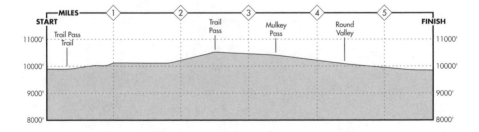

1.8 Unsigned junction with unmaintained trail.

2.5 Trail Pass, turn left.

3.4 Mulkey Pass, turn left.

4.4 Round Valley, continue straight, leaving trail.

5.3 Trail Pass Trail, turn right.

5.7 Cottonwood Pass Trailhead.

28 Big Whitney Meadow

A perfect weekend backpack or a convenient base camp at the hub of several routes to more remote Kern Plateau destinations.

Start: Cottonwood Pass Trailhead.
Total distance: 13 miles.
Difficulty: Moderate.
Total climbing: 3,090 feet.
Trail traffic: Moderate.
Best months: Late June through October.
Maps: USGS Cirque Peak and Johnson Peak quads; Forest Service Golden Trout and South Sierra Wilderness map.

Permits: Available in advance or at the Mount Whitney Ranger Station in Lone Pine. Quotas are in place.
Trailhead facilities: Camping, toilets, water. Nearest gas, groceries, and phones in Lone Pine.

Finding the trailhead: From Lone Pine on Interstate 395, drive west on Whitney Portal Road (the only traffic light in town) for 3 miles to Horseshoe Meadow Road. Turn left (south) and climb the steep, hairpin-turning road for 20 miles to a signed junction. Go straight ahead just past the junction to the campground and trailhead parking area.

The Hike

Big Whitney Meadow is laced with clear creeks teeming with golden trout and liberally sprinkled with wildflowers most of the season. The trail begins at a set of big interpretive signs near the toilets. Just beyond, another sign reminds travelers that the National Park Boundary is 8 miles ahead and that no pets or firearms are permitted beyond that point. The path is sandy and flat at first. At mile 0.3 it meets a junction at which you continue straight ahead (west). The right-hand fork goes northeast to the pack station and the Cottonwood Lakes Trailhead; the left (south) fork goes to Trail Pass. Skirt the north side of Horseshoe Meadow and ignore a second Trail Pass cutoff to the south. Rock-hop a little creek, climb a short distance, then jump the creek back to the other side again. The grade increases gradually on sandy footing until it begins some fairly steep switchbacks. Please heed the signs that remind hikers not to shortcut these switchbacks. Cross a creek in gully, return to the forest, and climb up the last few switchbacks to Cottonwood Pass at mile 2.9.

Just beyond, pass a junction with the Pacific Crest Trail (PCT) and descend straight ahead (southwest) through a meadow with a snow survey marker in the middle, then drop more steeply alongside willow-choked Stokes Stringer Creek.

Big Whitney Meadow is clearly visible below at the bottom of a long series of dusty switchbacks. These become longer and more gradual after you hop across the stream and continue to descend along its south side until you reach Stokes Stringer itself. There are a few campsites in the nearby forest. Recross two more branches of

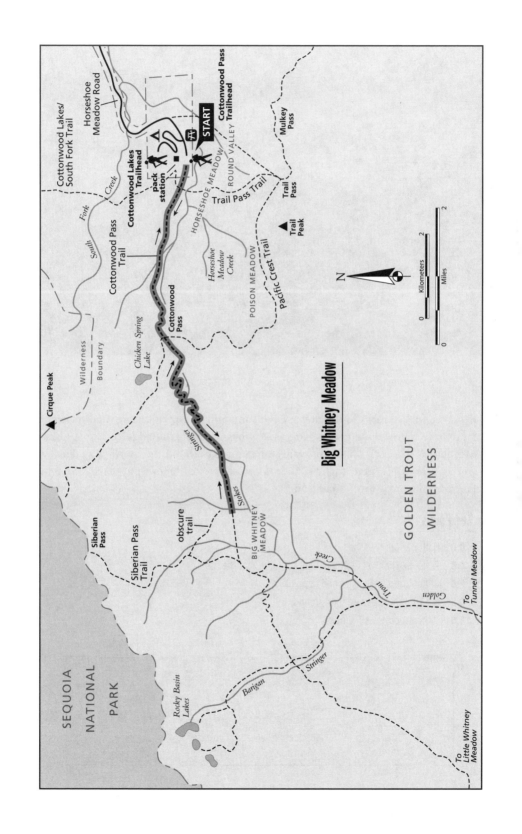

Big Whitney Meadow

Big Whitney Meadow from the Cottonwood Pass Trail

the creek on big rocks in the flowery, but sometimes slushy, meadow, then traverse a low, sandy hump dotted with lodgepole pines to reach the edge of Big Whitney Meadow at mile 6.5. There are plenty of campsites around the meadow's edge, but you will probably have to kick aside a few cow pies before pitching your tent. Retrace your steps to the trailhead.

Key Points

0.0 Cottonwood Pass Trailhead.

0.3 Trail Pass/pack station junction, continue straight (west).

2.9 Cottonwood Pass, continue straight.

6.5 Big Whitney Meadow, turn around.

13.0 Cottonwood Pass Trailhead.

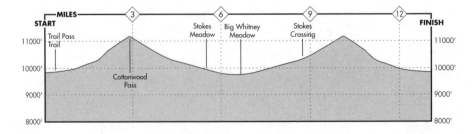

29 Rocky Basin Lakes

An angler's favorite out-and-back trek.

Start: Cottonwood Pass Trailhead.
Total distance: 26.4 miles.
Difficulty: Moderate to strenuous.
Total climbing: 4,230 feet.
Trail traffic: Light to moderate.
Best months: Mid-June through mid-October.
Maps: USGS Cirque Peak and Johnson Peak quads; Forest Service Golden Trout and South Sierra Wilderness map.

Permits: Required and available in advance or at the Mount Whitney Ranger Station in Lone Pine. Quotas are in effect.
Trailhead facilities: Camping, toilets, water. Nearest gas, groceries, and phones in Lone Pine.

Finding the trailhead: From Lone Pine on Interstate 395, drive west on Whitney Portal Road (the only traffic light in town) for 3 miles to Horseshoe Meadow Road. Turn left (south) and climb the dizzying, hairpin-turning road for 20 miles to a signed junction. The right fork goes to the Cottonwood Lakes Trailhead. Go straight ahead just past the junction to the campground and trailhead parking area.

The Hike

The trail begins at a set of big interpretive signs near the toilets. Just beyond, another sign reminds travelers that the National Park Boundary is 8 miles ahead and that no pets or firearms are permitted beyond that point. The path is sandy and flat at first. At mile 0.3 it meets a junction at which you continue straight ahead (west). The right-hand fork goes northeast to the pack station and the Cottonwood Lakes Trailhead; the left (south) fork goes to Trail Pass. Skirt the north side of Horseshoe Meadow and ignore a second Trail Pass cutoff to the south. Rock-hop a little creek, climb a short distance, then jump the creek back to the other side again. The grade increases gradually on sandy footing until it begins some fairly steep switchbacks. Please heed the signs that remind hikers not to shortcut these switchbacks. Cross a creek in gully, return to the forest, and climb up the last few switchbacks to Cottonwood Pass at mile 2.9.

Continue straight ahead (southwest), passing a junction with the Pacific Crest Trail (PCT), descending through a meadow with a snow survey marker in the middle. Begin a long series of switchbacks down along the north side of Stokes Stringer Creek toward Big Whitney Meadow, clearly visible below. About halfway down, cross the creek and continue to descend along its south side until you reach Stokes Stringer itself, beside which are a few campsites. Cross two more branches of the creek burbling through a sometimes slushy meadow using conveniently spaced boulders, then

The first of the remote, reputedly trout-filled Rocky Basin Lakes

traverse a low, sandy hump dotted with lodgepole pines to reach the edge of Big Whitney Meadow. There are plenty of campsites all around its periphery.

Cross two tributaries of Golden Trout Creek on another set of boulders, traverse another sandy rise in the middle of the meadow, then hop a final creek to reach forest once again. Watch for Cirque Peak to the northeast and Johnson Peak to the southwest. Walk just a few yards into the forest to reach a junction with the signed Siberian Pass Trail at mile 7.1. Go straight ahead a short distance farther to a second junction with the trail to Tunnel Meadow at mile 7.2. Keep right (southwest) this time. Climb over a ridge on moderate switchbacks and descend to Barigan Stringer at mile 10.0. At the signed junction, turn right (north) and follow the pretty creek upstream to pass an even prettier meadow blooming with wildflowers.

At mile 11.2 the trail splits. The left fork is marked HORSE TRAIL; the right, FOOT TRAIL. The horse trail is the better choice by far, even for hikers. It is slightly longer, but is more gradual and much easier to follow. The foot trail is not shown on the topo. Climb a few dry switchbacks, pass a grassy pond almost completely silted in, negotiate a few more switchbacks on granite slabs, and pass a few more small meadows.

Once you reach a tiny pond nestled in a pocket in the rocks (dry late in the season), only a few more minutes' laborious ascent brings you to a ridgetop at 10,900

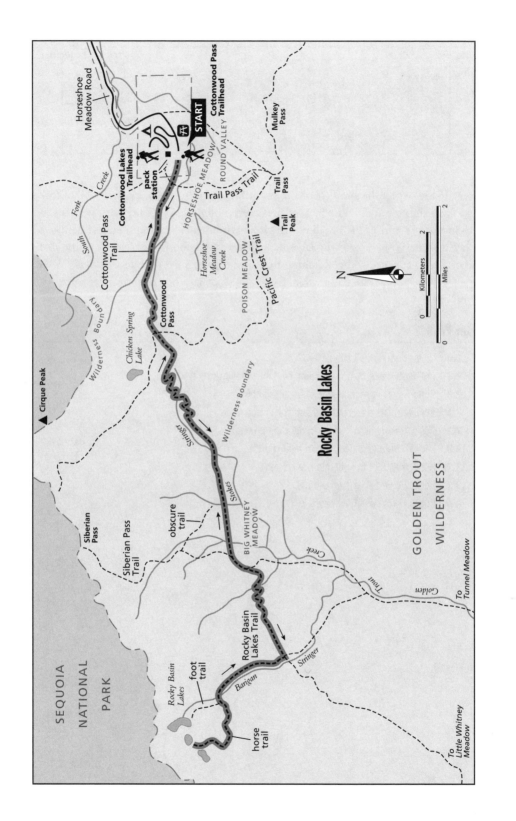

Rocky Basin Lakes

SEQUOIA NATIONAL PARK

Cirque Peak

Horseshoe Meadow Road

Horseshoe Meadow

Cottonwood Lakes Trailhead

START

Cottonwood Pass Trailhead

pack station

Cottonwood Pass Trail

South Fork Cottonwood Creek

Wilderness Boundary

Chicken Spring Lake

Cottonwood Pass

Stringer

Wilderness Boundary

HORSESHOE MEADOW

Horseshoe Meadow Creek

POISON MEADOW

Trail Pass Trail

ROUND VALLEY

Mulkey Pass

Trail Pass

Trail Peak

Pacific Crest Trail

Siberian Pass

Siberian Pass Trail

obscure trail

Stokes

BIG WHITNEY MEADOW

Golden Trout Creek

Rocky Basin Lakes

foot trail

horse trail

Barigan Stringer

Rocky Basin Lakes Trail

GOLDEN TROUT WILDERNESS

To Tunnel Meadow

To Little Whitney Meadow

N

Kilometers 0 2

Miles 0 2

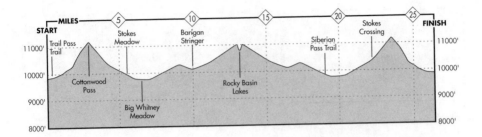

feet, below which lie the first of the beautiful blue-green Rocky Basin Lakes (mile 13.2). A sign reminds campers that fires are prohibited here. There are several lakes to investigate within the broad glacial cirque, and plenty of campsites. Just be sure to stay at least 100 feet from the lakeside and stow your food out of reach of the marmots (who are sure to be watching from the tops of surrounding boulders). When you have explored the basin, caught your limit, or run out of time, return the way you came.

Key Points

0.0 Cottonwood Pass Trailhead.

0.3 Trail Pass/pack station junction, continue straight (west).

2.9 Cottonwood Pass, continue straight (southwest).

7.1 Siberian Pass Trail, continue straight.

7.2 Rocky Basin Lakes Trail, keep right (southwest).

10.0 Barigan Stringer junction, turn right (north).

11.2 Horse trail/foot trail junction, keep left.

13.2 Rocky Basin Lakes, turn around.

26.4 Cottonwood Pass Trailhead.

30 Tunnel Meadow

A loop backpack with two passes, vast meadows, great fishing, and some local cowboy history.

Start: Cottenwood Pass Trailhead.
Total distance: 24.2 miles.
Difficulty: Moderate to strenuous, depending on how long you take.
Total climbing: 2,610 feet.
Trail traffic: Moderate near Cottonwood and Trail Passes, otherwise light.
Best months: Mid-June to mid-October.

Maps: USGS Cirque Peak, Johnson Peak, and Kern Peak quads; Forest Service Golden Trout and South Sierra Wilderness map.
Permits: Required and available in advance or at the Mount Whitney Ranger Station in Lone Pine. Quotas are in effect.
Trailhead facilities: Camping, toilets, water. Gas, groceries, and phones in Lone Pine.

Finding the trailhead: From Lone Pine on Interstate 395, drive west on Whitney Portal Road (the only traffic light in town) for 3 miles to Horseshoe Meadow Road. Turn left (south) and climb the dizzying, hairpin-turning road for 20 miles to a signed junction. The right fork goes to the Cottonwood Lakes Trailhead. Go straight ahead just past the junction to the campground and trailhead parking area.

The Hike

The trail begins at a set of big interpretive signs near the toilets. Just beyond, another sign reminds travelers that the National Park Boundary is 8 miles ahead and that no pets or firearms are permitted beyond that point. The path is sandy and flat at first. At mile 0.3 it meets a junction at which you continue straight ahead (west). The right-hand fork goes northeast to the pack station and the Cottonwood Lakes Trailhead; the left (south) fork goes to Trail Pass. Skirt the north side of Horseshoe Meadow and ignore a second Trail Pass cutoff to the south. Rock-hop a little creek, climb a short distance, then jump the creek back to the other side again. The grade increases gradually on sandy footing until it begins some fairly steep switchbacks. Please heed the signs that remind hikers not to shortcut these switchbacks. Cross a creek in gully, return to the forest, and climb up the last few switchbacks to Cottonwood Pass at mile 2.9.

Just beyond, pass a junction with the Pacific Crest Trail (PCT) and proceed straight ahead (southwest) through a meadow with a snow survey marker in the middle, then begin a steeper descent alongside willow-choked Stokes Stringer Creek. Big Whitney Meadow is clearly visible below at the bottom of a long series of dusty switchbacks. Hop across the stream and continue to descend along its south side until you reach Stokes Stringer itself; there are a few campsites in the nearby

Golden Trout Creek winds its way through a meadow on the Tunnel Meadow Trail.

forest. Cross two more branches of the creek running through a sometimes slushy meadow using conveniently spaced boulders, then traverse a low, sandy hump dotted with lodgepole pines to reach the edge of Big Whitney Meadow at mile 6.5. There are plenty of campsites all around its periphery. Cross two tributaries of Golden Trout Creek on another set of boulders, traverse another sandy rise in the middle of the meadow, then hop a final creek to reach forest once again. To the northeast you can spot big, bare Cirque Peak at the end of the Sierra Crest, and to the southwest you'll catch a glimpse of partly forested Johnson Peak. Walk just a few yards into the forest to reach a junction with the Siberian Pass Trail at mile 7.1. At the signed junction, go straight ahead (southwest); the right (north) fork goes to Siberian Outpost. At mile 7.2 meet a second fork in the trail. Keep left (south) here; the right fork heads west toward Rocky Basin Lakes.

Follow along the west side of Golden Trout Creek, no more than a trickle here, at the very edge of Big Whitney Meadow. The soft, cow-trampled sand makes it easy to lose the trail. Ignore any of the apparent paths that wander up the sandy slope toward the forest and stay near the meadow's edge and the stream. Soon the banks of the creek begin to narrow, the meadow pinches out, and the stream picks up speed, tumbling over rocks into pools lined with shooting stars, ranger's buttons, cinquefoil, and buttercups. Beautiful golden trout are easy to spot in the deep quiet places. At mile 10.0, just where another little stream flows into Golden Trout Creek is a junction with a second trail to Rocky Basin Lakes, this one via Barigan Stringer. Keep left (south), following along the west bank of Golden Trout Creek. (The Golden Trout Wilderness map erroneously shows the trail on the eastern side of the creek.)

At mile 12.2 where the trail seems to disappear and the bank becomes too steep and high for progress along the west side, cross the creek on a combination of rocks and logs. If you have crossed at the right spot, you will see blazes on the trees and a tempting, but clearly illegal campsite on the eastern side. Walk along the creek until you reach the Bullfrog junction at mile 13.2, a short distance beyond which is found the Tunnel Meadow Guard Station. This is the lowest point of the route at about 8,900 feet and the point at which you turn northeast to complete the loop, but before you do so, make a short detour of only 100 yards to investigate the guard station and the site of the infamous tunnel.

In the 1880s farmers living downstream on the South Fork of the Kern noticed that Golden Trout Creek and the South Fork flowed side by side in this area and, at one point, almost came together. They hatched a plan to blast a tunnel between the two streams and divert water from Golden Trout Creek into the South Fork to increase its volume. The tunnel collapsed almost as soon as it was dug, and the diversionary ditches filled in. Lawsuits ended any attempt to rebuild it. The remains of the ditches can still be seen alongside the trail, and the dip in the path between the Bullfrog Trail junction and the guard station is the spot where the tunnel used to be. The Tunnel Meadow Guard Station itself was at one time the central point of communication by phone lines among the cow camps scattered around the area. Some of the wires are still up, and coils of phone line can be found here and there along wilderness trails. The station is still used by the Forest Service but no longer has a ranger in permanent summer residence.

After exploring the guard station, go back to the Bullfrog junction and take the northeast fork toward Bullfrog Meadow. The trail enters the corridor of the Wild and Scenic South Fork of the Kern River on fairly flat, sandy terrain alongside a meadow partly shaded by lodgepoles.

At mile 14.2 pass a junction with a path that heads left (northwest) toward Big Whitney Meadow and Rocky Basin Lakes. This trail is the southern end of a short-cut route between Golden Trout Creek and the Kern River, the other end of which is so obscure that you probably did not see it at all on your way here. It is not shown at all on the Golden Trout Wilderness map. Continue straight ahead (northeast) for a short distance to pass an enormous camping area with a corral for horses. Before the wilderness was established, there was a small airstrip nearby. Soon the meadow

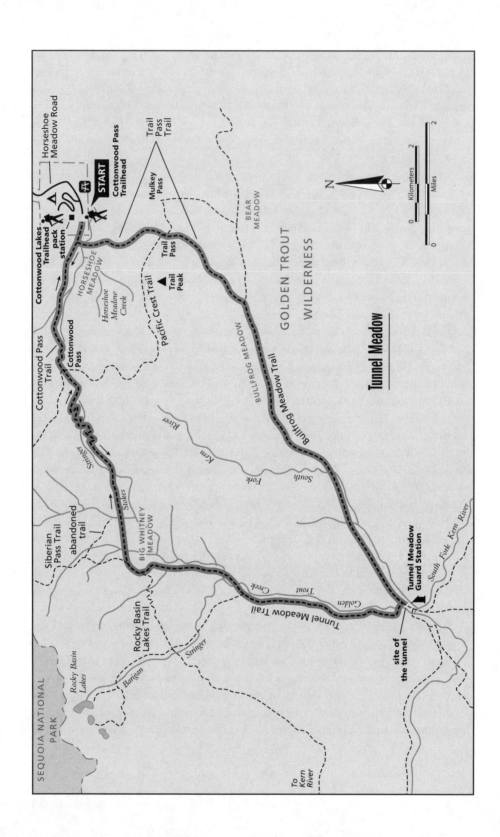

Tunnel Meadow

beside you pinches out and the stream flows more swiftly past some smaller, more pleasant campsites. The Bullfrog Meadow Trail climbs a little gully and hops the South Fork of the Kern, at this point no more than a trickle. Continue climbing along its eastern bank. The gully opens into a little meadow where the South Fork goes on north, but you continue east along another tiny, spring-fed creeklet. Finally water and shade are left behind and the trail crosses over a sandy saddle with scattered lodgepoles, then descends into Bullfrog Meadow. A long tedious slog in soft, deep sand follows along an ugly series of parallel grooves worn into the earth by the pounding of too many feet and hooves.

It is a relief to leave this difficult, though oddly beautiful wasteland at a junction at mile 19.1 and follow the north (left) path toward Trail Pass; the right (east) fork heads toward Bear Meadow and Mulkey Pass; the Trail Pass Trail winds upward through lodgepoles, junipers, and foxtail pines, first on a moderate grade, then more steeply. A little spring with corn lilies and willows provides much-needed refreshment about 500 feet below the top. From here climb a few final switchbacks to the crest at 10,487 feet to an intersection with the Pacific Crest Trail at mile 21.7. Continue straight ahead (north) passing under the remains of an old phone line. Head down the shallow draw until the trail makes a switchback to the left (southwest) and passes the remains of an old trail at mile 22.4, seldom used or maintained, that cuts off to the right, skirting the east side of Round Valley. Keep left, crossing a flowery, spring fed creek, and drop easily onto the sandy edge of Horseshoe Meadow, carpeted with tiny but brilliant magenta monkey flowers early in the season. The grassy meadow soon resumes and a flattened log provides a dry-foot crossing over the stream. Here you meet the Cottonwood Pass Trail junction at mile 23.9 where you turn right (east) to find yourself back at the Cottonwood Pass Trailhead at mile 24.2.

Key Points

0.0 Cottonwood Pass Trailhead.

0.3 Trail Pass/pack station junction, continue straight (west).

2.9 Cottonwood Pass, continue straight (southwest).

7.1 Siberian Pass Trail, continue straight.

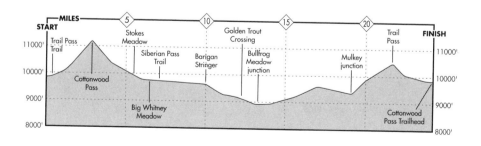

7.2 Rocky Basin Lakes Trail north, keep left (south).

10.0 Rocky Basin Lakes Trail south (Barigan Stringer), keep left (south).

12.2 Golden Trout Creek crossing.

13.2 Bullfrog Meadow junction/Tunnel Meadow, turn left (northeast).

14.2 Big Whitney/Rocky Basin shortcut, continue straight (northeast).

19.1 Bullfrog/Trail Pass junction, keep left (north).

21.7 Trail Pass, continue straight.

22.4 Unsigned junction with unmaintained trail.

23.9 Cottonwood Pass/pack station junction. This is the end of the loop. Turn right.

24.2 Cottonwood Pass Trailhead.

31 Cottonwood Pass to the Kern River

A one-way hike to a major intersection near the center of the wilderness and to one of the two bridges across the Kern. It can be used as one leg of a number of extended backpacks within the wilderness, or beyond to Sequoia National Park.

Start: Cottonwood Pass Trailhead.
Total distance: 44.4 miles.
Difficulty: Moderate to strenuous, depending on your pace.
Total climbing: 1,950 feet.
Trail traffic: Moderate.
Best months: Mid-June to mid-October.
Maps: USGS Cirque Peak, Johnson Peak, Kern Peak and Kern Lake quads; Forest Service

Golden Trout and South Sierra Wilderness map.
Permits: Required and available in advance or at the Mount Whitney Ranger Station in Lone Pine. Quotas are in effect.
Trailhead facilities: Camping, toilets, water. Gas, groceries, and phones in Lone Pine.

Finding the trailhead: From Lone Pine on Highway 395, drive west on Whitney Portal Road (the only traffic light in town) for 3 miles to Horseshoe Meadow Road. Turn left (south) and climb the dizzying, hairpin-turning road for 20 miles to a signed junction. The right fork goes to the Cottonwood Lakes Trailhead. Go straight ahead just past the junction to the campground and Cottonwood Pass Trailhead parking area.

The Hike

The trail begins at a set of big interpretive signs near the toilets. Just beyond, another sign reminds travelers that the National Park Boundary is 8 miles ahead and that no pets or firearms are permitted beyond that point. The path is sandy and flat at first. At mile 0.3 it meets a junction at which you continue straight ahead (west). The right-hand fork goes northeast to the pack station and the Cottonwood Lakes Trailhead; the left (south) fork goes to Trail Pass. Skirt the north side of Horseshoe Meadow and ignore a second Trail Pass cutoff to the south. Rock-hop a little creek, climb a short distance, then jump the creek back to the other side again. The grade increases gradually on sandy footing until it begins some fairly steep switchbacks. Please heed the signs that remind hikers not to shortcut these switchbacks. Cross a creek in gully, return to the forest, and climb up the last few switchbacks to Cottonwood Pass at mile 2.9.

Pass a junction with the Pacific Crest Trail and proceed straight ahead (southwest) through a meadow with a snow survey marker in the middle, then begin a steeper descent along Stokes Stringer Creek. Big Whitney Meadow is clearly visible below at the bottom of a long series of dusty switchbacks. Hop across the stream and continue to descend along its south side until you reach Stokes Stringer itself.

The bridge over the Kern River at the Sequoia National Park boundary

Cross two more branches of the creek running through a meadow, then traverse a low sandy hump to reach the edge of Big Whitney Meadow at mile 6.5. Cross two tributaries of Golden Trout Creek, traverse another sandy rise in the middle of the meadow, then hop a final creek to reach forest once again. Walk just a few yards into the forest to reach a junction with the Siberian Pass trail at mile 7.1. Go straight ahead (southwest.) The right (north) fork goes to Siberian Outpost. At mile 7.2 meet a second fork in the trail. Keep left (south) here. The right fork heads west toward Rocky Basin Lakes.

Follow the west side of Golden Trout Creek. The cow-trampled sand makes it easy to lose the trail. Ignore any of the apparent paths that wander up the sandy slope toward the forest and stay near the meadow's edge and the stream. At mile 10.0, there is a junction with a second trail to Rocky Basin Lakes, this one via Barigan Stringer. Keep left (south) following the west bank of Golden Trout Creek. (The Golden Trout Wilderness map erroneously shows the trail on the eastern side of the creek.)

At mile 12.2, cross the creek on a combination of rocks and logs. If you have crossed at the right spot, you will see blazes on the trees. Walk along the creek until you reach the Bullfrog junction at mile 13.2. The trail goes through a gate, then makes an odd little dip before arriving at Tunnel Meadow Guard Station. The dip is all that remains of a tunnel that was dug between Golden Trout Creek and the South Fork of the Kern River. In the 1880s farmers downstream on the South Fork hoped to divert water from Golden Trout Creek into the river to increase its volume. The tunnel collapsed, diversion ditches partially filled in, and lawsuits ended the project.

The Tunnel Guard Station itself was at one time the central point of communication by phone lines among the cow camps scattered around the area. Some of the wires are still up, and coils of phone line can be found here and there along wilderness trails. The station is still used by the Forest Service, but no longer has a ranger in permanent summer residence. Just past the guard station at mile 13.4 is another junction. The left fork heads southeast toward Ramshaw Meadows, Kern Peak, and the South Fork of the Kern. Keep right, following alongside a series of fence posts. Where the posts make a right turn, so do you. There is actually an unmarked junction here (at mile 13.7) that is easy to miss. The faint trail heading due south toward Bear Meadow is not maintained and soon disappears. As soon as you have turned southwest to follow the fence, wade Golden Trout Creek and make your way through a willow thicket to the forest beyond.

At mile 14.3 keep right at the next signed junction. Both forks ultimately reach Little Whitney Meadow, your next objective, but the right (northwest) route is the shorter and better-marked way around the rough jumble of volcanic rocks known as the Malpais (badlands). This lava flow is the most recent in the region, less than 5,000 years old. The Swiss cheese texture of the rocks comes from gas bubbles in the lava while it was still molten. Continue on through the sandy forest, passing southwest of little Groundhog Meadow. Hop a little tributary of Golden Trout Creek and hike along its northern bank on trail lined with tiny lupines whose silvery foliage is interspersed with pussy-paws and wallflowers. The ridge to the north confines trail and creek to a narrow notch alongside the lava flow. Watch for a small inconspicuous sign on a tree to the right of the trail marked KERN RIVER. Turn left here and wade Golden Trout Creek, or search a few yards upstream and downstream to find a log crossing. If you are here early in the year, look for the seldom seen white McCloskey's violets near the creekside. Little Whitney Meadow is just ahead at mile 17.2. There is good camping near the meadow at a big packer site with log chairs and a corral. A couple of picturesque ranchers' cabins are tucked into a forest corner across the meadow.

Follow alongside the fence enclosing the meadow on wet, sloppy footing, passing a sign that confirms that you are headed toward the Kern. Go through a gate to a junction at mile 17.6. The left fork goes to Volcano Meadow, the southern route around the Malpais Lava Flow; the right, to the Kern River. The 7.5-minute topo shows the trail crossing Golden Trout Creek a short distance after this junction, but stay on the south side; the way has been rerouted to save you two extra crossings.

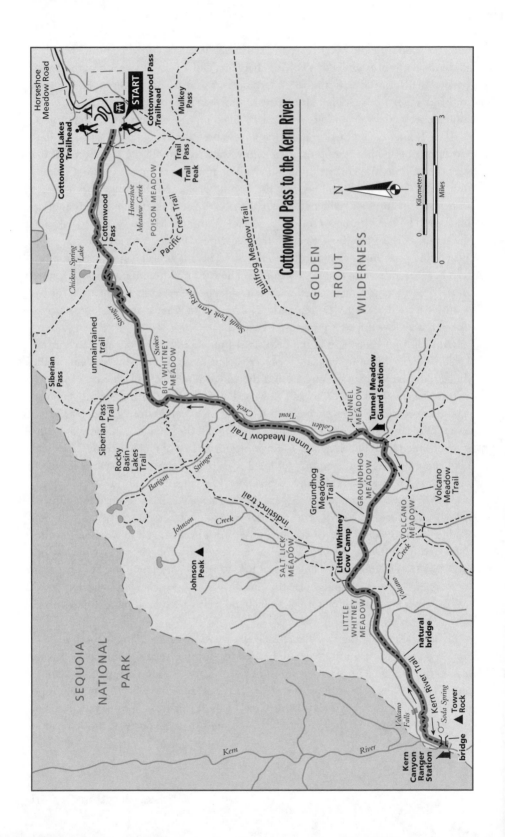

Cottonwood Pass to the Kern River

SEQUOIA NATIONAL PARK

GOLDEN TROUT WILDERNESS

Horseshoe Meadow Road

Cottonwood Lakes Trailhead

START

Cottonwood Pass Trailhead

Mulkey Pass

Trail Pass

Trail Peak

Horseshoe Meadow Creek

POISON MEADOW

Pacific Crest Trail

Bullfrog Meadow Trail

Cottonwood Pass

Chicken Spring Lake

Stringer

Siberian Pass

unmaintained trail

Siberian Pass Trail

Rocky Basin Lakes Trail

Stokes

BIG WHITNEY MEADOW

South Fork Kern River

Golden Trout Creek

TUNNEL MEADOW

Tunnel Meadow Guard Station

Tunnel Meadow Trail

Barigan

Stringer

indistinct trail

Johnson Creek

Johnson Peak

SALT LICK MEADOW

Groundhog Meadow Trail

Little Whitney Cow Camp

GROUNDHOG MEADOW

VOLCANO MEADOW

Volcano Meadow Trail

LITTLE WHITNEY MEADOW

Volcano Creek

natural bridge

Kern River Trail

Soda Spring

Tower Rock

Volcano Falls

Kern Canyon Ranger Station

bridge

Kern River

N

Kilometers 3

Miles 3

0

0

About 0.5 mile beyond the junction, cross a tributary that makes its way through a lava boulder field. As you descend through the forest, springs seep to the surface to nourish a pretty little meadow. As the path steepens, the waters flow together to make a rushing creek that leaps and tumbles down through an exquisite garden of wild roses, geraniums, blue-eyed grass, monkey flowers, and larkspur.

The Groundhog Meadow Trail crosses this creek on a natural bridge made of travertine, a rock produced by the evaporation of hot mineral-rich water—a sure sign that there used to be a hot spring here. The falls below the crossing are even prettier than the ones above, but you will have to make a short detour below the bridge to see them. Begin the final descent to the Kern on a series of steep switchbacks above the gorge of Golden Trout Creek. At roughly the midpoint of the descent, watch for the long, spectacular series of drops that make up Volcano Falls off to your right. You get only one chance: Once the trail rounds a corner, you lose sight of them. Continue downward among Jeffrey pines, ceanothus, and manzanita to pass beneath a cliff of basalt columns, a smaller version of the Devil's Postpile. This is where the Malpais lava flowed down over the cliff to the Kern and cooled so quickly and uniformly that the rock cracked into (mostly) hexagonal columns. You can see that the bottoms of the columns end a distance above the level of the river, showing how much farther the river has cut down into its bed since the lava cooled.

A few more steep, rocky switchbacks take you down to a sunny manzanita-covered flat, which you traverse for about a mile before reaching the big bridge across the Kern River (mile 22.2). This is the low point on the hike at 6,400 feet. The best camping is across the bridge on the west side. Don't expect solitude, and watch where you step to avoid rattlesnakes. This is the border of Sequoia National Park. A sign directs those traveling with pets or firearms who plan to head south to Kern Lake to keep left and cross Coyote Creek to avoid entering the park, though this ford can be tricky early in the season. There is a big log upstream that is much safer. The nearby Kern Canyon Ranger Station is staffed in summer. If you want to visit, hike west uphill from the river and keep left at a junction with a spur trail to Soda Spring and left again at the Funston Meadow junction. Beyond the ranger station the Coyote Pass Trail heads west across Coyote Creek, and the Kern Lake Trail goes north. To return to Cottonwood Pass Trailhead follow the same route.

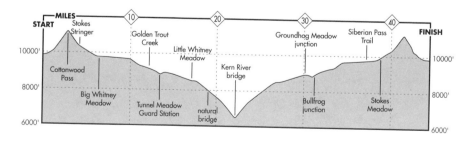

Key Points

0.0 Cottonwood Pass Trailhead.

0.3 Trail Pass/pack station junction, continue straight (west).

2.9 Cottonwood Pass, continue straight (southwest).

7.1 Siberian Pass Trail, continue straight.

7.2 Rocky Basin Lakes Trail north, keep left (south).

10.0 Rocky Basin Lakes Trail south (Barigan Stringer), keep left (south).

12.2 Golden Trout Creek crossing.

13.2 Bullfrog Meadow junction near Tunnel Meadow.

13.4 Ramshaw Meadow junction, keep right.

13.7 Unmarked Bear Meadow junction, turn right.

14.3 Groundhog Meadow junction, keep right (northwest).

17.1 Golden Trout Creek crossing.

17.2 Little Whitney Meadow.

17.6 Volcano Meadow junction, keep right (southwest).

22.2 Bridge at the Kern River.

44.4 Cottonwood Pass Trailhead.

32 Kern Peak

A loop hike with optional variations to 11,510-foot Kern Peak for views of the Southern Sierra and high desert unsurpassed anywhere in the Golden Trout Wilderness.

Start: Cottonwood Pass Trailhead.
Total distance: 35.2 miles.
Difficulty: Strenuous.
Total climbing: 5,400 feet.
Trail traffic: Light.
Best months: Late June to October.
Maps: USGS Cirque Peak, Johnson Peak, and Kern Peak quads; Forest Service Golden Trout and South Sierra Wilderness map.

Permits: Required and available in advance or at the Mount Whitney Ranger Station in Lone Pine.
Trailhead facilities: Camping, toilets, water. Nearest gas, groceries, and phones in Lone Pine.

Finding the trailhead: From Lone Pine on Interstate 395, drive west on Whitney Portal Road (the only traffic signal in town) for 3 miles to Horseshoe Meadow Road. Turn left (south) and climb the dizzying, hairpin-turning road for 20 miles to a signed junction with the Cottonwood Lakes Trailhead Road. Go straight ahead just past the junction to the campground and trailhead parking area.

The Hike

This is the easiest route to Kern Peak by trail, though the route gets little maintenance beyond Tunnel Meadow and in a few places is indistinct or altogether absent. You should be fairly competent at reading your topo map. The hike is described here as a loop—which makes the approach to the peak a bit easier to follow and provides some variety—but you can start in either direction, and descend the same way you came up. Part of the loop is not shown at all on the Forest Service Golden Trout Wilderness map, and even the USGS quad shows the location of part of the trail as "approximate." (To confuse the matter even further, the Sequoia National Forest map shows the "approximate" loop and omits the one shown on the Golden Trout Wilderness map altogether.)

The trail begins at a set of big interpretive signs near the toilets. Just beyond, another sign reminds travelers that the National Park Boundary is 8 miles ahead and that no pets or firearms are permitted beyond that point. The path is sandy and flat at first. At mile 0.3 it meets a junction at which you continue straight ahead (west). The right-hand fork goes northeast to the pack station and the Cottonwood Lakes Trailhead; the left (south) fork goes to Trail Pass. Skirt the north side of Horseshoe Meadow and ignore a second Trail Pass cutoff to the south. Rock-hop a little creek,

Approaching the rocky summit of 11,510-foot Kern Peak

climb a short distance, then jump the creek back to the other side again. The grade increases gradually on sandy footing until it begins some fairly steep switchbacks. Please heed the signs that remind hikers not to shortcut these switchbacks. Cross a creek in gully, return to the forest, and climb up the last few switchbacks to Cottonwood Pass at mile 2.9.

Pass a junction with the Pacific Crest Trail and proceed straight ahead (southwest) through a meadow with a snow survey marker in the middle, then begin a steeper descent along Stokes Stringer Creek. Big Whitney Meadow is clearly visible below at the bottom of a long series of dusty switchbacks. Hop across the stream and continue to descend along its south side until you reach Stokes Stringer itself. Cross two more branches of the creek running through a meadow, then traverse a low sandy hump to reach the edge of Big Whitney Meadow at mile 6.5. Cross two tributaries of Golden Trout Creek, traverse another sandy rise in the middle of the meadow, then hop a final creek to reach forest once again. Walk just a few yards into the forest to reach a junction with the Siberian Pass trail at mile 7.1. Go straight ahead (southwest.) The right (north) fork goes to Siberian Outpost. At mile 7.2 meet a second fork in the trail. Keep left (south) here. The right fork heads west toward Rocky Basin Lakes.

Follow the west side of Golden Trout Creek. The cow-trampled sand makes it easy to lose the trail. Ignore any of the apparent paths that wander up the sandy slope toward the forest and stay near the meadow's edge and the stream. At mile 10.0, there is a junction with a second trail to Rocky Basin Lakes, this one via Barigan Stringer. Keep left (south) following the west bank of Golden Trout Creek. (The Golden Trout Wilderness map erroneously shows the trail on the eastern side of the creek.)

At mile 12.2, cross the creek on a combination of rocks and logs. If you have crossed at the right spot, you will see blazes on the trees. Walk along the creek until you reach the Bullfrog junction at mile 13.2; the Tunnel Meadow Guard Station lies a bit farther. Just beyond the station is a signed junction at mile 13.3. Follow the left fork toward the Kern River and Kern Peak. Just a few yards past this junction, find another more decrepit sign indicating Kern Peak to the right (south). Ignore this one and keep left (southeast) instead, heading toward Ramshaw Meadows. Climb a saddle between two red cinder cones and pass through a gate. To your left (east) the Kern River winds off into the distance through Ramshaw Meadows toward Olancha Peak (12,120 feet) on the skyline. Follow the still-obvious trail on down into the northwest corner of Ramshaw Meadows, then watch for the faint trace of a trail junction about 200 yards after crossing Kern Peak Stringer Creek. Early in the season the creek may be divided into several branches. The junction appears beyond the last and largest of these at mile 14.3. This trail is not shown on the Golden Trout Wilderness map. Turn right (west).

The Kern Peak Trail fades almost immediately, but you can keep on track by following the creek upstream and southward, taking care to stay alongside the main watercourse, ignoring or hopping over any smaller tributaries feeding into it. You might have to make your way through some scratchy willows as the walls of the notch through which the creek flows slowly close in. Keep a sharp eye out for blazes on trees alongside the stream; you will be hopping from one side to the other now and then. Once you have spotted the first blaze, it's easy to stay on course until you reach the top. The route is sometimes quite steep. At a little green meadow, hop the creek one last time, ending up on the east side, and resume climbing now on easily followed switchbacks under a pure stand of foxtail pines.

The Kern Peak Trail veers slightly southwest of the summit at first. Through the boulders and pines you can occasionally spot the crown with a rakishly slanted cap (the roof of an old lookout tower) cocked over its brow. The trail goes around the "back" or west side of the peak, shifts direction to head southeast, and leaves the foxtails behind. Where it turns due north again for the final approach to the main summit, you'll find a spectacularly scenic rocky shoulder where you are sure to pause and gasp, from both the thin air and the awesome expanse of peaks and ridges marching off into the distance. Now your goal is in sight—the platform of the ruined old lookout at the top.

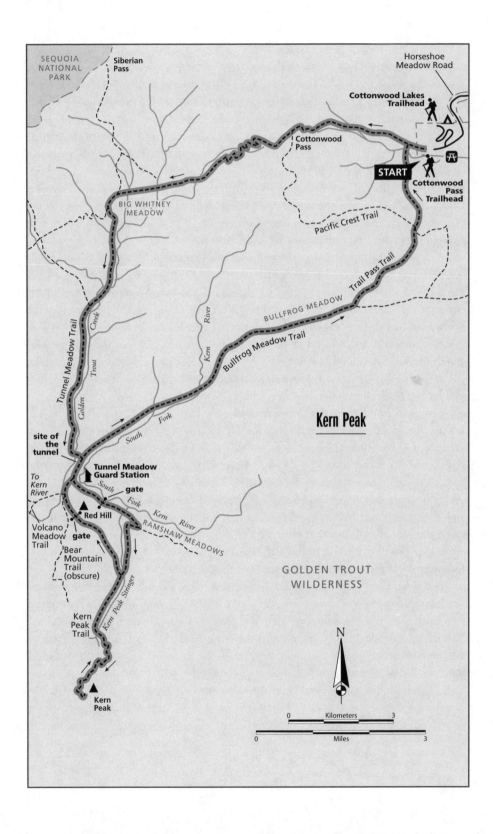

SEQUOIA
NATIONAL
PARK

Siberian
Pass

Horseshoe
Meadow Road

Cottonwood Lakes
Trailhead

Cottonwood
Pass

START

Cottonwood
Pass
Trailhead

Pacific Crest Trail

BIG WHITNEY
MEADOW

Trail Pass Trail

BULLFROG MEADOW

Bullfrog Meadow Trail

Kern   River

Tunnel Meadow Trail

Trout   Creek

Golden

South   Fork

Kern Peak

site of
the
tunnel

Tunnel Meadow
Guard Station

South   Fork

gate

To
Kern
River

Kern   River

Red Hill

RAMSHAW MEADOWS

Volcano
Meadow
Trail

gate

Bear
Mountain
Trail
(obscure)

GOLDEN TROUT
WILDERNESS

Kern
Peak
Trail

Kern Peak Stringer

Kern
Peak

N

0   Kilometers   3

0   Miles   3

When you reach the top, the views in every direction are simply stunning, probably the finest in the wilderness. You can see the Great Western Divide soaring above the Kern Canyon on one side; on the other lies the main Sierra Crest, culminating in Mount Whitney, highest point in the continental United States at almost 14,500 feet. Across the Owens Valley to the east are the Panamint Mountains, crowned by Telescope Peak, beyond which lies Death Valley, lowest point in the United States. If the weather is clear, you might even catch a glimpse of the transverse ranges of Southern California.

When you are ready to return, reverse your steps and follow the trail back down the notch alongside Kern Peak Stringer Creek. You can return to Tunnel Meadow the way you came, but to complete the loop, when the trail alongside the creek begins to level out, keep to the left (west) side of the creek, gradually veering away from the bank, still following blazes. You will occasionally spot sections of telephone line running toward the Tunnel Meadow Guard Station. Should you lose the path altogether, just aim for the low point of the notch between a granitic hill on the left (west) and the Red Hill volcanic cone on the right (east).

From the top of the notch, head straight downhill, passing through an open gate and following occasional yellow-painted can lids nailed on trees. These unconventional blazes are found sometimes on one side of a tree, sometimes on the other, so you might have to glance over your shoulder now and then to locate the ones you have passed. These markers are helpful since countless hooves have obliterated the trail on the ground.

Just after the grade flattens out, the yellow trail markers disappear and a willowy meadow can be spied ahead through the trees. At about the same time, you should pick up the Bear Meadow Trail where it meets the main Tunnel Meadow Trail running northeast along the east side of Golden Trout Creek. The unmarked junction of these two trails is found where the fence makes its right-angled turn. From here turn right and retrace your steps to the junction just south of the Tunnel Meadow Guard Station at mile 24.3.

Walk north past the guard station, dipping through the trench below the collapsed tunnel to meet the Bullfrog Meadow junction at mile 24.2. Continue straight ahead (northeast), passing a junction at mile 25.4 with a path that heads left (northeast) toward Big Whitney Meadow and Rocky Basin Lakes that is not shown on the Golden Trout Wilderness map. In a short distance pass an enormous camping area with a corral for horses. Soon the meadow beside you pinches out and the stream flows more swiftly past some smaller, more pleasant campsites. The Bullfrog Meadow Trail climbs a little gully and hops the South Fork of the Kern, at this point no more than a trickle. Follow along its eastern bank until the gully opens into a little meadow, where the South Fork goes on north, but continue east along another tiny, spring fed creeklet. Finally, water and shade are left behind and the trail crosses over a sandy saddle with scattered lodgepoles, then descends into Bullfrog Meadow.

A long tedious slog in soft, deep sand follows along an ugly series of parallel grooves worn into the earth by the pounding of too many feet and hooves.

It is a relief to leave this difficult, though oddly beautiful, wasteland at a junction at mile 30.3 and follow the north (left) path toward Trail Pass. The right (east) fork heads toward Bear Meadow and Mulkey Pass. The Trail Pass Trail winds upward through lodgepoles, junipers, and foxtail pines, first on a moderate grade, then more steeply. A little spring with corn lilies and willows provides much needed refreshment about 500 feet below the top. From here climb a few final switchbacks to the crest at 10,487 feet to an intersection with the Pacific Crest Trail at mile 32.9.

Continue straight ahead (north) passing under the remains of an old phone line and head down the shallow draw until the trail makes a switchback to the left (southwest) and passes the remains of an old trail at mile 33.6, seldom used or maintained, that cuts off to the right, skirting the east side of Round Valley. Keep left, crossing a flowery, spring fed creek, and drop easily onto the sandy edge of Horseshoe Meadow, carpeted with tiny but brilliant magenta monkey flowers early in the season. The footing becomes grassy meadow and a flattened log provides a dry foot crossing over a branch of Horseshoe Meadow Creek. Here you meet the Cottonwood Pass Trail junction at mile 35.6 where you turn right (east) to find yourself back at the Cottonwood Pass Trailhead at mile 35.9.

Key Points

0.0   Cottonwood Pass Trailhead.

0.3   Trail Pass/pack station junction, continue straight (west).

2.9   Cottonwood Pass, continue straight (southwest).

7.1   Siberian Pass Trail, continue straight.

7.2   Rocky Basin Lakes Trail north, keep left (south).

10.0 Rocky Basin Lakes Trail south (Barigan Stringer), keep left (south).

12.2 Golden Trout Creek crossing.

13.2 Bullfrog Meadow junction near the Tunnel Meadow Guard Station.

13.3 Junction south of guard station, keep left (southeast).

14.3 Kern Peak Stringer turnoff, turn right (west).

18.7 Kern Peak, turn around.

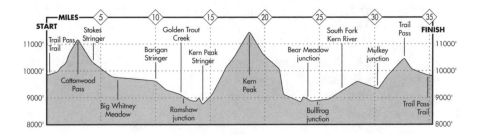

21.7 Faint trail, lead left (northwest).

24.0 Bear Meadow Trail junction, turn right.

24.2 Return to Tunnel Meadow Guard Station, turn right (northeast).

25.8 Big Whitney/Rocky Basin shortcut, continue straight (northeast).

30.3 Mulkey Pass/Trail Pass junction, keep left (north).

32.7 Trail Pass, continue straight.

33.4 Unsigned junction with unmaintained trail.

34.9 Cottonwood Pass/pack station junction. This is the end of the loop. Turn right.

35.2 Cottonwood Pass Trailhead.

33 Chicken Spring Lake

An out-and-back weekend backpack or a vigorous day hike to a true High Sierra glacial cirque lake.

Start: Cottonwood Pass Trailhead.
Total distance: 7 miles.
Difficulty: Moderate.
Total climbing: 1,340 feet.
Trail traffic: Moderate.
Best months: Mid-June through October.
Maps: USGS Cirque Peak quad; Forest Service Golden Trout and South Sierra Wilderness map.

Permits: None for a day hike; required and available in advance or at the Mount Whitney Ranger Station in Lone Pine for overnight trips. Quotas are in effect.
Trailhead facilities: Camping, toilets, water. Nearest gas, groceries, and phones in Lone Pine.

Finding the trailhead: From Lone Pine on Interstate 395, drive west on Whitney Portal Road (the only traffic signal in town) for 3 miles to Horseshoe Meadow Road. Turn left (south) and climb the dizzying, hairpin-turning road for 20 miles to a signed junction. Go straight ahead just past the junction to the campground and trailhead parking area.

The Hike

This outing involves lots of altitude gain in a short distance. If you're not already acclimatized to high elevations, you are likely to suffer symptoms of altitude sickness if you take this one too fast. The trail begins at a set of big interpretive signs near the toilets. Just beyond, another sign reminds travelers that the National Park Boundary is 8 miles ahead and that no pets or firearms are permitted beyond that point. The path is sandy and flat at first. At mile 0.3 it meets a junction at which you continue straight ahead (west). The right-hand fork goes northeast to the pack station and the Cottonwood Lakes Trailhead; the left (south) fork goes to Trail Pass. Skirt the north side of Horseshoe Meadow and ignore a second Trail Pass cutoff to the south. Rock-hop a little creek, climb a short distance, then jump the creek back to the other side again. The grade increases gradually on sandy footing until it begins some fairly steep switchbacks. Please heed the signs that remind hikers not to shortcut these switchbacks. Cross a creek in gully, return to the forest, and climb up the last few switchbacks to Cottonwood Pass at mile 2.9.

Just beyond the pass turn right (northwest) onto the Pacific Crest Trail (PCT). Contour around a flowery little meadow on a bouldery hillside through a stand of thriving foxtail pines mingled with some dead, gracefully twisted golden snags. After a hike of only minutes, the granite cirque that contains the lake opens up on the right at mile 3.5. A spur of about 100 feet takes you to the lakeside at 11,250 feet. You will probably have to share the lakeshore with other campers (especially on weekends), but there are plenty of sites scattered among the boulders. Hang your

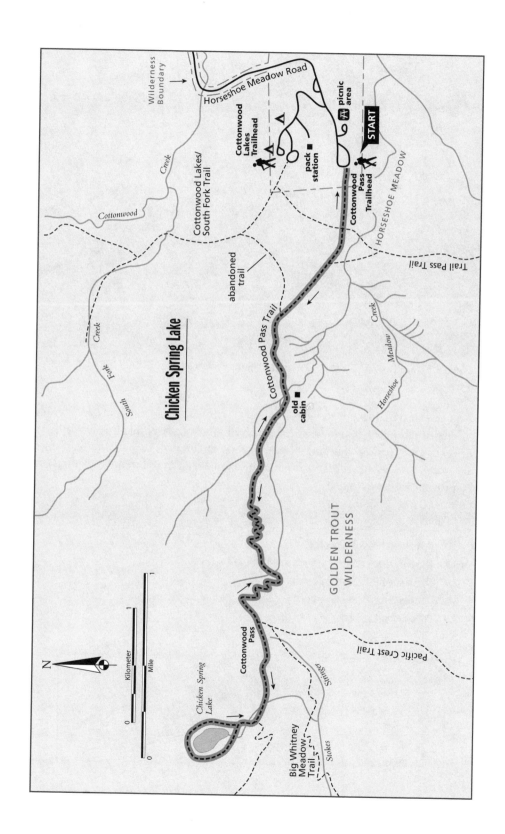

Chicken Spring Lake

N

Wilderness Boundary

Horseshoe Meadow Road

Cottonwood Lakes Trailhead

pack station

picnic area

START

Cottonwood Pass Trailhead

HORSESHOE MEADOW

Trail Pass Trail

Creek

Cottonwood

Cottonwood Lakes/South Fork Trail

abandoned trail

Cottonwood Pass Trail

South Fork Creek

Creek

old cabin

Horseshoe Meadow Creek

GOLDEN TROUT WILDERNESS

Cottonwood Pass

Pacific Crest Trail

Chicken Spring Lake

Big Whitney Meadow Trail

Stokes

Siberian

Kilometer

Mile

0   1

Chicken Spring Lake is a spectacular but heavily used weekend destination.

food properly or, better yet, carry a canister. There are bears, marmots, and several species of squirrels here, all of which love trail mix and other hiker snacks and can be remarkably patient and enterprising in their attempts to swipe yours. You must also carry a stove if you plan to spend the night: Fires are prohibited at the lake. Return the way you came.

Key Points

0.0   Cottonwood Pass Trailhead.

0.3   Trail Pass/pack station junction, continue straight (west).

2.9   Cottonwood Pass, turn right (northwest).

3.5   Chicken Spring Lake, turn around.

7.0   Cottonwood Pass Trailhead.

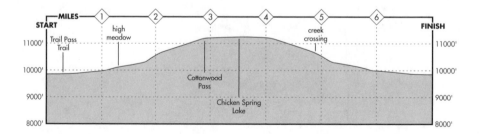

34 Siberian Outpost

A loop backpack through high open country with great views.

Start: Cottonwood Pass Trailhead.
Total distance: 17.6 miles.
Difficulty: Moderate to strenuous, depending on your pace.
Total climbing: 1,300 feet.
Trail traffic: Light to moderate.
Best months: Mid-June through October.
Maps: USGS Cirque Peak and Johnson Peak quads; Forest Service Golden Trout and South Sierra Wilderness map.
Permits: Required and available in advance or at the Mount Whitney Ranger Station in Lone Pine. Quotas are in effect.
Trailhead facilities: Camping, toilets, water. Nearest gas, groceries, and phones in Lone Pine.

Finding the trailhead: From Lone Pine on Interstate 395, drive west on Whitney Portal Road (the only traffic signal in town) for 3 miles to Horseshoe Meadow Road. Turn left (south) and climb the dizzying, hairpin-turning road for 20 miles to a signed junction. Go straight ahead just past the junction to the campground and trailhead parking area.

The Hike

The trail begins at a set of big interpretive signs near the toilets. Just beyond, another sign reminds travelers that the National Park Boundary is 8 miles ahead and that no pets or firearms are permitted beyond that point. The path is sandy and flat at first. At mile 0.3 it meets a junction at which you continue straight ahead (west). The right-hand fork goes northeast to the pack station and the Cottonwood Lakes Trailhead; the left (south) fork goes to Trail Pass. Skirt the north side of Horseshoe Meadow and ignore a second Trail Pass cutoff to the south. Rock-hop a little creek, climb a short distance, then jump the creek back to the other side again. The grade increases gradually on sandy footing until it begins some fairly steep switchbacks. Please heed the signs that remind hikers not to shortcut these switchbacks. Cross a creek in gully, return to the forest, and climb up the last few switchbacks to Cottonwood Pass at mile 2.9. Just beyond the pass turn right (northwest) onto the Pacific Crest Trail. Contour around a meadow on a bouldery hillside. After a hike of only minutes, the granite cirque that contains the Chicken Spring Lake opens up on the right at mile 3.5.

Leaving the lakeside, wind your way up out of the cirque and pause at its lip for views back down to the lake. Beyond it to the south and west is spread a grand panorama that takes in Big Whitney Meadow, Kern Peak, Templeton Mountain, and Olancha Peak. Ahead to the northwest sprawl barren Siberian Outpost, the Boreal Plateau, and, beyond, the Great Western Divide. The trail of soft, energy-sapping sand winds its way along a dry ridge, then contours around the inner side of another cirque, this one sheltering a little meadow. This is a good place to camp if Chicken

Sweeping views from the Siberian Pass Trail toward Big Whitney Meadow

Spring Lake is crowded. The map shows a pond in its center and another one above it on a rocky shelf. These are dry late in the year, but there is always a little creek flowing through. Climb out of this cirque to find the wild and aptly named Siberian Outpost spread out before you, with Mount Langley as a backdrop. This is the highest point on the loop at 11,400 feet. At mile 6.3 a sign marks the entrance to Sequoia National Park.

Descend gently for a mile past the park border to a marked trail junction at mile 7.2. Turn left (west) toward Siberian Pass. Cross two gravelly stringers with bouquets of tiny alpine wildflowers sprinkled among the grasses early in the year. While these meadows are damp most of the time, the water is found only in seeps and trickles and is not a good source for filling water bottles. At mile 8.1 you reach Siberian Pass at 10,850 feet and reenter the Golden Trout Wilderness. Now the trail descends on long, tedious switchbacks down a dry, forested gully with not much to see until you reach Big Whitney Meadow. Watch for a vague, unmarked junction at mile 10.0. Both forks will take you to Big Whitney Meadow, but the left fork—the one that follows the gully—is not maintained and is no longer shown on the 7.5-minute topo. Take the right fork, leaving the gully and crossing over a forested saddle between two rounded hills. The path trends south at first, then curves southwest to

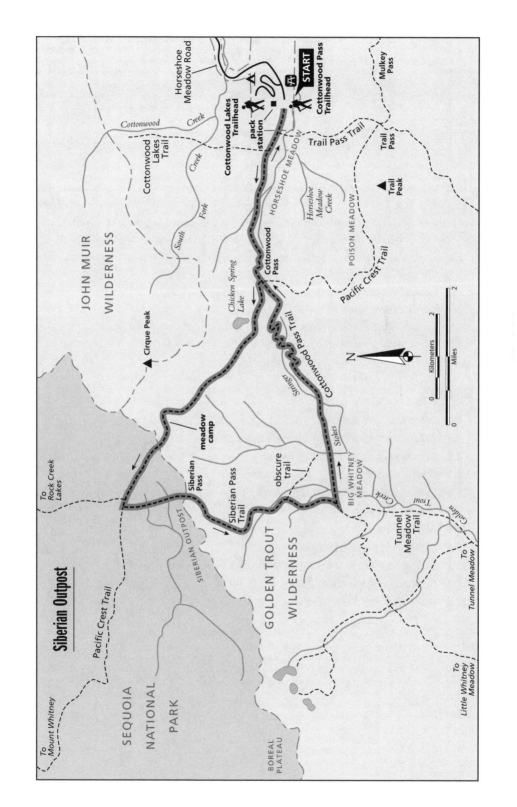

Siberian Outpost

START

Cottonwood Pass Trailhead

Cottonwood Lakes Trailhead

pack station

Horseshoe Meadow Road

Cottonwood Creek

Cottonwood Lakes Trail

South Fork

Creek

Chicken Spring Lake

Cottonwood Pass

HORSESHOE MEADOW

Horseshoe Meadow Creek

Trail Pass Trail

Trail Pass

Trail Peak

POISON MEADOW

Pacific Crest Trail

JOHN MUIR WILDERNESS

Cirque Peak

meadow camp

Cottonwood Pass Trail

Stringer

Stokes

Siberian Pass

Siberian Pass Trail

obscure trail

BIG WHITNEY MEADOW

Golden Trout Creek

Tunnel Meadow Trail

To Rock Creek Lakes

SIBERIAN OUTPOST

Pacific Crest Trail

GOLDEN TROUT WILDERNESS

SEQUOIA NATIONAL PARK

To Mount Whitney

BOREAL PLATEAU

To Tunnel Meadow

To Little Whitney Meadow

Mulkey Pass

N

Kilometers   0   2

Miles   0   2

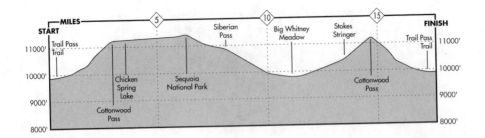

meet the junction with the Cottonwood Pass Trail at mile 11.1. Turn left and head eastward across Big Whitney Meadow over alternating sand and grasses splattered with daubs of bright paintbrush, lupine, woolly daisy, monkey flower, yampah, and gentian, hopping three branches of Golden Trout Creek on rocks. Your goal, Cottonwood Pass, is easy to recognize on the ridgeline by the green V shape of meadow below the top.

Cross over a forested hump, pass a sign pointing the way to Cottonwood Pass and Horseshoe Meadow, then rock-hop the creek in Stokes Stringer. There are campsites nearby in the forest if you are not ready to go home yet. Switchback up the draw to the meadow just below the pass, and reach the pass itself at mile 14.7. From here descend to the Cottonwood Pass Trailhead.

Key Points

0.0 Cottonwood Pass Trailhead.

0.3 Trail Pass/pack station junction, continue straight (west).

2.9 Cottonwood Pass, turn right (northwest).

3.5 Chicken Spring Lake.

6.3 Sequoia National Park boundary.

7.2 Siberian Pass junction, turn left (west).

8.1 Siberian Pass.

10.0 Unmarked junction, keep right.

11.1 Big Whitney Meadow, turn left (east).

14.7 Cottonwood Pass, continue straight.

17.6 Cottonwood Pass Trailhead.

35 Golden Trout Camp

An out-and-back day hike to the northern border of the wilderness.

Start: Cottonwood Lakes Trailhead.
Total distance: 4 miles.
Difficulty: Easy.
Total climbing: 200 feet.
Trail traffic: Moderately heavy.
Best months: May through November, or any-time Horseshoe Meadow Road is open.

Maps: USGS Cirque Peak quad; Forest Service Golden Trout and South Sierra Wilderness map.
Permits: None.
Trailhead facilities: Camping, rest rooms, water, bear boxes. Nearest groceries, gas, and phones in Lone Pine.

Finding the trailhead: From Interstate 395 in Lone Pine, turn west onto Whitney Portal Road, the only stoplight in town. Drive through the lumpy, rounded Alabama Hills, scene of innumerable western movies, toward Mount Whitney for 3 miles to the Horseshoe Meadow Road. Turn left (south). The dizzying, cliff-hugging road climbs hairpin switchbacks for 20 miles to a signed junction. Turn right here, toward Cottonwood Lakes (not Cottonwood Pass). In about 0.25 mile find a pack station, equestrian campground and corrals, hiker campground, and backpacker parking area with a set of interpretive panels at the trailhead.

The Hike

Golden Trout Camp, operated by the Thacher School in Ojai, California, is used by the Audubon Society and other educational organizations for nature programs. The beginning of this trail isn't depicted quite accurately on the topo or the Golden Trout map, but it is well traveled and easy to follow. Set out northwestward from the big signs at the trailhead with information about safety, Leave No Trace camping, and golden trout. Hiking on flat, sandy trail through a stand of foxtail pines, pass a sign cautioning that the boundary of Sequoia National Park lies 7 miles ahead, where pets and firearms are prohibited. Just beyond the sign enter the Golden Trout Wilderness.

At mile 0.2 meet a junction with the horse trail joining this one from the pack station. The mountain to your left with the bald top is Trail Peak. The path makes a little curve to the right and begins a gentle descent, picking up more lodgepole pines and abandoning foxtail pines along the way. Birdsong and a hint of green to your right foretell the appearance of Cottonwood Creek. Stroll along the streamside for a few hundred yards, enjoying a garden of ranger's buttons, cinquefoil, and dozens of other flowers before crossing Cottonwood Creek's south fork on a flattened log.

The Golden Trout Camp Trail begins to climb almost imperceptibly, then more definitely as it passes below a sheer granite tower on the left. At the same time,

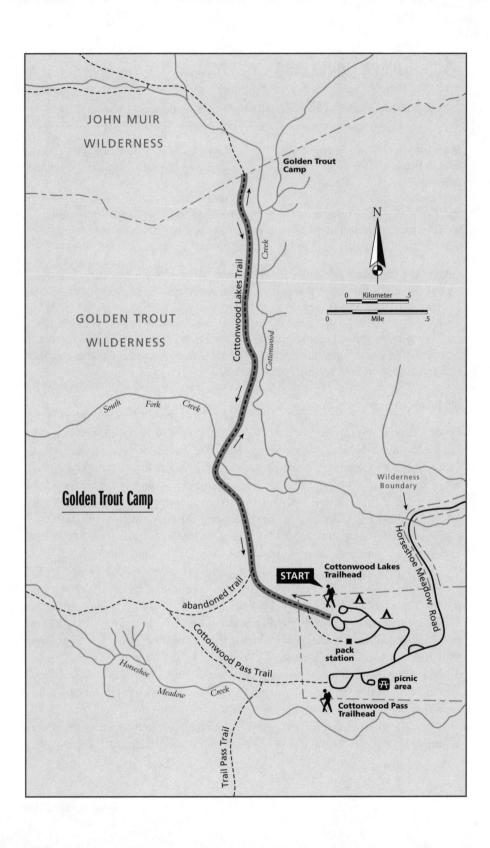

JOHN MUIR
WILDERNESS

**Golden Trout
Camp**

GOLDEN TROUT

WILDERNESS

Cottonwood Lakes Trail

Creek

Cottonwood

South   Fork   Creek

Golden Trout Camp

N

0   Kilometer   .5

0   Mile   .5

Wilderness
Boundary

Horseshoe Meadow Road

abandoned trail

START   **Cottonwood Lakes
Trailhead**

Cottonwood Pass Trail

pack
station

Horseshoe

Meadow   Creek

picnic
area

**Cottonwood Pass
Trailhead**

Trail Pass Trail

Cirque Peak from the "front yard" of Golden Trout Camp

another fork of the creek becomes audible on the right. Hike over a low rise under-lain by rock from the shoulder of the granite tower. The trail becomes wider and the forest grows flatter and more open, as does the meadow beside it. Above the meadow to the right, an outcrop of snaggly granite teeth protrudes from a ridge. Below this a fence that marks the boundary of Golden Trout Camp runs across the meadow. A final short uphill pull brings you to a sign that just says TRAIL to the left. The gate to the camp with its log and tent cabins is just to the right at mile 2.0. A short distance past the camp on the main trail is the border of Sequoia National Park. Return the way you came.

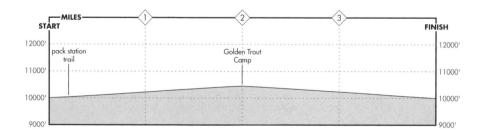

Key Points

0.0 Cottonwood Lakes Trailhead.

0.2 Trail to pack station.

2.0 Golden Trout Camp, turn around.

4.0 Cottonwood Lakes Trailhead.

South Sierra Wilderness

mmediately to the south of the Golden Trout Wilderness—and sharing many of its attractions—lies the South Sierra Wilderness. Created in 1984 under the California Wilderness Act, it encompasses only 82,000 acres, compared to the Golden Trout's 303,200. Still, it provides a valuable wildlife corridor, interrupted only by Kennedy Meadows Road between the Golden Trout Wilderness to the north and the Domelands Wilderness to the south. It also serves as a buffer for the protected Wild and Scenic South Fork of the Kern River, its main stream. It shares Olancha Peak (12,123 feet) on its northern boundary with the Golden Trout Wilderness, and reaches its lowest elevation at Kennedy Meadows (6,100 feet). You will find the same golden trout, wildflower gardens, granite peaks, volcanic features, and of course the South Fork of the Kern River, but with only 30 miles of trails it offers hikers a much wilder, more remote sojourn. It is seldom patrolled, and trails, except for the Pacific Crest Trail, are infrequently maintained, so you'll have to be able to take care of yourself and will need at least minimal route-finding skills.

It is overall a drier place than the Golden Trout Wilderness; many of its stream-beds are empty by late summer, though the South Fork of the Kern is never too far away and there are dozens (possibly hundreds) of year-round seeps and springs. The vegetation is primarily piñon-juniper woodland, with islands of other conifers at higher elevations and along watercourses.

Like the Golden Trout Wilderness, it is administered by the Sequoia National Forest on the west and the Inyo National Forest on the east. All the trails described here begin in the Inyo National Forest. A wilderness permit is required, but if you do not expect to arrive when ranger stations are open, you can call ahead to have a permit left outside for you. There is no charge.

The South Sierra is accessible by road only from the south via Kennedy Meadows and by secondary Forest Service roads from the southwest. Four-wheel-drive vehicles have an additional point of entry from the Monache Meadows region to the northwest. There are two steep and rugged trails that climb up the eastern escarpment from Interstate 395 to the east but no vehicle access at all.

This part of the Sierra Nevada is remote, spare, and beautiful. It provides a wilderness experience more challenging and therefore more satisfying than many of the more popular parts of the range.

36 Olancha Pass

An out-and-back day hike and an approach to Olancha Peak and the Pacific Crest Trail (PCT).

Start: Sage Flat Trailhead.
Total distance: 10.8 miles.
Difficulty: Strenuous as a day hike.
Total climbing: 3,300 feet.
Trail traffic: Light to moderate.
Best months: Late June through October, though water is scarce after July.
Maps: USGS Haiwee Pass quad; Forest Service Golden Trout and South Sierra Wilderness map.
Permits: Wilderness permits are not required for a day hike. Required and available in advance or at the Mount Whitney Ranger Station in Lone Pine for overnight.
Trailhead facilities: None. Nearest water, gas, groceries, and phones in Olancha.

Finding the trailhead: From the town of Olancha on Interstate 395, drive south for 6 miles to Sageflat Road. Turn right (west). A short distance up the road is a sign that reads OLANCHA PASS TRAIL. Drive 5 more miles to a grove of live oaks and turn left at a stock chute to a corral, hitching posts, and a cabin. The trailhead is marked by a big map and a self-registration box (not for wilderness permits).

The Hike

Carry plenty of water and keep an eye out for rattlesnakes. The Olancha Pass Trailhead sign is hidden from the parking area by a cabin in a grove of oak trees and silktassel bushes. These shrubs resemble manzanita but have gray bark instead of red, along with flowers of greenish gray dangling tassels instead of little white bells. They are also known as cinchona or quinine bushes and are historically important because their bark contains quinine, the only defense against malaria available to European explorers (and exploiters) of the Tropics.

The trail climbs through sagebrush and piñon pines. The Sierran escarpment just to the north of the trail displays an especially colorful mixture of light and dark granitic rocks. Go through a wire gate and enter a pasture of sorts. Be sure to close the gate behind you. On the other side there is a signpost with no sign on it. Follow the wire fence along the slope above the creek then exit the pasture through another gate. There is another trail parallel to yours on the left down in a creekbed that looks shadier and more inviting than the one you are on, but it is used by cattle and is a muddy, smelly mess. The upper trail is better maintained and easier going.

Pass a few defunct telephone poles and, at mile 1.7, reach a junction with a sign that directs cattle to the left, horses and hikers to the right. As you switchback up the right fork, you can see more and more of the Haiwee Reservoir to the east and beyond it the Coso and Inyo Mountains. The higher mountains beyond these are

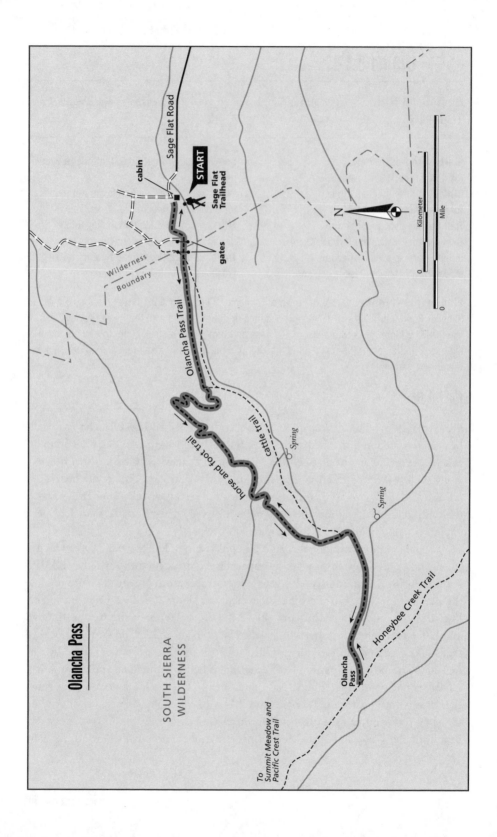

Olancha Pass

SOUTH SIERRA
WILDERNESS

Sage Flat Road

cabin

START

Sage Flat
Trailhead

gates

Wilderness
Boundary

Olancha Pass Trail

cattle trail

Spring

horse and foot trail

Spring

Honeybee Creek Trail

Olancha
Pass

To
Summit Meadow and
Pacific Crest Trail

N

Kilometer

Mile

0

0

Haiwee Reservoir in the Owens Valley from the Olancha Pass Trail

the Panamints, which overlook the lowest point in the continental United States in Death Valley. On your own side of the valley to the south, a beautiful serrated granite ridge painted with brilliant green lichens juts out into the desert from the steep Sierra escarpment.

At mile 4.4 the cow trail and horse trail rejoin below a little saddle among mountain mahogany and a few white firs and Jeffrey pines. This saddle is *not* the pass. Bear right (west), climbing still, alongside a gully to a sluggish but permanent little seep near a ruined water trough. A short pull over the brow of a sagebrush-covered hump brings you to the pass and a signed junction at 9,220 feet (mile 5.4). The route that heads southeast toward Haiwee Pass is the Honeybee Creek Trail (see Hike 40).

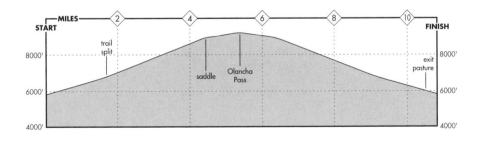

The trail northwest toward Monache Meadows leads to a junction with the Pacific Crest Trail. Unless your plans take you farther into the mountains, return the way you came.

Key Points

0.0   Sage Flat Trailhead.

1.7   Cow trail and horse/foot trail split, keep right.

4.4   Cow and horse/foot trails rejoin, bear right (west).

5.4   Olancha Pass, turn around.

10.8   Sage Flat Trailhead.

37 Olancha Pass to the Pacific Crest Trail

A one-way route to the Pacific Crest Trail (PCT).

Start: Sage Flat Trailhead.
Total distance: 14.4 miles.
Difficulty: Moderate.
Total climbing: 3,300 feet.
Trail traffic: Light to moderate.
Best months: Late June through October.
Maps: USGS Haiwee Pass and Monache

Mountain quads; Forest Service Golden Trout and South Sierra Wilderness map.
Permits: Required and available in advance or at the Mount Whitney Ranger Station in Lone Pine.
Trailhead facilities: None. Nearest gas, food, and phones in Olancha.

Finding the trailhead: From the town of Olancha on Interstate 395, drive south for 6 miles to Sageflat Road. Turn right (west). A short distance up the road is a sign that reads OLANCHA PASS TRAIL. Drive 5 more miles to a grove of live oaks and turn left at a stock chute to a corral, hitching posts, and a cabin. The trailhead is marked by a big map and a sign-in box.

The Hike

The trail begins by climbing through sagebrush and piñon pines. Go through a wire gate and enter a pasture of sorts. Be sure to close the gate behind you. On the other side there is a signpost with no sign on it. Follow the wire fence along the slope above the creek then exit the pasture through another gate. There is another trail parallel to yours on the left down in a creekbed that looks shadier and more inviting than the one you are on, but it is used by cattle and is a muddy, smelly mess. The upper trail is better maintained and easier going.

At mile 1.7 reach a junction with a sign that directs cattle to the left, horses and hikers to the right. At mile 4.4 the cow trail and horse trail rejoin below a little saddle. This saddle is *not* the pass. Bear right (west) climbing, alongside a gully to a sluggish, but permanent, little seep near a ruined water trough. A short pull over the brow of a sagebrush-covered hump brings you to the top of the Olancha Pass and a signed junction at 9,220 feet (mile 5.4).

From the junction at the top, head northwest through open forest and sagebrush to Summit Meadow. This long narrow stretch is green and flowery early in the summer, dry and golden later on, but seldom, if ever, filled with water as it appears to be on the topo. Near the end of the meadow is an elaborate packer's camp and a corral at mile 6.4. An unmarked and unmaintained trail in back of the camp makes a shortcut uphill to the Pacific Crest Trail where climbers cut off to climb Olancha Peak, but nowadays the route described here is the more popular and easier one. Continue on the Summit Meadow Trail, veering left around the upper end of Summit Meadow to reach a signed junction at mile 6.7. If your route on the PCT is

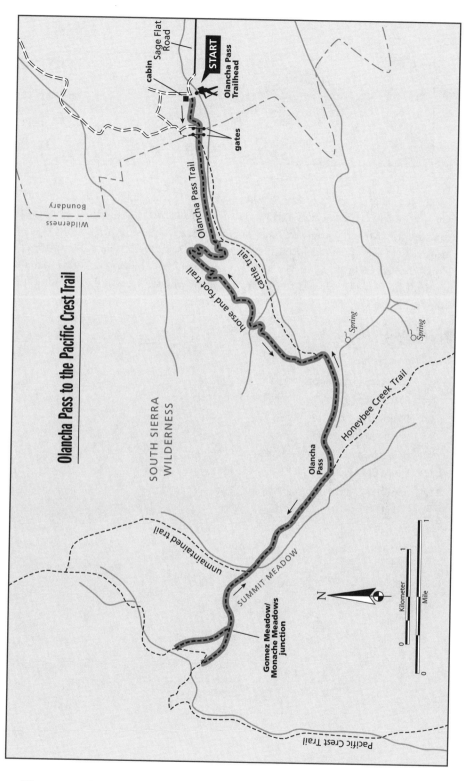

Olancha Pass to the Pacific Crest Trail

START

Sage Flat Road

cabin

Olancha Pass Trailhead

gates

Olancha Pass Trail

Wilderness Boundary

cattle trail

horse and foot trail

Spring

Spring

SOUTH SIERRA WILDERNESS

Honeybee Creek Trail

Olancha Pass

unmaintained trail

SUMMIT MEADOW

Gomez Meadow/ Monache Meadows junction

N

Kilometer

Mile

Pacific Crest Trail

◀ *The summit of Olancha Peak (12,123 feet) from the Pacific Crest Trail*

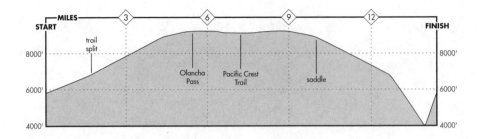

northward, take the right fork to Gomez Meadow. If you plan to go south, continue left toward Monache Meadows. Both trails eventually arrive at the PCT. The northern, Gomez Meadow, route is quite straightforward. The southern route is crisscrossed with cow paths and a bit obscure, but you will stay on track if you descend along the left bank of a little rivulet that gradually becomes more substantial and soon meets Cow Creek and the PCT. To return to Sage Flat Trailhead follow the same route back.

Key Points

0.0   Sage Flat Trailhead.

1.7   Cow trail and horse/foot trail split, keep right.

4.4   Cow and horse/foot trails rejoin, bear right (west).

5.4   Olancha Pass, turn right (northwest).

6.4   Unmarked shortcut trail.

6.7   Gomez Meadow/Monache Meadows junction.

7.2   Pacific Crest Trail.

14.4   Sage Flat Trailhead.

38 Haiwee Pass

A vigorous out-and-back day hike or a quick way to connect with the Pacific Crest Trail (PCT) from the Owens Valley.

Start: Haiwee Pass Trailhead.
Total distance: 8.8 miles.
Difficulty: Strenuous as a day hike.
Total climbing: 3,000 feet.
Trail traffic: Light.
Best months: May to June and mid-September to October. If you plan to use this route to reach the PCT, the South Fork of the Kern is too dangerous to cross before midsummer, and July and August in the Owens Valley are hot.

Maps: USGS Haiwee Pass quad; Forest Service Golden Trout and South Sierra Wilderness map.
Permits: None required for a day hike. Required and available in advance or at the Mount Whitney Ranger Station in Lone Pine for an overnight.
Trailhead facilities: None. Nearest gas, food, minimal groceries, and phones in Pearsonville or Olancha.

Finding the trailhead: From Interstate 395 drive 8 miles north from Coso Junction or 9 miles south from Olancha to Haiwee Canyon Road. Turn west and go 3 miles on a dirt road to the end. There is room for only two cars at the trailhead, but there are several turnouts for parking along the road.

The Hike

This is a favorite of deer hunters in fall. You should probably allow more time than you think you will need for this hike. The distance isn't long, but the footing is soft and deep from the passage of countless cattle and horses. A big sign marks the Haiwee Pass Trailhead, directing your steps close alongside the spring-fed creek into a canyon. The canyon floor quickly becomes so narrow that you are obliged to hop back and forth over the stream eight times. Several tributaries feeding the main stream add to the number of crossings. The trail is easy to follow, but the undergrowth is dense and the elevation low, so watch out for snakes.

The way along the creek must have been a rich all-you-can-eat buffet at the right times of year for the Native people who used this route over the Southern Sierra. There are piñon nuts, acorns, chia seeds, wild grapes, rose hips, cattails, sedges, and more. There is a pharmacy here, too: willow, coffeeberry, ephedra, mint, mugwort, and many others. In about 1.5 miles, the Haiwee Pass Trail leaves the creek and passes a final seep in the form of a soda spring that forms a red mineral pond surrounded by green grasses. It then climbs steeply through a shady grove of oaks to a flat resting spot and tackles a set of switchbacks up a sagebrush- and rabbitbrush-covered slope before it enters more piñon forest. It swings northeast, then north, then southwest again to avoid dropping too deeply into a couple of tributary gorges,

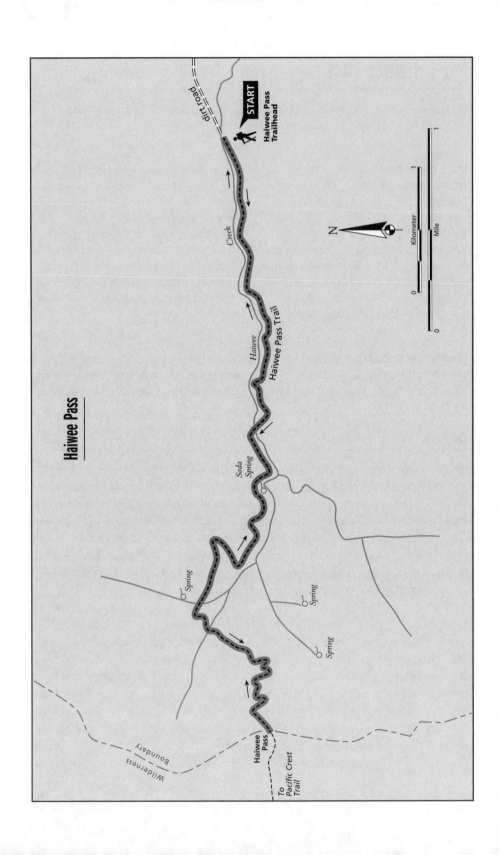

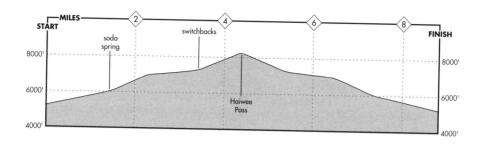

then resumes its westward course, zigzagging up to the pass and the wilderness boundary at mile 4.4. The pass itself, at 8,200 feet, is something of an anticlimax. There is no view but there are some unusually massive old piñon pines, Jeffrey pines, and junipers, and the feathery fruits of the mountain mahogany are especially beautiful in autumn. If you do not plan to continue on to the Pacific Crest Trail, return the way you came.

Key Points

0.0 Haiwee Pass Trailhead.

4.4 Haiwee Pass.

8.8 Haiwee Pass Trailhead.

39 Haiwee Pass to the Pacific Crest Trail

A quick way to connect with the Pacific Crest Trail (PCT) from the east.

Start: Haiwee Pass Trailhead.
Total distance: 19.4 miles one way.
Difficulty: Moderate.
Total climbing: 3,500 feet.
Trail traffic: Light.
Best months: September through October. The South Fork of the Kern River is dangerous to cross before midsummer, and July and August in the Owens Valley where this hike begins are hot.

Map: USGS Haiwee Pass and Monache Mountain quads; Forest Service Golden Trout and South Sierra Wilderness map.
Permits: Required and available in advance or at the Mount Whitney Ranger Station in Lone Pine.
Trailhead facilities: None. Nearest gas, food, and phones in Pearsonville or Olancha.

Finding the trailhead: From Interstate 395 drive 8 miles north from Coso Junction or 9 miles south from Olancha to Haiwee Canyon Road. Turn west and go 3 miles on dirt to the end. There is room for only two cars at the trailhead, but there are several turnouts for parking along the road.

The Hike

A big sign marks the trailhead directing your steps along the creek into a canyon. The canyon floor quickly becomes so narrow that you are obliged to hop back and forth over the stream eight times. The trail is easy to follow, but the undergrowth is dense and the elevation low so watch out for snakes. In about 1.5 miles, the trail leaves the creek and passes a red mineral pond. It then climbs steeply to a flat resting spot and then up a set of switchbacks. The trail swings northeast, then north, then southwest again to avoid dropping too deeply into a couple of tributary gorges, then resumes its westward course zigzagging up to Haiwee Pass and the wilderness boundary at mile 4.4. Descend the eroded and somewhat overgrown trail through mountain mahogany and rabbitbrush to the Honeybee Trail at mile 5.3, where a sign points right (north) to Olancha Pass and Summit Meadow. Note that the topo shows two parallel trails heading in the same direction, but the westernmost one has been abandoned and the junction is no longer visible. Keep left (west) and begin dropping more steeply on rocky, eroded switchbacks into the gorge of the South Fork of the Kern, where the green river running through golden willows is especially striking in fall. At mile 6.1 reach a campsite beside the river. It is obviously heavily used, though it is too near the water to be legal and too sloping to be comfortable. The trail swings

The Kern River ford on the Haiwee Pass Trail should not be attempted early season.

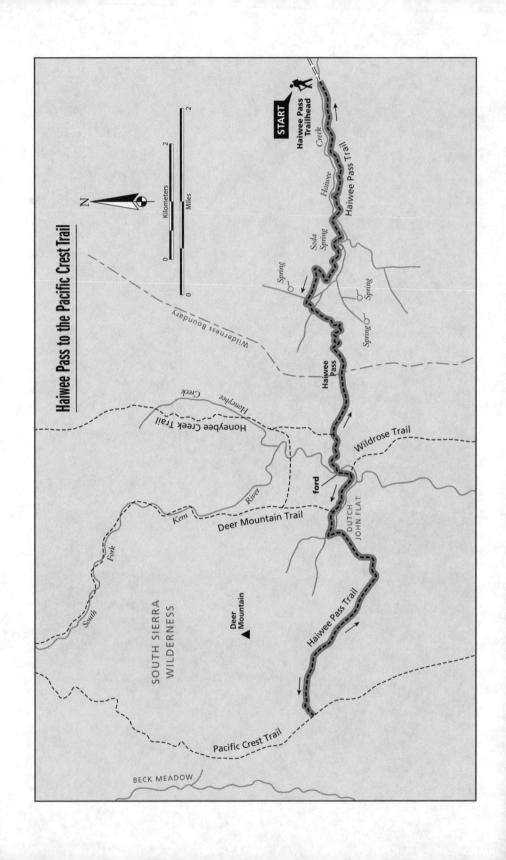

Haiwee Pass to the Pacific Crest Trail

START
Haiwee Pass Trailhead

Haiwee Creek

Haiwee Pass Trail

Soda Spring

Spring

Spring

Spring

Wilderness Boundary

Haiwee Pass

Wildrose Trail

Honeybee Creek Trail

Honeybee Creek

ford

Deer Mountain Trail

Kern River

South Fork

DUTCH JOHN FLAT

SOUTH SIERRA WILDERNESS

Deer Mountain

Haiwee Pass Trail

Pacific Crest Trail

BECK MEADOW

N

Kilometers
Miles
0   2
0   2

left here, heads downstream for about 100 yards, and fords the river at an obvious sandy crossing. If you glance back uphill to your left just before the crossing, you will spot a sign on a tree marking the Wildrose Trail, which heads back to Kennedy Meadows (Hike 42).

On the west side of the river is a vandalized trail sign that used to read HAIWEE TRAIL AND DUTCH JOHN FLAT. Climb out of the riverbed, switchbacking once to the left (west) and follow a willow-choked, spring-fed trickle away from the river. At the point where another creek flows in from the west to meet this one, you can just glimpse, off to the left, a developed camp, complete with rickety picnic table, a stone oven, and piles of rusting junk. Just beyond, at mile 6.7, is an indistinct junction where a sign propped against the base of a Jeffrey pine indicates that Trail 37E01 and the PCT lie to the left (west). A few yards beyond this, a second sign—this one still attached to its tree—confirms that you are indeed on 37E01. The right fork is the Deer Mountain Trail and is marked with a sign a few yards past the junction.

Now follow a little gully uphill, skirting the north side of Dutch John Flat, a broad golden sheet of rabbitbrush punctuated with widely spaced Jeffrey pines. Where two creekbeds, often dry, come together on your left, the trail makes an abrupt left turn (south) and cuts across the flat. The dense growth almost obscures the trail in spots. Beyond the meadow where the sparse forest resumes, the path climbs to the top of a saddle at 8,000 feet. From here follow the main stream gully down a wide forested bowl to pick up another usually dry creekbed, and descend, steeply at first, then more gradually, slogging through deep sand to meet the PCT at mile 9.7. To return to Haiwee Pass Trailhead follow the same route back.

Key Points

- **0.0**   Haiwee Pass Trailhead.
- **4.4**   Haiwee Pass.
- **5.3**   Honeybee Trail, keep left (west).
- **6.1**   South Fork Kern River, crossing.
- **6.7**   Dutch John Flat, turn left (west).
- **9.7**   Pacific Crest Trail.
- **19.4** Haiwee Pass Trailhead.

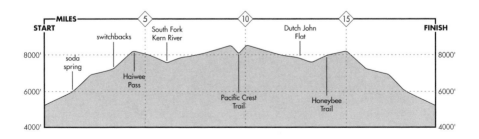

40 Honeybee Creek Trail

A shuttle hike great for early or late season, with solitude guaranteed.

Start: Haiwee Pass Trailhead.
Total distance: 29.9 miles.
Difficulty: Moderate.
Total climbing: 4,570 feet.
Trail traffic: Light.
Best months: June through October. Midsummer can be hot.

Maps: USGS Haiwee Pass quad; Forest Service Golden Trout and South Sierra Wilderness map.
Permits: Required and available in advance or at the Mount Whitney Ranger Station in Lone Pine or at the Blackrock Ranger Station.
Trailhead facilities: None. Nearest gas, food, and phones in Pearsonville or Olancha.

Finding the trailhead: From Interstate 395 drive 8 miles north from Coso Junction or 9 miles south from Olancha to Haiwee Canyon Road. Turn west and go 3 miles on dirt to the end. There is room for only two cars at the trailhead, but there are several turnouts for parking along the road. Leave your other vehicle at the Olancha Pass Trailhead as described in Hike 36, Olancha Pass. (The shuttle is a short one—less than 15 miles each way.)

The Hike

A big sign marks the trailhead directing your steps along the creek into a canyon. The canyon floor quickly becomes so narrow that you are obliged to hop back and forth over the stream eight times. The trail is easy to follow, but the undergrowth is dense and the elevation low so watch out for snakes. In about 1.5 miles, the trail leaves the creek and passes a red mineral pond. It then climbs steeply to a flat resting spot and then up a set of switchbacks. The trail swings northeast, then north, then southwest again to avoid dropping too deeply into a couple of tributary gorges, then resumes its westward course zigzagging up to Haiwee Pass and the wilderness boundary at mile 4.4. Descend the eroded and somewhat overgrown trail from the pass through mountain mahogany and rabbitbrush to the Honeybee Trail junction at mile 5.3, where a sign points right (north) to Olancha Pass and Summit Meadow. Note that the topo shows two parallel trails heading in the same direction, but you will only see one. The westernmost one has been abandoned. You are less than a mile from the South Fork of the Kern River if you want to make a side trip.

Hike upward through a wide gulch to top a broad saddle on trail partly overgrown by sagebrush. A metal blaze on a Jeffrey pine at the top will let you know you're on track. Down the other side, drop into a narrow gorge. The trail has mostly been eroded away, but there are still a few sections to indicate where it was. Partway down the slot, pass a little seep fragrant with mint. At the bottom, another little trickle flows down yet another gully at right angles to yours on its way to the South Fork of the Kern not far below to your left. Hop this tiny stream and follow the trail

Feathery fruit of mountain mahogany shrubs above Honeybee Creek

up and over another ridge, then drop down to meet Honeybee Creek. This year-round stream, fed by numerous springs, flows through a cool, quiet glade, blooming with great masses of pink wild roses early in the season, glowing with golden willows in fall. Your sudden presence is likely to disturb dozens of quail families that shelter in the dense vegetation, setting off an explosion of frantic flapping. Turn right to follow the east bank of the creek upstream, passing a campsite, then hop across to the west side and slop through a very soggy grassy area fed by hidden springs.

Now ascending gradually, leave the seeps behind to cross a low rise; beyond this lies a last campsite beside a final, isolated spring. Climb over the saddle between Round Mountain to the right (east) and a little bump to the left, through sunny open country. To the west the South Fork of the Kern meanders lazily through Monache Meadows. Beyond Round Mountain, drop to cross a wide brushy swale and climb up a gradually steepening ridgeline to skirt the east side of an unnamed peak, the highest point on this hike at 9,320 feet. Then follow the ridgeline back down again to Olancha Pass at mile 10.6. A short pull over a sagebrush covered hump takes you down to a gully where you hop a little seep near a ruined water trough. Bear left (west) descending the slope while the gully with the little stream drops away to your right. Reach a little saddle among mountain mahogany, a few

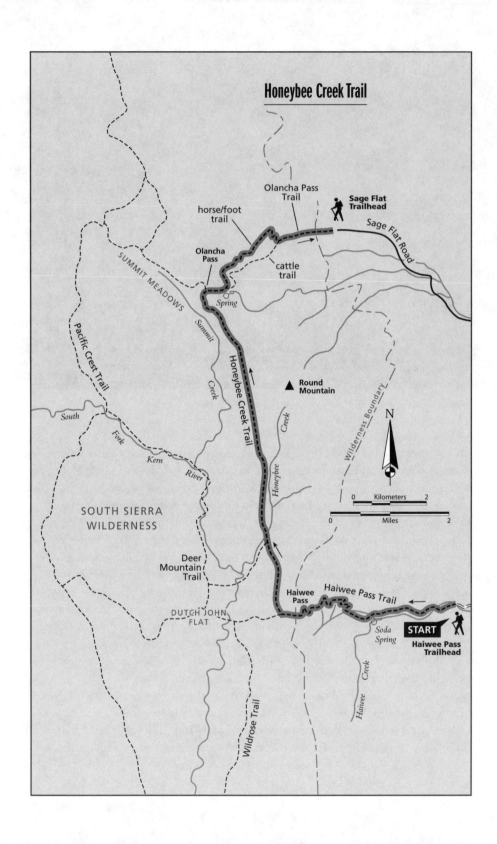

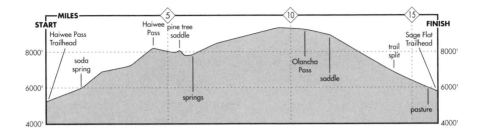

white firs, and Jeffrey pines. Drop down to the left (east) to meet a junction at mile 12.6 where there are two trails, both of which descend to the Sage Flat Trailhead. The right fork is used by cattle, and soon becomes muddy and smelly. Use the left fork, which is intended for horses and hikers and is much better maintained.

As you switchback downhill you get a good look at the Haiwee Reservoir below, and beyond it the Coso and Inyo Mountains. The higher peaks behind these are the Panamints that overlook the lowest point in the continental United States in Death Valley. On your own side of the valley to the south, a beautiful serrated granite ridge painted with brilliant green lichens juts out into the desert from the steep Sierra escarpment. At mile 15.3, pass a few defunct telephone poles to reach a junction where the cattle and horse trails rejoin, though the cattle usually ignore the sign and continue down the gully to the right. You should keep left, higher up the slope, to enter a pasture through a wire gate. Follow the wire fence and exit via a second gate. Be sure to close the gates behind you. Now descend through sagebrush and piñon pines to meet the Sage Flat Trailhead beside an old cabin in a grove of oak trees at mile 17.0.

Key Points

0.0   Haiwee Pass Trailhead.

4.4   Haiwee Pass.

5.3   Honeybee Trail junction, turn right (north).

10.6 Olancha Pass.

11.6 Cow and horse/foot trail splits, turn left (north).

14.3 Cow and horse/foot trail rejoin, turn left (east).

16.0 Sage Flat Trailhead.

41 Wildrose Meadow

An out-and-back day hike to a pretty spring with plenty of wildflowers.

Start: Wildrose Trailhead.
Total distance: 6 miles.
Difficulty: Easy to moderate.
Total climbing: 1,200 feet.
Trail traffic: Light.
Best months: Mid-May through October, whenever Ninemile Canyon Road is open.
Maps: USGS Crag Peak and Long Canyon quads; Forest Service Golden Trout and South Sierra Wilderness map.

Permits: None needed for a day hike. For an overnight, required and available at the Blackrock Ranger Station or the Mount Whitney Ranger Station in Lone Pine.
Trailhead facilities: None. Nearest groceries, gas, phones, and water 1 mile back at the Kennedy Meadows Store.

Finding the trailhead: From Interstate 395 north of Pearsonville, turn west onto Ninemile Canyon Road. At the Chimney Peak Fire Station, it turns into Kennedy Meadows Road (Forest Road 22S05). At Kennedy Meadows keep right onto Forest Road 21S08 and go about a mile to a dirt road heading east (right) marked WILD ROSE TRAIL 36E01—½ MILE. The road is badly rutted, and if you do not have a high-clearance vehicle you might want to park as soon as you can find a wide enough spot to pull out. You can also leave your car at the FIRE SAFE camping area across the main road just a few yards to the north and walk the extra 0.5 mile along the dirt road to the trailhead. Keep right at all splits of the dirt road until you reach the sign marked WILD ROSE TRAIL 36E01.

The Hike

This trail doesn't get much use, so you're guaranteed solitude, but neither does it get much maintenance, so you must stay alert and keep your map ready in case of confusion. There are ducks and blazes here and there, but the piñon pines beside the trail do their best to heal over any injuries to their bark, so the blazes are sometimes indistinct. Occasionally clumps of prickly pear cactus remind you that this is semi-desert country; the ground is rocky and sandy, with sparse understory to hold water. Rainfall and snowmelt run off rapidly and carve gullies that are hard to distinguish from trail, especially since some gullies and trails are meant to coincide. It's a short, fun, and interesting route-finding adventure with lots of unusual wildflowers.

The trail climbs moderately eastward at first, then swings northeast, dipping in and out of dry stream courses until it gains a bigger, straighter watercourse than the rest and turns to follow this one upward through the remains of an old gate toward a saddle. Along the way, early in the season, startling splashes of brilliant canary yellow interrupt the subdued gray of the piñon pine forest. These are *Fremontodendron,* honoring the western explorer John C. Frémont. Their common name, flannelbush, comes from the soft, woolly texture of the flowers and foliage. A little farther up, the

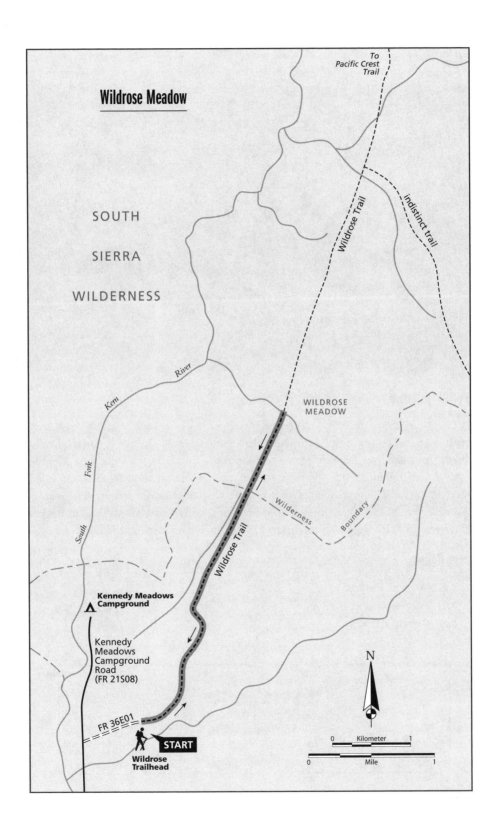

Wildrose Meadow

To
Pacific Crest
Trail

SOUTH

SIERRA

WILDERNESS

Wildrose Trail

indistinct trail

River

Kern

WILDROSE
MEADOW

Fork

Wilderness   Boundary

South

Wildrose Trail

**Kennedy Meadows
Campground**

Kennedy
Meadows
Campground
Road
(FR 21S08)

N

FR 36E01

START

**Wildrose
Trailhead**

0   Kilometer   1

0   Mile   1

Approaching Wildrose Meadow from the south

path is graced by some truly immense old Jeffrey pines. At the top of the saddle is a badly vandalized sign marking your entry into the South Sierra Wilderness. On the way down the other side, you are treated to a dramatic view of Olancha Peak, straight ahead. Wildrose Meadow lies in a bowl at the bottom at mile 3.0. Springs provide year-round water for the wild profusion of willows, rosebushes, and other flowers, and there is good camping nearby. Retrace your steps to the trailhead.

Key Points

- **0.0** Wildrose Trailhead.
- **3.0** Wildrose Meadow.
- **6.0** Wildrose Trailhead.

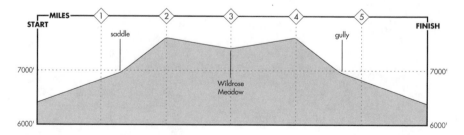

42 Wildrose Trail

A little-used loop backpack for those who love solitude and wildflowers.

Start: Wildrose Trailhead.
Total distance: 20.9 miles.
Difficulty: Moderate.
Total climbing: 1,800 feet
Trail traffic: Light on the Wildrose section, light to moderate on the Pacific Crest Trail section.
Best months: June through October, though the South Fork of the Kern may be too deep and swift to cross during spring runoff.

Maps: USGS Long Canyon, Haiwee Pass, and Crag Peak quads; Forest Service Golden Trout and South Sierra Wilderness map.
Permits: Available at the Blackrock Ranger Station or from the Mount Whitney Ranger Station in Lone Pine.
Trailhead facilities: None but primitive camping. Nearest groceries, gas, phones, and water 1 mile back at Kennedy Meadows Store.

Finding the trailhead: From Interstate 395 north of Pearsonville, turn west onto Ninemile Canyon Road. At the Chimney Peak Fire Station, it turns into Kennedy Meadows Road (Forest Road 22S05). At Kennedy Meadows keep right onto Forest Road 21S08 and go about a mile to a dirt road heading east (right) marked WILD ROSE TRAIL 36E01—½ MILE. The road is badly rutted and if you do not have a high-clearance vehicle you might want to park as soon as you can find a spot wide enough to pull out. You can also leave your car at the FIRE SAFE camping area across the road just a few yards to the north and walk the extra 0.5 mile along the dirt road to the trailhead. Keep right at all splits of the dirt road until you reach the sign marked WILD ROSE TRAIL 36E01.

The Hike

The trail climbs eastward moderately at first, then swings northeast dipping in and out of dry stream courses until it gains a bigger, straighter watercourse. It follows this upward through the remains of an old gate toward a saddle. At the top of the saddle is a badly vandalized sign marking your entry into the South Sierra Wilderness. Wildrose Meadow lies in a bowl at the bottom at mile 3.0. The willows and rose bushes are so dense here that you might want to put on your long pants to get to the other side of the meadow. The open grassland is briefly interrupted by a short stretch of forest, then the trail traces another long straight arm of a second meadow. The footing is sandy, deep, and slow, but the fabulous show of wildflowers in early season here makes up for the effort. There are carpets of bright blue lollipop-shaped nama, yellow buckwheat, red paintbrush, and white popcorn flowers, to mention only a few. After passing through another old fence, the path returns to the forest and continues northeast, crossing back and forth over, and sometimes running down the middle of a shallow dry creek bed. The way opens into a sagebrush-lined bowl dotted with juniper trees and crosses a bigger, more deeply eroded, arroyo that occasionally

Rose hips, a rich source of vitamin C, ripen in late summer.

carries a trickle of water. The topo shows a junction with another trail at the point where these two watercourses join, heading southeast back to Long Canyon, but it seems to have become abandoned and overgrown.

The trail climbs again to a broad saddle clothed in mountain mahogany, junipers, and piñon pines at 7,700 feet, then drops into an eroded creek bed trending slightly northwest. Follow this, occasionally using pieces of trail that run alongside the streambed, but most of the time staying in the dry wash itself. Pass a very tiny seep, and in a few minutes, cross another, deeper creek bed with a little more moisture in it. Continue straight ahead, climbing to a flat saddle then dropping down on switchbacks toward the noisy rush of the South Fork of the Kern River at mile 7.3. A sign on a Jeffrey pine to the right of the trail indicates the HAIWEE PASS TRAIL AND OWENS VALLEY to the right (upstream). On the ground, in front of the same tree, the broken bottom half of the sign points back the way you came along the WILD ROSE TRAIL. After soaking your feet and enjoying the nearly constant birdsong, cross the river if the water is low enough to do so safely. If it is not, return the way you came.

Fording the river is easiest if you keep to the sandy bottom as the rocks are extremely slippery. Once on the other side (west), find a vandalized trail sign that used to say HAIWEE TRAIL AND DUTCH JOHN FLAT. Climb out of the riverbed, switch-

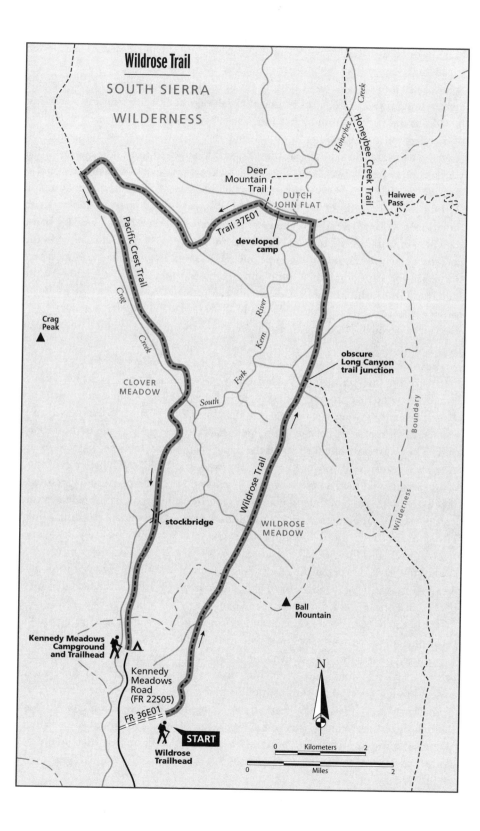

Wildrose Trail

SOUTH SIERRA
WILDERNESS

Honeybee Creek

Deer
Mountain
Trail

DUTCH
JOHN FLAT

Honeybee Creek Trail

Haiwee
Pass

Trail 37E01

developed
camp

Pacific Crest Trail

Crag Creek

Crag
Peak

Kern River

South Fork

CLOVER
MEADOW

obscure
Long Canyon
trail junction

Wilderness Boundary

Wildrose Trail

stockbridge

WILDROSE
MEADOW

Ball
Mountain

Kennedy Meadows
Campground
and Trailhead

Kennedy
Meadows
Road
(FR 22S05)

FR 36E01

START

Wildrose
Trailhead

N

0   Kilometers   2

0   Miles   2

backing once to the left (west), and follow alongside a willow-choked, spring-fed trickle. At the point where another creek flows in from the west to meet this one, you can just glimpse a developed camp off to the left, complete with rickety picnic table, a stone oven, and piles of rusting junk, all of which is too near the water. Just beyond, at mile 7.9, is an indistinct junction where a sign propped against the base of a Jeffrey pine indicates TRAIL 37E01 and the PACIFIC CREST TRAIL to the left (west). A few yards beyond this, a second sign, still attached to its tree, confirms that you are indeed on TRAIL 37E01. The right fork is the Deer Mountain Trail and is marked with a sign a few yards past the junction. Now follow a little gully uphill skirting the north side of Dutch John Flat, a broad golden sheet of rabbit brush punctuated with widely spaced Jeffery pines. Where two creekbeds, often dry, come together on your left the trail makes an abrupt left turn (south) and cuts across the flat. The dense growth almost obscures the trail in spots. Beyond the meadow where the sparse forest resumes, the path climbs to the top of a saddle at 8,000 feet, the highest point on the hike. From there follow the main stream gully down a wide forested bowl to pick up another usually-dry creekbed. Descend steeply at first, then more gradually, slogging through deep sand to meet the Pacific Crest Trail at mile 10.8.

Turn left (south) on the PCT and descend along the west side of a pine-shaded notch, passing the spring that is the source of seasonal Crag Creek. Ignore any unmarked paths that cross to the west side of the creek bed. The topo mistakenly shows the trail crossing Crag Creek, though the Golden Trout Wilderness map is correct. Keep the creek bed on your right, ignoring side paths made by wandering cattle. The forest now opens to reveal the upper section of Clover Meadow. Skirt the meadow's eastern side, passing through an area burned in 1980, where a profusion of sun-loving wildflowers have moved in. The meadow itself is pretty and green, usually dotted with cattle, and there is a shady spot for camping on the far side near the stream (often no more than a trickle late in the summer). Below the meadow, at mile 13.8, hop the creek and follow the path as it dips in and out of usually dry gullies crossing back and forth over blocked sections of an old trail no longer in use. Pass around the back of a rocky ridge, winding your way through clumps of royal blue flowered sage, stirring up an aroma that is almost overpowering and descend to meet the South Fork of the Kern River at mile 16.4.

Cross the river on a good bridge and follow its downstream course alongside the usual riparian vegetation of willows, wild roses, and horsetails. There are several illegal campsites here (too near both water and trail) as well as tire tracks of proscribed vehicles. The trail eventually veers away from the riverside and continues south, passes through a gate and climbs through piñon forest to reach the Pacific Crest Trailhead at mile 18.4 at the rear of the Kennedy Meadows campground. Walk through the campground to the road (21S08) and follow it south until you reach the Wildrose Trail spur road (36E01) on the left at mile 20.4. From here hike up the dirt road to your car at the trailhead at mile 20.9.

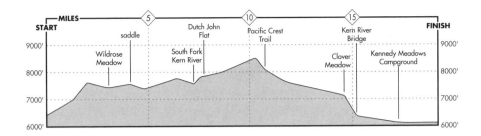

Key Points

0.0 Wildrose Trailhead.

3.0 Wildrose Meadow.

7.3 South Fork Kern River crossing.

7.9 Dutch John Flat, keep left (west).

10.8 Pacific Crest Trail, turn left (southeast).

17.2 Kennedy Meadows Campground.

19.2 Junction Kennedy Meadows Campground Road (21S08) and road to trailhead.

The Pacific Crest Trail

The Pacific Crest Trail, dedicated in 1993, is part of the National Trails System authorized by Congress in 1968. It begins at the Mexican border and runs through the most scenic parts of the western states for 2,650 miles to the Canadian border. Hiking the entire trail takes a long summer season, but you can sample a superlative section of it as it passes through the South Sierra and Golden Trout Wildernesses—from Kennedy Meadows to the border of Sequoia National Park just south of Mount Whitney—in about a week.

Most PCT through-hikers begin in Mexico and hike north, following the summer snowmelt to reach Canada in fall. They usually get to the Golden Trout region before June, and sometimes find the deep snow and swift, high river crossings challenging, if not impossible. The Golden Trout/South Sierra Wilderness section of the famous trail is described here in the usual south-to-north direction, but you will probably have a more enjoyable hike if you wait another month before setting out. The Pacific Crest Trail Association has lots of good information about current trail conditions and trip planning. You can contact the group at 5325 Elkhorn Boulevard, Sacramento, California Highway 95842; (916) 349–2109; or online at www.pcta.org.

43 Pacific Crest Trail

An extended shuttle backpack along the Sierra Crest.

Start: Pacific Crest Trailhead at Kennedy Meadows.
Total distance: 45.8 miles.
Difficulty: Strenuous if you hike the entire distance in less than a week; moderate if you take longer.
Total climbing: 8,900 feet.
Trail traffic: Moderate in late spring as through-hikers pass through. Otherwise light to moderate.
Best months: Mid-June through October.

Maps: USGS Crag Peak, Long Canyon, Haiwee Pass, Monache Mountain, Olancha, Templeton Mountain, Johnson Peak, and Cirque Peak quads; Forest Service Golden Trout and South Sierra Wilderness map.
Permits: Required and available in advance or at the Mount Whitney Ranger Station in Lone Pine.
Trailhead facilities: Camping, water, and toilets. Nearest gas, phone, and groceries 3 miles back at the Kennedy Meadows Store.

Finding the trailhead: From Interstate 395 north of Pearsonville, turn west onto Ninemile Canyon Road. At the Chimney Peak Fire Station, this turns into Kennedy Meadows Road (Forest Road 22S05). At Kennedy Meadows keep right onto Forest Road 21S08 and drive about 3 miles to the end of the road at Kennedy Meadows Campground. At the north end of the campground is a parking lot for hikers only.

If you plan to arrange a car shuttle, leave one vehicle at the Cottonwood Pass Trailhead (see section 6), then drive to Kennedy Meadows. The Pacific Crest Trail (PCT) leaves the Golden Trout Wilderness in a roadless area 2.6 miles north of Cottonwood Pass.

The Hike

The Pacific Crest Trail enters the South Sierra Wilderness just beyond the Kennedy Meadows Campground at 6,240 feet. Begin at the trailhead sign that displays more or less accurate mileages across the road from the parking lot. Head north in piñon forest, pass through and close a gate, and pick up the gurgle or roar (depending on the season) of the South Fork of the Kern River. Follow along its eastern bank past the usual riparian vegetation of willows, wild roses, and horsetails. In the drier, sunny soil on the other side of the trail grows tall fuzzy milkweed, whose intricate, almost bizarre flowers are worth a close inspection. They are poisonous to almost every animal but the larvae of the monarch butterfly. You will also see, unfortunately, several illegal campsites (too close to both water and trail) as well as tire tracks of proscribed vehicles. At mile 2.0 cross the bridge to the west side of the river and ascend around the back of a rocky ridge to wind your way through clumps of royal-blue-flowered sage, whose aroma is almost overpowering. The PCT dips into and out of usually dry gullies, crossing back and forth over blocked sections of an old trail that is no longer in use. Hop over Crag Creek, a mere trickle late in the season, and traverse

The Pacific Crest Trail through Kennedy Meadows

a shrubby slope to arrive at the edge of pretty green Clover Meadow, usually dotted with cattle (mile 4.6). The area around the meadow was burned in 1980, and the opening of the forest has invited a profusion of sun-loving wildflowers to move in. There is a shady spot for good camping in the forest at the meadow's edge.

The PCT passes around the east side of an upper section of the meadow, climbing easily. The Golden Trout and South Sierra Wilderness map is more accurate than the provisional topo in this region. The latter shows the trail crossing Crag Creek in the middle of the upper part of Clover Meadow, but in fact the PCT sticks to the east side of the meadow and plunges into a notch shaded with Jeffrey pines without crossing Crag Creek at all. Partway up, the old, now abandoned trail, which is still used by cattle, joins the PCT, and the footing becomes deep and soft. The climb becomes much steeper now, too.

The trail passes the spring that is the source of Crag Creek and finally reaches a saddle and a junction with the Haiwee Pass Trail at 8,080 feet (mile 7.6). If you sit quietly here for a short time, you may see, and will surely hear, an odd association of scrub jays and Clark's nutcrackers, sharing the same habitat. Scrub jays are usually found at lower elevations; Clark's nutcrackers, at timberline. Like all jays they have raucous, scolding voices.

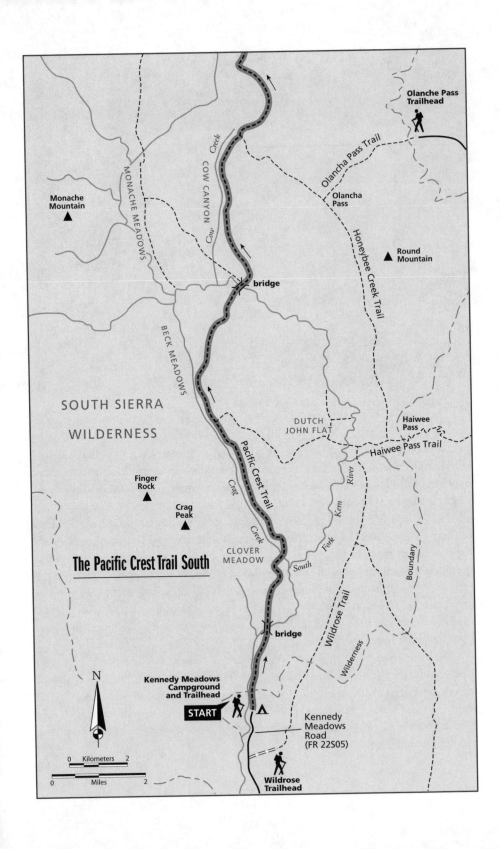

Olanche Pass
Trailhead

Olancha Pass Trail

Olancha
Pass

Round
Mountain

Monache
Mountain

MONACHE MEADOWS

COW CANYON

Creek

bridge

Honeybee Creek Trail

BECK MEADOWS

SOUTH SIERRA

WILDERNESS

DUTCH
JOHN FLAT

Haiwee
Pass

Haiwee Pass Trail

Pacific Crest Trail

Finger
Rock

Crag
Peak

Crag

Creek

CLOVER
MEADOW

South

Fork

Kem River

Boundary

The Pacific Crest Trail South

bridge

Wildrose Trail

Wilderness

N

Kennedy Meadows
Campground
and Trailhead

START

Kennedy
Meadows
Road
(FR 22S05)

0   Kilometers   2

0   Miles   2

Wildrose
Trailhead

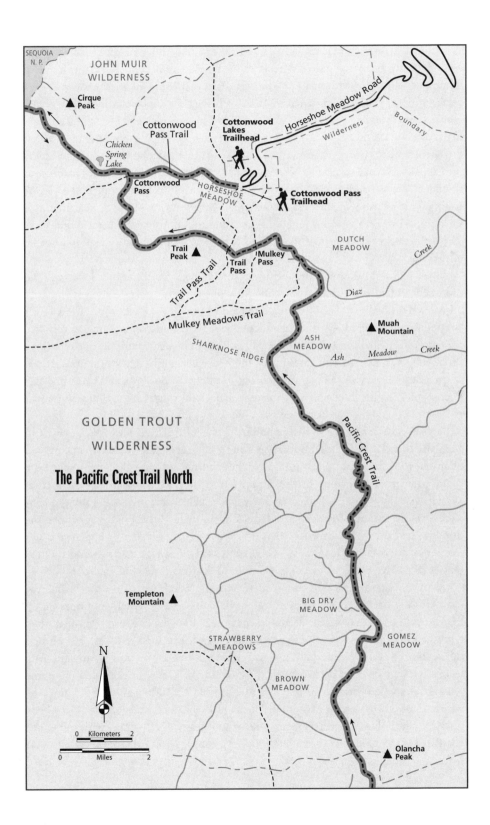

SEQUOIA N. P.

JOHN MUIR
WILDERNESS

▲ Cirque Peak

Cottonwood Pass Trail

Cottonwood Lakes Trailhead

Horseshoe Meadow Road

Wilderness   Boundary

Chicken Spring Lake

Cottonwood Pass

HORSESHOE MEADOW

Cottonwood Pass Trailhead

DUTCH MEADOW

Creek

Trail Peak ▲

Mulkey Pass

Trail Pass Trail

Trail Pass

Diaz

Mulkey Meadows Trail

SHARKNOSE RIDGE

ASH MEADOW

▲ Muah Mountain

Ash   Meadow   Creek

GOLDEN TROUT

WILDERNESS

The Pacific Crest Trail North

Pacific Crest Trail

Templeton Mountain ▲

BIG DRY MEADOW

GOMEZ MEADOW

STRAWBERRY MEADOWS

BROWN MEADOW

N

0   Kilometers   2

0   Miles   2

▲ Olancha Peak

A short distance down the other side of the saddle, the expanse of Beck Meadows gradually becomes visible. The horizon beyond it is defined by the rounded humps of Monache Mountain to the left, Round Mountain to the right, and—between them in the far distance—Mount Whitney, the highest point in the continental United States at almost 14,500 feet. The trail passes several dilapidated signs marked PCT 2000. Just beyond the last of these, at mile 8.0, the route splits. The left fork heads out into the meadow. Your path keeps to the right (east). In a few minutes Olancha Peak, at 12,123 feet, juts up to the northwest. A glance over your shoulder to the south reveals a good view of Crag Peak (left) and Finger Rock (right). This portion of the hike above Beck Meadows can be dry, but there is a spring (marked on the topo) piped into a cattle trough just at the base of the slope. The artificial structures across the meadow are private property and should not be disturbed.

The PCT follows the slope northeast, up and away from the meadow, gains the top of the ridge that culminates in Deer Mountain, then makes a long switchback down to the northeast. Soon the snaking path of the South Fork of the Kern River comes into view below. Cross an abandoned jeep road and, after a couple of dips and rises, drop down to the bridge at mile 11.5. There are small campsites up the slope above the river. Even if you cannot stay, there are pleasant beaches along this stretch of the river where you can loaf or picnic and watch the swallows and black phoebes swoop and dive for insects. If you are very lucky, you might get a glimpse of a pair of mountain bluebirds cruising the meadow.

Across the river, find a signed junction at mile 11.6. The right fork goes back to Kennedy Meadows via Dutch John Flat. Your trail heads left (northwest), making use of an old road for a few yards until it reaches another signpost directing you to the right, away from the river. In this area, as at Clover Meadow, the Golden Trout Wilderness map is more reliable than the topo, which shows the trail heading northwest through the meadow, crossing Cow Creek. In fact, the PCT stays above the meadow, first through sagebrush, then into the welcome shade of junipers and Jeffrey pines, curving northward into Cow Canyon. The canyon narrows and the trail crosses to the west side of Cow Creek, then back over to the east again.

A few hundred yards after the second crossing, watch for a post that marks the third crossing back to the west. Multiple cattle trails, one of which continues on up the east side of the creek, can lead you into messy tangles of brush. Arrive at, then ignore, an unsigned junction with a trail that cuts back to the southwest. Just beyond this, a sign on a big Jeffrey pine that says simply TRAIL steers you northward. At a second TRAIL sign, hop back over to the east side of Cow Creek and climb a few switchbacks, which bring you to a junction at mile 15.3. Turn right (east) here; the left fork goes to Monache Meadows. After a little more climbing, cross Cow Creek yet again and follow a little tributary stream southeast to a junction with the Olancha Pass Trail at mile 15.7. Keep left, following the sign toward Gomez Meadow. At mile 15.8, meet a second cutoff to the Olancha Pass Trail and keep left again. The trail winds moderately upward through fairly open forest, rises, dips, passes a PCT sign, and continues climbing up alongside a spring-fed creek full of rosebushes. The Jeffrey pines are gradually replaced by lodgepoles as you gain altitude. At the point where the PCT makes a little jog to the left to skirt another trickle densely lined with tall corn lilies, pause to contemplate the tall rock pile on your left. This one and several others beyond it are stained white with the droppings of raptors (birds of prey), which find these sites perfect perches from which to keep a lookout for the smaller birds and rodents that depend on the year-round spring water nearby.

The trail continues to climb through sagebrush from which umbrella-like bunches of white flowers on tall stalks protrude. This is the linear-leaved angelica, a member of the carrot family. The way becomes more level as the PCT tops a broad saddle, then skirts a wide bowl at the base of which lie Monache Meadows with conical Monache Mountain squatting in the middle. As you cross over the shoulder of a rocky ridge, you catch your first neck-craning look at the top of Olancha Peak just ahead. A little farther on, a magnificent panorama of the Sierra Crest opens up, including Mounts Langley and Whitney, Kern Peak, and the Toowa Range rising above the smoothly rounded hump of Templeton Mountain. The trail now describes another arc along the slope above Brush Meadow to reach another ridge in a pure stand of foxtail pines at mile 19.2. This is the obvious cutoff point, at 10,540 feet, from which to scramble up the bouldery slope to the top of Olancha Peak (12,123 feet). From here the trail makes several switchbacks down off the ridge, then begins to descend more gently into lodgepole forest carpeted with silvery little lupines. As it passes Brown Mountain, it leaves the South Sierra Wilderness to enter the Golden Trout Wilderness at mile 19.6.

Follow the PCT along the hillside, losing elevation steadily, enjoying vistas of Brown and Strawberry Meadows and another section of the South Fork of the Kern. The route winds in and out of forest, roller-coasters up and down over low ridges, then crosses a creek at mushy Gomez Meadow. Leave the lower end of the meadow on a raised section of trail to keep your boots dry, then trace a wide curve around to the west to skirt Big Dry Meadow. Cross another low, forested hump to reach the mouth of Death Canyon at mile 25.4. There are several good campsites near the creek, and a signed spur trail goes to corrals a short distance upstream. The elevation here is less than 9,000 feet and a long dry climb awaits you, so be sure to fill up with water before you proceed.

Ascend on mostly comfortably graded switchbacks through open, sandy patches of junipers, mountain mahogany, and manzanita. Isolated gray spikes of Kern frasera, a member of the gentian family, poke up through the soil here and there. They seem dull and unremarkable at a distance, but a closer examination reveals delicate greeny-white flowers crowded along the stem. As you climb, the bulk of Olancha Peak ceases to fill your entire field of vision back to the south and the isolated foxtail pines begin to coalesce into real forest.

The bridge over the Kern River near Monache Meadows

After a few final switchbacks among big piles of blocky granite boulders, reach the crest of the Sierra and the highest point on this hike at 10,700 feet and mile 29.3. Beyond the crenellated ramparts of granite and a dizzying 7,000 feet below sprawls the expanse of Owens Lake, a science-fiction landscape painted with swirls of color, sometimes silvery with a shallow layer of salty water. Before the streams that fed the lake were diverted to the city of Los Angeles, there was enough water for a paddle-wheeled steamer to ply back and forth across the lake carrying silver bullion from mines in the Inyo Mountains to the west side of the valley. Mule trains hauled it the rest of the way to Southern California.

A few wide switchbacks take you down off the crest to contour along its western slope into a saddle where an obvious path to the right (east) is marked with a sign that says CORRAL, FEED, WATER. Leaving the saddle, swing northeast. There are good views of Olancha and Kern Peaks as you climb to the top of another saddle amid more soaring granite spires. A little farther on you arrive at the best point in the wilderness to appreciate the Shark's Nose thrusting itself above the surface of Sharknose Ridge. Drop to another low point with another public corral sign directing hikers and equestrians in need of water or a place to camp to the east toward a finger of Ash Meadow. There is a cleaner, more pleasant water supply from a spring about 75 yards down the gulch to the opposite (west) side of the trail. The terrain levels out a bit near Ash Meadow, which is often churned to a smelly morass by grazing cattle. Beyond the meadow is a good view of Mount Langley; a little farther on lies a third public corral sign. Where the PCT makes a dogleg to the southwest, you are treated to a grander panorama that sweeps from Trail Peak, Sharknose Ridge, and far up Mulkey Meadow to the distant peaks of the Great Western Divide. Now leave the ridge you have been skirting to level out between stringers of Mulkey Meadows to the west and Diaz Meadow to the east. The area is crisscrossed by innumerable paths left by cattle wandering back and forth between the two meadows, so keep your topo handy in case you get confused.

Hike northwest above the drainage of Diaz Creek, climbing to pass the edge of Dutch Meadow at mile 35.9. Ascend rather steeply via switchbacks at first, then ascend more slowly, meandering through another magical rock garden of granite sculptures set off by rugged golden foxtail pines. The trail arcs around a bowl above Mulkey Meadows, whose spidery stringers creep up into the gullies between the surrounding ridges. Springs feed many of these little streams, which will eventually become Mulkey Creek. Soon you arrive at Mulkey Pass at mile 37.2. Ranchers moving their cattle into and out of the high meadows in summer use this pass, so the footing is sandy and slow until you begin to contour around the south side of a low peak to meet Trail Pass at mile 38.1. This is the shortest and easiest route down to the trailhead at Horseshoe Meadow for through-hikers who want to resupply in Lone Pine.

Climb a few long switchbacks, then contour around the north side of Trail Peak. Hop a tiny stream and wind through a dense stand of willows, then pass through a broad notch between the base of Trail Peak and long, narrow Poison Meadow, where there is a mediocre campsite. Swing south around another ridge and pause to enjoy a great view over almost the entire southern Kern Plateau. Beyond Bullfrog and Mulkey Meadows just below you sprawl Templeton Meadows and, beyond, Strawberry Meadows. Templeton Mountain sits right in the middle. Beyond these Kern Peak rises from the near end of the Toowa Range, and Olancha Peak looms above the ridgeline to the far left.

The route swings north to skirt a charming little meadow blooming with a patchwork of different-colored wildflowers. There is an especially fine campsite among foxtail pines on a sort of little island on the northwest side of the meadow, but don't count on finding water here late in the summer. Climb between two raggedy granite crags and make your way around the northeast side of the ridge of which Cottonwood Pass is a part to reach the Cottonwood Pass Trail a few steps west of Cottonwood Pass at mile 43.2.

From here the PCT skirts the top of a little meadow, then contours around a bouldery hillside to enter the Chicken Spring Lake basin at mile 43.8. To reach the lakeshore follow the little spur that leads north just a few steps off the main trail.

There is plenty of camping in this dramatic glacial cirque, but you are sure to have company on weekends, both two- and four-legged. There are rodents of all kinds—marmots, Belding ground squirrels, golden-mantled ground squirrels, chipmunks—many of which will chew holes into your pack if you leave food in it. There is also a healthy population of Clark's nutcrackers—beautiful birds but notorious camp robbers.

The trail ascends rather abruptly out of the cirque. The footing is deep sand, and the going can be hot, dry, and exhausting, but is compensated for by another sweeping panorama of Big Whitney Meadow with Kern Peak beyond. Wind along the "back" (southeast) side of Cirque Peak (the big cirque for which the peak is named is on the other side), then drop a short distance into another, smaller cirque and contour around its inside surface. The topo shows a small pond in the bottom, but this has almost completely silted in, leaving only a little green meadow with a creek running through it. There are a few small campsites here. The trail climbs back out of this bowl, rounds a ridge, and drops down a few switchbacks. Ahead lies the high, wide, desolate Siberian Outpost below the even higher and more desolate Boreal Plateau. Far beyond broods the Great Western Divide. The Pacific Crest Trail leaves the Golden Trout Wilderness on a sandy, sparsely forested switchback at a sign at about 11,400 feet (mile 45.8). To return to your car (if you've set up this hike as a shuttle), retrace your steps to the Cottonwood Pass junction and drop down over the pass to Horseshoe Meadow.

Key Points

0.0   Pacific Crest Trailhead at Kennedy Meadows.

2.0   Kern River Bridge.

4.6   Clover Meadow.

7.6   Haiwee Pass Trail, continue straight.

8.0   Beck Meadows, keep right (east).

11.5 South Fork Bridge.

11.6 Trail junction, keep left (northwest).

15.3 Monache Meadows junction, turn right (east).

15.7 South Olancha Pass Trail junction, keep left.

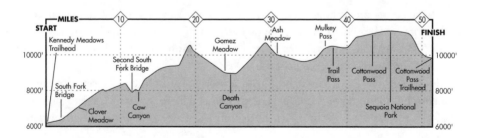

15.8 North Olancha Pass Trail junction, keep left.

19.2 Olancha Peak cutoff, continue straight.

19.6 Golden Trout/South Sierra Wilderness boundary.

25.4 Death Canyon.

29.3 Owens Valley overlook.

35.9 Dutch Meadow.

37.2 Mulkey Pass.

38.1 Trail Pass.

43.2 Cottonwood Pass.

43.8 Chicken Spring Lake turnoff.

45.8 Sequoia National Park boundary.

48.4 Cottonwood Pass, turn left (east).

51.0 Trail Pass/pack station junction, continue straight (east).

51.3 Cottonwood Pass Trailhead.

Appendix A: Hike Finder

Giant Sequoias
1. Tule River/Eastside Trail Loop
2. McAnlis Trail
3. Shake Camp and the Tule River
6. Summit Lake Loop

Backcountry Lakes
4. Maggie Lakes
5. Summit Lake
6. Summit Lake Loop
12. Silver Knapsack Trail
14. Little Kern Lake
16. Central Wilderness Grand Tour
17. Bullfrog Lakes
18. Silver Lake
19. Coyote Lakes
20. Northern Golden Trout Tour
29. Rocky Basin Lakes
33. Chicken Spring Lake
34. Siberian Outpost
43. Pacific Crest Trail

Waterfalls and Major Cascades
1. Tule River/Eastside Trail Loop
2. McAnlis Trail
3. Shake Camp and the Tule River
6. Summit Lake Loop
14. Little Kern Lake
15. Doe Meadow and Kern Flat Loop
16. Central Wilderness Grand Tour
31. Cottonwood Pass to the Kern River

Lots of Alpine Country: Ridges, Passes, and Plateaus
12. Silver Knapsack Trail
16. Central Wilderness Grand Tour
17. Bullfrog Lakes
18. Silver Lake
19. Coyote Lakes
20. Northern Golden Trout Tour

24. Cottonwood Pass
29. Rocky Basin Lakes
32. Kern Peak
33. Chicken Spring Lake
34. Siberian Outpost
43. Pacific Crest Trail

Early Season (before July) Trails
1. Tule River/Eastside Trail Loop
2. McAnlis Trail
3. Shake Camp and the Tule River
7. Grey Meadow Loop
8. Jerkey Meadow Trailhead to the Little Kern River
9. Lewis Camp Trail to the Little Kern River
10. Trout and Willow Meadows
13. Forks of the Kern
21. Casa Vieja Meadows
22. Jordan Hot Springs
36. Olancha Pass
38. Haiwee Pass
40. Honeybee Creek Trail
41. Wildrose Meadow

Wildflowers
4. Maggie Lakes
5. Summit Lake
6. Summit Lake Loop
12. Silver Knapsack Trail
15. Doe Meadow and Kern Flat Loop
16. Central Wilderness Grand Tour
17. Bullfrog Lakes
18. Silver Lake
19. Coyote Lakes
20. Northern Golden Trout Tour
22. Jordan Hot Springs
23. Redrock Meadow/Templeton Mountain Loop
30. Tunnel Meadow
31. Cottonwood Pass to the Kern River
41. Wildrose Meadow
42. Wildrose Trail

Hikes That Require Some Route-Finding Experience

11. Lion Meadows Loop
12. Silver Knapsack Trail
16. Central Wilderness Grand Tour
20. Northern Golden Trout Tour
23. Redrock Meadow/Templeton Mountain Loop
30. Tunnel Meadow
31. Cottonwood Pass to the Kern River
32. Kern Peak
40. Honeybee Creek Trail
42. Wildrose Trail

Easiest Day Hikes

2. McAnlis Trail
13. Forks of the Kern
21. Casa Vieja Meadows
25. Trail Pass
35. Golden Trout Camp
41. Wildrose Meadow

Author's Favorites

1. Tule River/Eastside Trail Loop
5. Summit Lake
17. Bullfrog Lakes
18. Silver Lake
22. Jordan Hot Springs
24. Cottonwood Pass
31. Cottonwood Pass to the Kern River
32. Kern Peak
43. Pacific Crest Trail

Appendix B: Further Reading

Browning, Peter. *Place Names of the Sierra Nevada*. Berkeley, Calif.: Wilderness Press, 1991.

Cutter, Ralph. *Sierra Trout Guide*. Truckee, Calif.: Frank Amato Publications, 1991.

Harvey, Thomas H., Howard S. Shellhammer, and Ronald E. Stecker. *Giant Sequoia Ecology: Scientific Monograph Series No. 12*. Washington, D.C.: U.S. Department of the Interior, Washington, D.C., 1980.

Horn, Elizabeth L. *Sierra Nevada Wildflowers*. Missoula, Mont.: Mountain Press Publishing Co., 1998.

Lanner, Ronald M. *Made for Each Other: A Symbiosis of Birds and Pines*. New York: Oxford University Press, 1996.

Moore, James G. *Exploring the Highest Sierra*. Stanford, Calif.: Stanford University Press, 2000.

Odion, Dennis C., Tom L. Dudley, and Carla D'Antonio. "Cattle Grazing in Southeastern Sierran Meadows: Ecosystem Change and Prospects for Recovery" from *Plant Biology of Eastern California,* edited by Clarence A. Hall Jr. and Victoria Doyle-Jones. Berkeley: University of California, 1988.

Paruk, Jim. *Sierra Nevada Tree Finder*. El Portal, Calif.: Yosemite Association, 1997.

Preston, Gilbert. *Wilderness First Aid*. Helena, Mont.: Falcon Publishing, 1997.

Schaffer, Jeffrey P., Ben Schifrin, Thomas Winnett, and Ruby Johnson Jenkins. *The Pacific Crest Trail, Volume 1*. Berkeley, Calif.: Wilderness Press, 1995.

Schneider, Bill. *Bear Aware*. Helena, Mont.: Falcon Publishing, 1996.

Schneider, Bill, and Russ Schneider. *Backpacking Tips*. Helena, Mont.: Falcon Publishing, 1998.

Smith, Ginny Schumacher. *The Deepest Valley*. Los Altos, Calif.: Walter Kaufman Inc., 1978.

Storer, Tracy I., and Robert L. Usinger. *Sierra Nevada Natural History*. Berkeley: University of California Press, 1966.

Swedo, Suzanne. *Wilderness Survival*. Helena, Mont.: Falcon Publishing, 1998.

Weeden, Norman. *A Sierra Nevada Flora*. Berkeley, Calif.: Wilderness Press, 1996.

Weise, Karen. *Sierra Nevada Wildflowers*. Helena, Mont.: Falcon Publishing, 2000.

Whitney, Stephen. *A Sierra Club Naturalist's Guide to the Sierra Nevada*. San Francisco: Sierra Club Books, 1979.

About the Author

Suzanne Swedo, director of W.I.L.D., teaches wilderness survival and natural sciences at universities, museums, and organizations such as Yosemite Association and the Sierra Club. She has backpacked the mountains of every continent and led groups into the wilderness for more than twenty-five years. Her books include *Wilderness Survival, Hiking Yosemite National Park, Best Easy Day Hikes Yosemite National Park,* and *Adventure Travel Tips* (Falcon Press). She lives in Van Nuys, California.